POST-SOVIET GRAFFITI

Free Speech in Authoritarian States

For more than a decade, Alexis Lerner combed the alleyways, under-passes, and public squares of cities once under communist rule, from Berlin in the west to Vladivostok in the east, recording thousands of cases of critical and satirical political street art and cataloging these artworks linguistically and thematically across space and time. Complemented by first-hand interviews with leading artists, activists, and politicians from across the region, *Post-Soviet Graffiti* provides theoretical reflection on public space as a site for political action, a semiotic reading of signs and symbols, and street art as a form of text.

The book answers the question of how we conceptualize avenues of dissent under authoritarian rule by showing how contemporary graffiti functions not only as a popular public aesthetic, but also as a mouth-piece of political sentiment, especially within the post-Soviet region and post-communist Europe. A purposefully anonymous and accessible artform, graffiti is an effective tool for circumventing censorship and expressing political views. This is especially true for marginalized popu-lations and for those living in otherwise closed and censored states.

Post-Soviet Graffiti reveals that graffiti does not exist in a vacuum; rather, it can be read as a narrative about a place, the people who live there, and the things that matter to them.

ALEXIS M. LERNER is an assistant professor of political science at the US Naval Academy.

Post-Soviet Graffiti

Free Speech in Authoritarian States

ALEXIS M. LERNER

UNIVERSITY OF TORONTO PRESS
Toronto Buffalo London

© University of Toronto Press 2025
Toronto Buffalo London
www.utorontopress.com

ISBN 978-1-4875-0787-9 (cloth)   ISBN 978-1-4875-3713-5 (EPUB)
ISBN 978-1-4875-2542-2 (paper)   ISBN 978-1-4875-3712-8 (PDF)

Library and Archives Canada Cataloguing in Publication

Title: Post-soviet graffiti : free speech in authoritarian states / Alexis M. Lerner.
Names: Lerner, Alexis M., author.
Description: Includes bibliographical references and index.
Identifiers: Canadiana (print) 20240533828 | Canadiana (ebook) 20240533909 |
    ISBN 9781487525422 (paper) | ISBN 9781487507879 (cloth) |
    ISBN 9781487537128 (PDF) | ISBN 9781487537135 (EPUB)
Subjects: LCSH: Graffiti—Political aspects—Former Soviet republics. | LCSH: Street
    art—Political aspects—Former Soviet republics. | LCSH: Freedom of speech—Former
    Soviet republics. | LCSH: Public spaces—Political aspects—Former Soviet republics. |
    LCSH: Post-communism—Political aspects—Former Soviet republics. | LCSH: Graffiti
    artists—Former Soviet republics—Interviews. | LCSH: Political activists—Former
    Soviet republics—Interviews. | LCSH: Politicians—Former Soviet republics—Interviews.
Classification: LCC GT3913.42 .L47 2025 | DDC 751.7/3091717—dc23

Cover design: Heng Wee Tan
Cover image: Alexis Lerner

We wish to acknowledge the land on which the University of Toronto Press operates. This
land is the traditional territory of the Wendat, the Anishnaabeg, the Haudenosaunee, the
Métis, and the Mississaugas of the Credit First Nation.

This book has been published with the help of a grant from the Federation for the
Humanities and Social Sciences, through the Awards to Scholarly Publications Program,
using funds provided by the Social Sciences and Humanities Research Council of Canada.

University of Toronto Press acknowledges the financial support of the Government of
Canada, the Canada Council for the Arts, and the Ontario Arts Council, an agency of the
Government of Ontario, for its publishing activities.

 Canada Council Conseil des Arts
for the Arts du Canada

 **ONTARIO ARTS COUNCIL**
CONSEIL DES ARTS DE L'ONTARIO
an Ontario government agency
un organisme du gouvernement de l'Ontario

Funded by the   Financé par le
Government   gouvernement
of Canada   du Canada

To MR, L, & G –
May you learn from the hidden transcript throughout
all your adventures.

And to the brave artists painting against authoritarian repression –
May your voices continue to be heard and to inspire change.

An artist can show things that
other people are terrified of expressing.
– Louise Bourgeois

Contents

Conclusion: The Future of Political Graffiti   199

Figures and Tables

Figures

Table

Preface and Acknowledgments

I returned to Moscow to finish this book. Over the last decade, I had written much of the material many times in the form of art show blurbs, op-eds, and academic papers, but now was the time to put all the pieces together. And Moscow was the place to do it. After all, this is the city where so many interviews began at midnight and lasted until dawn. This is the city whose nuances I learned about while living with residents of different neighborhoods: Ostankino with Marina and her son from Israel, Old Arbat with Bo and friends from Texas, and Elektrozavodskaia with the wonderful and generous Kitov family. The Hilton Leningradskaia, where I stayed often, began to feel like home, after I first went there in the early 2000s – filthy and sweat stained – having climbed Mount Elbrus in the north Caucasus.

This book was first inspired by the marginalized political sentiment painted on the walls across Saint Petersburg, which I would read along my daily commute through the city in 2009. On those early morning walks, I noticed stencils, stickers, murals, and freehand drawings about nuclear policy, alcoholism, the Axis siege of Leningrad, and jailed opposition activists. However, the project really took shape in Moscow, especially after the political climate changed in the winter of 2012. During that time, and in the years that followed, I observed that the political environment opened to allow a variety of critical voices to enter the city's public spaces. Starting around 2015, peaking around the election of 2018, and lasting to the present day, I witnessed how those voices were then co-opted and flooded out of heavily trafficked urban areas by corporate murals and government-sponsored graffiti festivals. In 2012, my interviewees were painting critiques of the state, but by 2018, they were painting *on behalf* of that same government. Some brave contentious voices emerged during the global COVID-19 pandemic years, albeit to a lesser degree. In 2020, my interviewees painted critiques about facemasks and harsh isolation policies. In 2022, they risked harsh punishment to paint critiques about the Kremlin's war in Ukraine.

I also saw the city change in other ways over those years. I was grateful when Russia expanded its vegetarian-friendly culinary scene and when Moscow extended its metro to Marina Roshcha, which changed the way the neighborhood's residents engaged with the rest of the city (and the way the rest of the city could engage with Marina Roshcha). I spent many long days camped out at Vinzavod's Hitrye Ludi cafe, chatting with artists and planning out data collection routes on its Wi-Fi (before our smartphones developed the capacity to do this for us). I saw the introduction and growth of companies like Gett and Airbnb in Russia (both pulled out alongside international sanctions in 2022), which meant that I no longer needed to hire my own rides from random passing drivers outside of Park Ostankino or Red Square (a common practice ten years ago in Russia and surely a concern for a young woman traveling alone) or rent a room without much accountability for its quality or accuracy.

I biked the Ring Road in the Moscow summer on extremely hot summer days, but I also saw many winters. I spent four Christmas seasons under the twinkling lights and ice cream cone churches around Red Square. I also traveled far beyond Moscow, learning firsthand that Siberia is the warmest place to be when it's cold, connecting with my dear departed grandmother by wearing her fur coat one November in Vladivostok, and visiting with loved ones in Tbilisi, Ždiar, Budapest, and beyond.

My family always felt close by during my fieldwork, whether metaphorically or literally. Skype, FaceTime, WhatsApp, Telegram, Signal, and other technologies improved the ease of connecting with interviewees and loved ones by great measures. My spouse, David, joined me on multiple fieldwork excursions, and I carried two of our three babies through Russia – the first across eight time zones from Moscow to Tyumen to Vladivostok and back. I love that I could share this special part of my life with each of them. I hope that I am teaching them to be adventurous and bold, while observant and streetwise, in their exploration of the world.

After all, this work was not always pleasant or safe. In Belarus, an officer tried to confiscate my camera and memory card as I photographed escalations during the clapping protests of July 2011; I witnessed firsthand the brutality inflicted by the Belarusian police as they arrested Lukashenko's protesters. In December 2013, when I arrived at the John F. Kennedy airport to fly to Russia for a fellowship sponsored by the Ministry of Culture of the Russian Federation, I was informed that my reservation did not include a return trip. A friend and I spent precarious nights sleeping on children's play structures in Mátészalka (the town of my grandmother's birth in eastern Hungary), on benches in Chop, Ukraine, and in a small camping tent in the Białowieża Forest on the Belarus–Poland border. In Berlin, Germany, another friend and I spent a day hiking through a forest just so that we could pay off some local street kids to climb up and around an abandoned Soviet radio tower. This research meant visiting many such places – abandoned parking garages, forsaken industrial centers, and deserted factories on the outskirts of town.

As a Hungarian-descended Jew and the grandchild of Holocaust survivors, I also found myself curious about the street narrative as it relates to local history, particularly in Eastern European states like Ukraine, Belarus, Poland, Latvia, and Lithuania. This interest added another, quite different, layer of danger to my work as I snooped around the small towns that surrounded the region's concentration camps and killing fields, and as I hopped fences to explore graffitied and desecrated Jewish cemeteries in places like Mukachevo, Ukraine, and Łódź, Poland. The Holocaust graffiti in Berlin was particularly haunting and, as one might imagine, self-aware. Its parallels in Kyiv, Lviv, Łódź, and Białystok were less so. Across the region, I met with young skinheads, self-described gangsters (once with a loaded gun resting on our dining table, no less), men in black with earpieces following closely in Belarus, and soldiers in army fatigues guarding our Siberian residence (whether they were guarding against others entering or us leaving, I remain uncertain).

These interactions and observations prompted me to include Chapter Ten as both a critique of antisemitic and xenophobic art throughout the region and as an autoethnography of sorts. I often wonder if it is possible for a descendant of Holocaust survivors to conduct truly unbiased research about the intersection between political art, national identity, and memory in Eastern and Central Europe. However, throughout my fieldwork, I learned that the Holocaust, in particular, looms so large in the region's history that it is not only impossible for anyone to ignore it but it also inevitably appears pervasively on the region's graffitied walls. The etching of my grandfather's name on the exterior wall of his childhood home in Munkács (now Mukachevo) may have led me to Transcarpathia, but it did not draw me to catalog the 2014 stencil in Berlin of the girl in striped pajamas jumping rope with barbed wire, nor the 2011 "Gas Chamber Crew" tag in Lviv (see these in Chapter Ten).

This point links back to the main idea behind this book: graffiti is a tool for reflecting publicly the issues that concern a community, whether those issues are shaped by an autocratic state concerned with its durability and wants to instill feelings of pride, or by a nationalist population that wants to control limited resources and deter unwanted neighbors. *Post-Soviet Graffiti* analyzes the street art that critiques political leaders, social issues, and ideological stances. Anyone with access to a spray can or a permanent marker can contribute to the graffitied discourse present in a city, and this book tries to be inclusive of this wide range of discourse.

Many kind and good people helped me to understand the graffitied narrative of the post-Soviet and post-communist European world. I met with government officials, academics, and opposition leaders and enjoyed one particularly lovely night at the Indian Diplomatic Estate in Moscow. Welcoming and generous Couchsurfing hosts and hostel employees provided me with interviews, told me about the best places in town to see street art, or brought me to meet the graffiti artists that they knew. The artists themselves were always thoughtful, sharp-minded, and eager to speak about their experiences. They deserve my greatest thanks. Over the years, many became close friends. And as a woman, often traveling alone, I always felt respected and protected by a group of creatives composed mostly of men. I am invested in their work but also in their safety, and throughout this book, I refer to them by their self-assigned pseudonyms.

I have so many individuals and organizations to thank. First, research support and grants from McGill University, Georgetown University, the University of Toronto, the Cosmos Club, and the Ministry of Culture of the Russian Federation sent me back to the region many times for fieldwork. I am equally grateful to those organizations that helped me to gain access to hard-to-reach spaces and individuals – from colleagues at Radio Free Europe/Radio Liberty in Washington, DC, and Prague, to Ravi, Ken, Nelson, and other colleagues I met through the Stanford US–Russia Forum. This book was also published with the help of a grant from the Federation for the Humanities and Social Sciences, through the Awards to Scholarly Publications Program, using funds provided by the Social Sciences and Humanities Research Council of Canada.

I was lucky to have institutional support – a desk, a mentor, a scholarly community, and a sounding board that let me workshop different iterations of this project – at the Leonard Davis Institute at the Hebrew University of Jerusalem from 2016 to 2017, at the Harriman Institute for Russian, Eurasian, and East European Studies at Columbia University from 2017 to 2019, at the University of Toronto where I earned my PhD in 2020, at the University of Western Ontario where I worked as a postdoctoral fellow from 2020 to 2021, at New York University's Jordan Center for the Advanced Study of Russia, where I was a visiting researcher from 2020 to 2022, and at the United States Naval Academy, where I became an assistant professor of political science in 2021. I presented this work, often with accompanying art shows, at the University of Michigan, Georgetown University, the University of Illinois at Chicago, Columbia University, Johns Hopkins University (SAIS), Indiana University, the

University of Western Ontario, and annual meetings of the Association of Slavic, East European, and Eurasian Studies (ASEEES), and the American Political Science Association (APSA), in addition to many other conferences over the years.

Friends and colleagues at each of these institutions and presentations provided excellent feedback, which enabled me to shape this project into what it is today. I wish to thank especially Emmanuel Teitelbaum, Ed Schatz, Keith Gessen, Catherine Evtuhov, Colleen Wood, Roger Kangas, Amanda Wooden, Sue Vice, Peggy Kohn, Maggie Paxson, Ajmal Burhanzoi, Nick Fraser, Tim Frye, Judge Michael Warren, Reid Standish, Egor Lazarev, Jeff Kopstein, Lisel Hintz, Brendan Doherty, Yana Gorokhovskaia, and Elizabeth Plantan for talking through ideas with me or offering feedback through close readings. Thank you to the Descriptive Research Conference team for giving me a platform and a community to think through what it means to be committed to ethnography in the contemporary political science discipline, and to Bill Lopez and the Adelante Writing Group for being a consistent source of accountability and support through this process. Thank you to Diana Nasreddine and Lisa Yost for providing research assistance. Thank you also to my literary team – Gillian Steinberg, Daniel Quinlan at the University of Toronto Press, and Lori Ames and her team at the PR Freelancer – I could not have done this without you! My gratitude also goes to Alison Hilton and Harley Balzer, both at Georgetown, who helped me to shape this nontraditional project and to keep it methodologically rigorous from the beginning.

I will never forget when I was an intern at RFE/RL's Central Newsroom in Washington, DC, and my mentor, Christian Caryl, sat me down before my first fieldwork trip to talk about navigating political threats, data theft, and the protection of my sources. As a former Moscow bureau chief for outlets like Newsweek and US News and World Report, he passed along insights and tools that remain with me today. I also thank the many friends who accompanied me through dark alleys and highway underpasses over the last decade: Arianne Swieca, Nic Van Beek, Zev Moses, Shriya Malhotra, Beau Lambert, Dorota Lech, Lili Pach, Aron Halasz, Valdis Silins, Kate McCurdy, and many who must remain clandestine. Special thanks to so many for their generous hospitality: to the Kitovs in Moscow, to Kroshka for hosting us in her beloved Tbilisi, to the Pach family in Budapest, to Jimbo Holden in Ždiar, and to Matt Kwasiborski in Prague.

Finally, thank you to my family for always supporting me and giving me the space that I needed to conduct this research. Thank you for being genuinely interested in and/or proud enough to come to my public lectures on the topic (especially the early ones!). Thank you to my spouse,

David, for supporting me from afar as I explored new cities, joining me on fieldwork trips (and for propping me up on your shoulders so that I could get a better photograph of a mural), giving thoughtful feedback on so many iterations of lectures and papers, celebrating the production of this book at every little stage, and for carrying the team whenever I went into the field after we became parents. Thank you for driving to DC with me to celebrate at the Cosmos Club when we just began dating, and for dancing with me in Moscow in the neighborhood around the Narkomfin building that, back then, felt like a second home.

Notes on the Text

On Naming Creators

Throughout this book, I reference graffiti and street artists as both artists and writers, as is customary within these communities. To adhere to ethical standards and to protect the anonymity of my interviewees, I refer to all artists by their self-assigned pseudonyms.

On "Post-Soviet"

This book is predominately about the political graffiti of the fifteen independent countries that were united during the twentieth century under the administration of the Soviet Union (USSR). This group of sovereign nations is often referenced as "post-Soviet," which problematically centers their primary unifying characteristic as having previously been affiliated with the USSR, rather than some alternative feature of this grouping of independent states, such as geography, regime type, or ethnic composition (see, for example, Erizanu, 2021; Dziewanska, Degot, and Budraitskis 2013; Ismailov 2018). I opt to use this terminology of "post-Soviet" because my work specifically engages contemporary public art both in relation to its Soviet predecessor, as well as in relation to the Russian Federation as a regional power in the present day. In short, discourse surrounding decolonization, nationhood, and the Soviet legacy is ever-present on city streets. I have also conducted related fieldwork in post-communist European and non-post-Soviet states, such as Germany, Hungary, Poland, and the Czech Republic, and I include comparative analyses of these states in the book. In the future, I plan to expand this study to consider the political graffiti in the states of the former Republic of Yugoslavia and Albania, but these states are not included in this book.

On Naming Cities

Gregor Thum says this best when he writes, "East Central European cities rarely have only one name. The city of Lviv, for instance, is known not only by its current Ukrainian name, but also as "Lvov" in Russian, "Lwów" in Polish, "Lemberg" in German, and "Lemberik" in Yiddish. Each of these variants is associated with one of the various national groups that have considered the city home and have called it by a name in their own language. Whenever historians write in a language that does not have an established name form for that place, they have to make difficult choices. Which of the variants should they use in order to avoid being accused of favoring one or another of the various national groups that have political or historical claims to the place?" (Gregor [2003] 2011, xi). Like Thum, I use the present-day name of cities and countries in English, such as Prague instead of Praha. In the rare case that I am making a reference to a historical national community, I use the city name applicable to that group and at that time (e.g., the Hungarian Munkács instead of the present-day Ukrainian Mukachevo).

On Graffiti vs. Street Art

Some art historians claim an aesthetic difference between graffiti and street art (the former, freehand scribblings, and the latter, intentional murals and intertextual stencils – see, for example, the debate between Riggle (2010) and Baldini (2016) in *The Journal of Aesthetics and Art Criticism*). However, I generally use the terms interchangeably, as my intention is to evaluate the changing position and theme of political, public art over time rather than to debate the aesthetic boundaries of its various forms. I also use the term "public art" as a synonym for street art, particularly regarding non-painted art such as any references to guerilla living greenery art and/or public performance.

On Technique

Contemporary graffiti artists employ a few principal techniques. The most common are colorful murals and freehand writing; typically, the former is defined as street art and the latter as graffiti, though the boundaries are blurred with the advent of stencils, wheatpastes, and other contemporary methods. Nevertheless, some specifics differentiate these methods and media. For example, stencils are typically cut from cardboard material with a razor in the outline of an intended design. Stencils allow an artist to paint a uniform image repetitively across the public space.

Wheatpaste and sticker art are other practical yet fruitful techniques, as graffiti artists can create them at home or at their studio, or order them to be made and delivered by a third party, for the purpose of quickly affixing them to an intended surface. Wheatpaste is essentially the art of postering without tape or tacks. A sticky paste mix, made from vegetable starch and water, allows an artist to affix the paper to an external surface. When the liquid adhesive dries, the poster is nearly impossible to rip off, even in inclement weather. Sometimes artists affix these posters with large rollers to cover a greater surface. The final notable technique is the airbrush, which aids artists in adding precise and detailed effects to their artwork. However, it tends to be one of the more time-consuming techniques and is less frequently used in everyday street art. Other creative media of expression include living greenery (moss graffiti), paint-filled fire extinguishers, posted papers with engaging prompts for passersby, drone graffiti, and public performance.

On Transliteration

All transliterations adhere to the American Library Association – Library of Congress' Transliteration Schemes for Non-Roman Scripts, with the exceptions of words that have their own standard spelling in English (e.g., Marina Roshcha instead of Mar'ina Roshcha) or those that have a self-assigned English transliteration (e.g., Хитрые Люди as Hitrye Ludi instead of Hitrie Ludi). To better correspond with English-language norms, I also use "y" instead of "i" as a suffix in transliteration when appropriate, to indicate that a noun is plural in English (e.g., *sportzaly* instead of *sportzali* and *fanaty* instead of *fanati*).

On Methods

I traveled to the region annually from 2009 to 2019. This end date was externally imposed, first by the COVID-19 global pandemic and then, as restrictions began to lift, with the Kremlin's war in Ukraine. On each trip, I spent between three and forty-five days in a city before moving on to the next location. I conducted repeat fieldwork trips to select cities over multiple years to track changes in the same locations over time.

On each of these fieldwork trips, I spent my time photographing all the pieces, murals, stencils, and stickers that I could observe throughout each city's highway underpasses, train yards, back alleys, and designated graffiti spots. I also spent this time interviewing graffiti artists, attending and giving relevant lectures, touring exhibitions and private home collections and at contemporary art collectives.

While acknowledging the dynamic nature of street art, I standardized my research by applying the same fieldwork methodology to each urban center. I visited six specific locations in each city: the downtown area, student districts, artist districts, sanctioned graffiti spots (e.g., places like Lennon Wall in Prague or Tsoi Wall in Moscow, where artists are free to come and paint), the market district, and the end of the transit line. Systematizing my fieldwork like this allowed me to more accurately compare and contrast my findings over time and across space, both within and between countries.

I mapped out each of these locations through pre-trip digital ethnography. Initially, I reached out to every person on the social media platform Couchsurfing.com who mentioned an interest in graffiti, street art, or public art. These early searches and communications were conducted in both English and in national languages. Active and responding individuals told me where, in their opinion, I could find the best graffiti or street art in their city, as well as where I might find typical student or artist neighborhoods, and I cross-validated their responses with those of other respondents to build a map of nearly every major regional urban center. Over the next ten years, these maps would guide me on my ethnographic research trips. Even as the project changed and expanded, I would still visit those early hotspots to document how the political art there changed over time. In some scenarios, these individuals offered to show me these places themselves, and on occasion, I asked someone to sit for an interview. I also asked whom else I ought to meet, and in many instances, these individuals facilitated introductions for me. After many years of using this snowballing interview technique, I conducted multiple repeat, in-depth, and open-ended interviews on topics related to political graffiti with top artists and crews as well as with activists and students from across the region. All interviews took place in English, Russian, or the national language via the assistance of a third party, based on the interviewee's preference.

When I returned home after a fieldwork trip, I manually coded each photograph for analysis based on several parameters: the medium (e.g., stencil, sticker, wheatpaste, mural, tag, freehand, or mixed); the crew or artist, if known; the surface or context (e.g., bus, business door, residential, bus stop, cement sidewalk, and so on); the content (e.g., text, character, inanimate design, mixed); the location (as described above); the status (e.g., legal or commissioned, illegal work, de facto legal); and the language (e.g., English, Russian, Belarusian, German, Hungarian, and so on). I also coded each image by its theme, separating references to political leaders from calls for vegetarianism, and critiques of state censorship policies from nostalgic murals about World War Two. I used seven thematic categories: political, social, political fascism, advertisements, religious, music, and sport. I rejected any images that did not match one of these categories of hard or soft politics, including declarations of love, seemingly apolitical gang affiliations, and crude bathroom misogyny.

On the Cover

The cover shows a graffiti stencil of Vladimir V. Putin, current president of the Russian Federation, holding a pair of scissors. He is pictured cutting the prefix "Post-" off of the term "Post-Soviet" – a symbolic reference to the Russian leader's territorial and ideological expansions into sovereign states such as Georgia, Belarus, and Ukraine. Putin's eyes are blocked by the word "Graffiti," as though it was a sticker affixed to the wall in that spot. The stencil was originally photographed in March 2012 on the external wall of the Vinzavod Contemporary Art Center in Moscow and reworked in 2023 by the University of Toronto Press. In the original piece, Putin is cutting the letter "R" from the word "Revolution," turning it into "evolution." The cover also shows the subtitle, *Free Speech in Authoritarian States*, and the name of the author, Alexis Lerner.

POST-SOVIET GRAFFITI

Chapter One

Introduction

On a particularly gray and hazy Muscovite dawn, Misha Most carefully painted Article 29 of the Russian Constitution onto a wall adjacent to the Kremlin: "Everyone shall be guaranteed the freedom of ideas and speech," he spelled out in thick, black letters near a still-empty parking lot. The old paint on the government building was chipping, and the cold nipped at his exposed skin. Most grimaced, wet his brush, and continued to write: "No one may be forced to express his views and convictions or to reject them," dripped a second bullet-point. A Kremlin guard stood facing away from Most with a look of dull boredom, not noticing the young man writing on the wall behind him. Most continued: "The freedom of mass communication shall be guaranteed, and censorship shall be banned." The constitutional passage was exhibited in the public sphere for three weeks before it was buffed by order of the Russian government.[1] Misha Most (a self-designated pseudonym) is a graffiti artist, and his wall painting – a subversive comment on the Kremlin's restrictions on speech and assembly – was an illegal work.

Graffiti and street art are effective tools for circumventing censorship and expressing political beliefs. This is especially true for marginalized populations and those living in otherwise closed and censored states. Graffiti's effectiveness comes from its inherent anonymity and accessibility. *Anonymity* permits artists and activists to share banned information, promote ignored causes, and discuss society's ills in the public sphere without consequence (assuming that one is not caught by the authorities). Graffiti is also *accessible* to all – regardless of income, political affiliation, power, and even literacy. Unlike gallery art, which requires free time and expendable income to create or view, graffiti can appear anywhere. At the same time, it can be as nuanced and as aesthetically pleasing as pieces in a museum. Using this discursive artform, graffiti artists reclaim their agency in public spaces to freely criticize leaders, policies, and societal norms understood to be untouchable by the mainstream media.

Graffiti as a tool, medium, and organizing principle takes on a uniquely subversive role under autocratic and hybrid authoritarian rule, such as in the contemporary Russian Federation. Consider, for example, a freehand political statement painted on the wall of a Moscow underpass in early 2012. During this time, Russian voters expressed feeling disenfranchised by Putin and his party, Edinaia Rossiia (in English, United Russia), after a September 2011 announcement that the prime minister would "trade places" with then-president Dmitry Medvedev in the coming election (Brooke 2011). At the same time, Russian voters expressed concern about electoral violations in the 2011 parliamentary race (Gutterman 2011). Despite an all-time low approval rating of 51 per cent in mid-December, voters lamented the dearth of adequate alternative presidential candidates – whether due to ballot curation or a preference for the perceived stability that Putin and his associates brought (Russia Public Opinion Research Center 2011). In 2012, Putin remained, ostensibly, the only choice.

Figure 1.1. Anonymous. "Who, if Not Putin?!" Freehand. March 2, 2012. Moscow, Russia. (Photo: Alexis Lerner)

In Figure 1.1, an anonymous artist mirrors this political conflict, asking who might lead the country, if not Putin. Located in a metro underpass near the upscale, centrally located Kitai Gorod (in English, China Town) neighborhood of Moscow, Russia, this writing touched upon two shared anxieties. First, what candidate would be preferable to Putin? In 2012, alongside A Just Russia's Mironov, who challenged Putin's rule, the opposition included the communist leader, Zyuganov, the billionaire businessman, Prokhorov, and the incendiary nationalist, Zhirinovsky. These alternative candidates were seen as lacking the real capacity to win enough votes to unseat the pseudo-incumbent leader. Second, could another candidate maintain stability as effectively as Putin? After all, some of the Russian president's legitimacy originates from the common trope that the consistent, even if autocratic, status quo of the "stable 2000s" stands in contrast to the violence and anarchy of the "turbulent 1990s" (Malinova 2021).

Another example that demonstrates the ability of street art to satirize political life appears in Figure 1.2. Here, a Moscow stencil offers a meta-criticism on Russia as an unfree society, using the phrases "I Love (the) Free Press" and "I Love Independent Courts." These tongue-in-cheek critiques, located directly outside of a major, downtown metro stop and train station in Moscow, attack corruption in Russia's judicial system and the censorship of its media. The use of a wall to express disdain about a restricted freedom of speech, or judicial authorities who maintain close if not dependent ties with the state, illustrates the unrestricted quality of the art form.

I first explored this topic while studying at Saint Petersburg State University during the summer of 2009. Every day, my housemate and I would walk the same streets from our apartment near the Moskovskii Train Station to our class: west on Nevskii Prospekt, over the Fontanka River, past the statue of Catherine the Great, the Gostinii Dvor outdoor mall, and the lawn in front of the Kazan Cathedral on the left (a popular gathering space at the time for Russia's young artists and activists), and past Griboedov Canal and the colorful domes of the Church of the Savior on the Spilled Blood on the right. We traversed Palace Square, where musicians and street entertainers performed on the cobblestones between the Alexander Column and the Winter Palace. By foot, we crossed the Dvortsovii Bridge that famously rises at night to allow ships to pass in the Neva River that runs beneath it.

Along this daily commute, I read the walls of Saint Petersburg. I saw freehand scribbles about animal rights and wheatpastes hostile to gentrification. I saw stickers about corrupt political leaders, with details about where and when to gather for the next opposition meeting. And I saw

Figure 1.2. Anonymous. "I Love Independent Courts. I Love (the) Free Press."
Stencil. March 12, 2012. Moscow, Russia. (Photo: Alexis Lerner)

stencils opposing Russia's nuclear program and protesting the arrest of activist Artëm Loskutov. I observed which political statements were removed by the city, which were ignored, and which incited a response from other artists.

Soon enough, I realized that the writing on the wall shared a narrative about Russian oppositional political sentiment that was less, if at all, apparent from other media channels. It seemed to me that a city's streets doubled as a stage where frank, anonymous, and unpunished dissent could circumvent censorship and even facilitate mobilization. I wondered about the global application of my observations. Was this form of expression unique to authoritarian states, or could graffiti be used as a medium for marginalized actors to express political sentiment under all political conditions?

Universe of Cases

Post-Soviet Graffiti: Free Speech in Authoritarian States is a cross-regional and longitudinal study of street art observed within the post-Soviet region and post-communist Europe, from Berlin, Germany, in the west to Vladivostok, Russa, in the east. The study begins in the spring of 2009 and ends, for the purposes of this book, in 2022. This region is immense and varies widely from neighborhood to neighborhood, let alone state to state or over time. In brief, the Soviet Union fell in December of 1991, leaving fifteen independent states in its hegemonic wake. In addition, the fall of the Soviet Union impacted political life in the Eastern Bloc countries – Hungary, Bulgaria, Albania – which were in the general Soviet sphere of influence. East Germany formally reunited with West Germany in 1990, Czechoslovakia split peacefully into the Czech Republic and Slovakia in 1993, and Yugoslavia broke into seven different states in the early 1990s, with most countries recognizing Kosovo's independence since 2008.

Born of a shared legacy of twentieth-century single-party rule, the fifteen post-Soviet states developed over time in myriad ways. On one end of this regime-type spectrum, Estonia, Lithuania, and Latvia are constitutional democracies and parliamentary republics with "free" ratings and respected votes of no confidence, a parliamentary motion that declares a lack of support in the ruling party and often results in an election, thereby indicating a high degree of institutional legitimacy and accountability for the ruling party (Freedom House 2023). Furthermore, the Baltic states adhere to the principles of human rights, including a free media and judicial independence. By both thin and thick definitions, the present-day Baltics are considered fully liberal democratic states.[2]

On the other end sit fully authoritarian states, which lack competitive elections, independent judiciaries, and human rights protections. These states are generally marked by the centralized and long-term political tenure of one leader or a small circle of elites. For example, Saparmurat "Turkmenbashi" Niyazov led independent Turkmenistan for sixteen years, Vladimir Putin has been either the president, acting president, or prime minister of the Russian Federation for twenty-four years (as of 2024), Nursultan Nazarbayev ruled Kazakhstan for nearly 28 years before his resignation in 2019, and Aleksandr Lukashenko continues to preside over Belarus after 30 years. Historically, these autocrats have achieved such longevity of rule by keeping elites loyal while relying on public repression – jail, murder, exile – to discourage public expressions of political discontent and to silence any challengers. More recent scholarship suggests that repression backfires if it empowers an independent security force or radicalizes dissenters (Chenoweth and Stephan 2011; Lachapelle 2022); therefore, we see more open authoritarian states using alternative tools like co-optation or judicial targeting to curate their political threats (Lerner 2021; Shen-Bayh 2018; Svolik 2012; Wintrobe 1998).[3]

Between these two ends of the spectrum are a collection of so-called hybrid states, including Georgia, Armenia, Ukraine, Kyrgyzstan, and European Union (EU) member states like Hungary and Poland. Hybridity, regarding regime type, is determined by the degree to which these states use democratic institutions to achieve authoritarian aims (Levitsky and Way 2010; Diamond 2002). There is substantial variation among hybrid regimes, and many do demonstrate both accountability and legitimacy for the executive branch. However, this is not always the case, and many incumbents continue to suppress their opposition by censoring the media or using targeted repression. It is this variation in regime type – from the exemplars of liberal democracy to quintessentially illiberal authoritarian states, with every degree of competitive regime in between – that makes the post-Soviet and post-communist European region a unique set of comparative cases.

Freedom of Speech in this Universe of Cases

The freedom of speech permits individuals to express themselves without censorship or consequence, a right often protected by law.[4] One commonly used vehicle for communicating political discontent is through traditional sources of media, including print media, broadcast news, and digital media. Media outlets can be used to inform the public about state behavior, to hold officials accountable, and to facilitate the political discourse and debate that is so central to free speech.

Authoritarian and closed hybrid states are likely to establish control over the media to prevent dissenting individuals and opposition groups from sharing unwanted information or voicing their opinions in this traditional public sphere. In these cases, the media is a key tool for gaining, losing, and centralizing power. By restricting certain individuals, ethnic groups, or social movements from using the media for certain types of political expression, the elite maintain their centralized authority. Further, by permitting a selection of curated options for news consumption, the state can control, hierarchically, what information is disseminated and, likewise, what is omitted. Therefore, in such cases, street art proves to be an effective tool for circumventing censorship. Before I evaluate differences in street art across the post-Soviet and post-communist regions, it is necessary to first address variation in media freedoms throughout these states.

The most free are the EU member states, which are subject to Article 11 of the Charter of Fundamental Rights of the European Union (2009). This law, enforceable by the European Commission, as well as the Court of Justice of the European Union, includes the following two components:

1 Everyone has the right to freedom of expression. This right shall include freedom to hold opinions and to receive and impart information and ideas without interference by public authority and regardless of frontiers.
2 The freedom and pluralism of the media shall be respected.

However, individual countries sometimes fail to adhere to the specifications outlined in the charter, thus causing tensions between member states and the union. In recent years, for example, Viktor Orban and the Fidesz Party in Hungary have engaged in increasingly illiberal, intolerant, and even autocratic actions: a complete overhaul of the constitution in 2011 in a way that undermined democratic institutions and privileged the ruling Fidesz party (Bánkuti et al 2012), the limiting of judicial independence by appointing politically aligned judges and initiating disciplinary proceedings against political opponents arbitrarily since coming into office (Kovács and Scheppele 2018), and the exploitation of anti-semitic tropes in public speeches, especially since 2017 (Kalmar 2020).[5]

Hungary's embrace of "illiberal democracy" (Orban 2014; Plattner 2019) also undermines media freedoms. In January 2011, the Fidesz government introduced its so-called Media Law, which sought to subject all published material on the internet and in print to government approval, thereby threatening Hungary's freedom of expression and the integrity of Hungarian independent media outlets. Radio in Hungary also suffered at this time, when the state cut funding to the long-time, left-liberal station Klubrádió. While Klubrádió overcame this deficiency temporarily through listener donations, the station was ultimately refused its tender in December 2011. By the spring of 2012, Klubrádió lost its frequency to Advenio, a private firm owned by Tamás Fellegi, a minister in prime minister Viktor Orban's cabinet, and Zsolt Nyerges, a Fidesz-employed lawyer. The EU assessed the Media Law as a restriction on Hungarian speech freedoms and encouraged Hungary's ruling party to reform or reject the ruling. The EU's concerns were serious enough to prompt an infringement hearing.

In 2018, the consolidation of nearly 500 independently owned media outlets under the newly established Central European Press and Media Foundation (KESMA) raised concerns. KESMA, which has close ties to the Orban administration, is believed to privilege pro-Fidesz political coverage (Horsley 2021). Then in 2023, the European Parliament Committee of Inquiry confirmed that the Hungarian state purchased Pegasus surveillance spyware in 2017, with the intended use of surveilling independent journalists and opposition figures (European Parliament 2023). In a 2023 report, the committee stated that the spyware was "grossly abused in Hungary" and that "people have been spied on with the objective of gaining even greater political and financial control over the public sphere and media market" (European Parliament 2023). The impact of surveillance spyware – and especially the zero-click attack that Pegasus has proven to be capable of – presents grave concerns for civil society. It jeopardizes the integrity of independent investigations, facilitates the spread of misinformation and disinformation, and silences political dissent through the inherent threat of consequences (Deibert 2023). Notably, a similar scandal occurred around the same time in Poland.

States outside the EU may have greater autonomy when setting and implementing their own media policies. Consider contemporary Russia, where many news outlets, especially televised programs, are state owned or have been bought by state-owned energy companies. Independent journals and newspapers exist, but their writers "run the risk of attack and even murder if they delve too deeply into sensitive subjects such as corruption, organized crime, or rights abuses" (BBC Monitoring 2012). Even the last free broadcaster – Ekho Moskvi, or Echo of Moscow, majority owned by the oil and gas company Gazprom – encountered state pressure during both the 2012 and 2018 presidential elections and was finally closed in 2022, due to its coverage of the Kremlin's war in Ukraine.

Table 1.1. Ranked Countries from Highest to Lowest Press Freedoms, according to their Press Freedom Index ranking in 2009 and 2023. A lower rank (1) indicates a greater degree of relative press freedom in a country in a given year. Data sourced from Reporters Without Borders.

	Ranking in 2009	Ranking in 2023
Lithuania	2	1
Estonia	1	2
Czech Republic	5	3
Latvia	3	4
Slovakia	8	5
Germany	4	6
Moldova	15	7
Armenia	13	8
Romania	9	9
Poland	7	10
Bulgaria	10	11
Hungary	6	12
Georgia	11	13
Ukraine	12	14
Kyrgyzstan	16	15
Kazakhstan	17	16
Uzbekistan	21	17
Azerbaijan	18	18
Tajikistan	14	19
Belarus	19	20
Russia	20	21
Turkmenistan	22	22

Meanwhile, in Belarus, the state owns and explicitly censors all national television stations. The newspaper industry may not be overtly controlled, but state-owned newspapers are subsidized, and opposition newspapers (like Narodnaia Volia) encounter crippling fines and seemingly inevitable shutdowns. Independent news websites are also under the threat of pervasive government surveillance and closure. For example, the popular human rights news platform Charter'97 has been the target of multiple attacks, including the deletion of its archives in 2011, blocked access in 2018, and believed physical attacks on its leadership, such the mysterious death of founder Aleh Byabenin in 2010 and journalist Pavel Sheremet in 2016.

Table 1.1 shows a ranking of *relative* press freedoms in twenty-two of the post-Soviet and post-communist European states in the years under review in this study.[6] This data comes from the Reporters Without Borders World Press Freedom Index, a dataset compiled from structured surveys with journalists, lawyers, and experts on media freedoms pertaining to each country as well as empirics on violence against journalists during the year in question. The index is updated each calendar year, with the most recent update examining press freedoms in 2023.

The numbers shown in Table 1.1 represent a ranking of the countries in the study *relative* to each other as well as over time. For the purposes of this table, a rank of 22 is the highest, indicating that the country's media freedoms fare extremely well, and a rank of 1 is the lowest, indicating high levels of abuses, censorship and self-censorship, a lack of independent and pluralistic outlets, and poor legislative and infrastructural support.

The purpose of this table is to provide some context regarding each country's press freedoms, relative over time and to other states in the region. While people in states with high press freedoms may find adequate outlets for sharing political discontent in the mainstream media, others in states with low press freedoms will surely be forced to identify alternative avenues for political expression.

Expressing Discontent

Street Protests

In states with restricted press freedoms, individuals or groups that wish to express their political sentiments are forced to seek alternative avenues of expression. There are a few viable options for alternative protest; the first is public demonstration – open-air rallies, punctuated with speeches by civil society leaders and marching *en masse*. Denizens of states like Ukraine and Armenia have taken to their respective streets in solidarity in recent years for greater political openness, accountable democratic practices, and the protection of human rights. Although the Euromaidan movement in 2013-2014 Kyiv, Ukraine, and the so-called Velvet Revolution in 2018 Yerevan, Armenia, were both successful in engendering electoral turnover and regime change, such demonstrations are not always effective. In 2011 and 2012, protesters in Hungary and Russia, respectively, held some of their countries' largest post-communist demonstrations, and protesters in Belarus in 2020 held the largest pro-democracy demonstrations in its post-Soviet history. However, despite charismatic leadership and global media backing, these demonstrations effected little change.

For example, on July 3, 2011, protesters in downtown Minsk, Belarus, attempted to "clap out" the then-seventeen-year authoritarian rule of Aleksandr Lukashenko. During organized protests, plain-clothed employees of the Belarusian state security forces – still colloquially referred to as the KGB, hearkening back to the Soviet domestic intelligence and security agency – arrested approximately four hundred protesters; even more were apprehended at their homes in the days following the meetings (BBC 2011). I was there that day, in front of the Minsk Railway Station and on the side streets around it, and witnessed many of these violent arrests personally. A week later, on July 13, protesters met in Yakub Kolas Square with their cell phone alarms set for 8:00 p.m., at which time a cacophony of alarms buzzed and rang together in solidarity. In response, plain-clothed officers threw demonstrators into waiting green "catcher vans" that resemble outdated versions of UPS trucks. Eventually, Belarusian authorities decreed that anyone with suspected intentions of protesting – even one person standing alone – could be arrested for opposition action (Mouzykantskii 2011).

While Russian street protests draw larger crowds and, until 2022, include fewer reports of indiscriminate, Minsk-style violence, they conclude with similar results: scores of arrests, costly fines, a frustrated populace, and political stagnation. On December 10, 2011, 50,000 Muscovites heeded corruption-hunting blogger and opposition leader Alexei Navalny's call and gathered in Bolotnaia Square with sarcastic banners and anti-Putin slogans. In the biggest demonstration since the fall of the Soviet Union, the masses united against government corruption and the alleged electoral fraud that took place during the December 4 parliamentary elections. Despite a massive turnout, no ballot recount took place. In response, and despite record low temperatures, 80,000 demonstrators met on Sakharov Avenue on December 24, shouting slogans about the "party of crooks and thieves," Navalny's nickname for president Putin's political party (Navalny 2011). Putin publicly recognized, yet disregarded, their cries as those of an inconsequential minority.

On March 4, 2012 – election day in Russia – thousands of riot police barricaded Moscow's downtown public squares with rows of metal detectors, ensuring that opposition demonstrations could not take place. As I illustrate in 1.3, 1.4, and 1.5, hundreds of military vehicles lined Red Square, Pushkinskaia Square, Maiakovskaia Square, Bolotnaia Square, and Teatral'naia Square, passively demonstrating the ruling regime's military might. Thirty thousand youth from the pro-Kremlin group "Nashi" were bussed to Moscow from around the country to patrol those areas where the military vehicles could not fit – the city's underground passageways, metro stations, and back streets – to "make sure nothing happened" (Jones 2011; Nashi Youth Interview 2012). Moscow's large and peaceful meetings on March 5 and March 10 also failed to yield viable presidential candidates or policy change.

Figure 1.3. Military vehicles line Moscow's sidewalks and public squares in anticipation of election day protests. 2012. Moscow, Russia. (Photo: Alexis Lerner)

Figure 1.4. Military vehicles wait in Red Square in anticipation of election day protests. 2012. Moscow, Russia. (Photo: Alexis Lerner)

Figure 1.5. Barricades block access to public squares to prevent mass gatherings in the days leading to election day. 2012. Moscow, Russia. (Photo: Alexis Lerner)

In 2022, in protest of the Kremlin's invasion of neighboring Ukraine, hundreds of thousands of Russians came to the streets. After one month of ongoing demonstrations, 15,000 Russians were arrested. Not only were Russian protesters up against repressive arrests and fines, but political opposition leadership was also under attack. The previously mentioned Alexei Navalny was sentenced to nine additional years in a maximum-security penal colony on allegations of embezzlement (he had already been sentenced to two and a half years of prison for alleged parole violations in February 2021). In February 2024, Navalny died in an arctic prison in northern Yamalo-Nenets Autonomous Region. His death is widely believed to be a murder, especially considering the recent assassination attempt on the political opposition leader in August 2020, when he was poisoned with a Novichok nerve agent (Faulconbridge and Light 2024). While individual Russians are still marching and speaking out, the dismantling of an organized opposition makes it difficult to organize mass antiwar and anti-Kremlin demonstrations.

The case of public protest in Hungary yielded a similar outcome. On January 2, 2012, tens of thousands of Hungarians marched in downtown

Budapest to protest the right-wing Fidesz party's newly passed constitution. The document, titled the "Basic Law," presented a single-party revision of the nation's history, restructured the electoral system in a way that strengthened the leading party's power, presented conservative ethical norms as law, and employed a nationalist undertone throughout in language interpreted as threatening to minorities and foreign-born citizens. The January protests did not result in a collaborative constitutional review, even after the EU and then-US secretary of state Hillary Clinton got involved. Instead, the new constitution reinforced the elite's ability to interfere in judicial matters, nationalized Hungary's main banks, and replaced Jewish and Roma cultural leaders with politically favored individuals.

The Cyber-Sphere

With demonstration-style meetings occurring frequently, and with heavy-handed rulers fighting to retain control with tools like censorship, policymaking, and command over the police and military to disperse protesters, dissenting citizens must uncover further avenues for political expression. A second viable option is to reach a connected audience using social networking platforms like LiveJournal, VKontakte, Instagram, TikTok, and X (formerly known as Twitter), which have emerged in recent years as effective mobilizing venues because they let users share information in real time over mobile devices under a pseudonym (despite policies from some of these platforms that seek to force users to use their legal names in all communications) (Breuer 2016). Yet, even on the internet, free speech has definite limits. On January 4, 2012, Belarusian president Lukashenko enacted an internet censorship law that restricts access to foreign sites, including news hubs like Radio Svoboda (the local Belarusian service of the American Radio Free Europe/ Radio Liberty initiative), social networking sites like Facebook, and consumerist portals like eBay. In late 2014, anti-government protests in Hungary materialized again, this time in response to the proposed "Internet Tax," which was believed to threaten free speech and the independence of internet-based companies, particularly in low-income areas (Halasz 2014). Legal restrictions like these prevent individuals and activists from using these platforms and networks to share fact-based information, to hold officials accountable, to be informed voters in an election, and to communicate plans for mobilization.

On the Russian internet, especially in recent times, bloggers and social network users are ubiquitous, inspired perhaps by Navalny's early activist briefings on LiveJournal and YouTube. While the state has shut down websites, the most impactful being the shutdown of Facebook and Instagram in 2022 during Russia's war in Ukraine, users continue to post political and antiwar content using secure and encrypted virtual private networks (VPNs) or by moving to alternate platforms, such as the Telegram messaging app. Nevertheless, even with strong end-to-end encryption and self-destructing messaging measures in place, no communication platform is completely secure. Political institutions and contracted hackers can access user data through legal means, by coercing service providers, or by exploiting vulnerabilities in the platform's security. Further, online hackers – whether contracted by the authorities or operating independently – can easily navigate locked portals, passwords, and IP addresses to threaten the security and privacy of activist users (Soldatov and Borogan 2015). Belarusian blogger Anton Motolko and Kazakh video-blogger Askar Shaigumarov know about this well, as both have complained of personal repression and the monitoring of their web followers (Human Constanta 2021; Freedom House 2018). In 2011, I witnessed the state repression of Motolko firsthand when undercover police took and smashed his high-end camera equipment during the Independence Day "Clapping Protests" in Minsk.

These examples of public repression occur in tandem with the saturation of social media platforms with pro-state news and sentiment. These authoritarian regimes have proven efficient at leveraging trolls and bots to flood the digital commons with divisive, fake, and/or inflammatory content. Disinformation and misinformation, targeted harassment, and subjectively pro-state materials are presented in a manner that forcefully drowns out the news reports, expert opinions, and commentary of independent journalists (Lerner 2021; Stukal et al. 2017; Gunitsky 2015).

Graffiti

A third viable avenue for free expression is graffiti. Illegalities aside, graffiti and street art are effective tools for circumventing state censorship and expressing political sentiment on a truly public stage. Anonymity and pseudonym-protected authorship help to safeguard the identity of particularly critical writers. Not only can graffiti appear anywhere, but it is also accessible to all individuals – both as creators and viewers – regardless of literacy, income, political affiliation, or power. As such, graffiti as a tool, medium, and organizing principle takes on a uniquely effective and subversive role under autocratic and hybrid rule.

There is precedent for the study of street art as a dominant avenue of political communication in this region, as the Soviet state also relied upon public murals to impart twentieth-century propagandic messaging about political loyalty and behavioral norms to its residents. The Soviet regime used these large-scale works, painted on walls in public spaces, to celebrate state achievements such as technological and agricultural advancements, to promote socialist values like collective labor and patriotism, national heroes like Lenin and Stalin, indoctrination about Marxist-Leninist ideology and the achievements of socialism, and cultural propaganda about the diversity and supremacy of Soviet heritage.

Today, savvy graffiti artists can push the limits of social norms and political correctness by using street art to criticize and question political leadership, corrupt practices, unpopular policies, or targeted repression or hate crimes. For example, in Saint Petersburg, one artist drew a freehand outline of an unlabeled can of Campbell's soup to critique the company's inability to immerse itself in the traditional Russian soup market. In Budapest, politically motivated graffiti coats the city's streets, deepening the partisan schism between political parties, such as Jobbik, Fidesz, the Hungarian Socialist Party (MSZP), or even the satirical Two-Tailed Dog Party.

In Riga, Latvia, artists use graffiti to complain about the negative effect of international capitalism on the state, with slogans attacking the thirty-seventh gathering of the Group of Eight (G8) – a meeting between eight countries with (what once was) the world's largest industrialized economies – or one stencil of three bankers with their arms raised in a heil position, a critique of their political behavior and preferences (Figure 1.6). The 2008 global economic crisis hit Latvia hard, and while it was later one of the first European states to regain its financial strength, the crisis served to deepen the country's existing socio-economic schisms. One artist went so far as to paint a stencil of Latvian civic identity – Milda, the freedom monument in Central Riga – going through a literal meat grinder as shown in Figure 1.7, thereby producing something bland and malleable, stripped of any existing cultural markers or nationalist interests (I discuss this piece further in Chapter Five).

In Berlin, Germany, artists like Italy's BLU use public art to comment on the failures of reunification and economic development. In Figure 1.8, I show a mural by BLU in the Kreuzberg district of Berlin that aims to bring attention to the dissolved tent city that used to rest at the foot of the murals. It shows a faceless male in professional clothing, wearing two Rolex watches connected by a gold chain, imagery that pokes fun at the economic growth and gentrification that has imprisoned East Germany to the West. To the right (not pictured), is a second mural that depicts two individuals that are trying to unmask each other while throwing up gang signs for the East and West side. Both murals were buffed in 2014.

Figure 1.6. Bankers making a Heil Hitler gesture. 2011. Riga, Latvia. (Photo: Alexis Lerner)

Figure 1.7. "Independence Through the Meat Grinder." A wheatpaste pokes fun at the colossal Lady Freedom monument in the center of Riga. The monument is said to represent Latvia's national identity and independence, and the artist shows how these unique features can be made indistinguishable through outside pressure. 2011. Riga, Latvia. (Photo: Alexis Lerner)

Figure 1.8. A faceless figure is chained to capitalism. 2013. Berlin, Germany. (Photo: Alexis Lerner)

I use each of these examples, and those throughout the book, to illustrate how political graffiti can be used to amplify often-marginalized perspectives on political, economic, and social matters. As a truly anonymous and accessible form of public art, graffiti is an effective tool for circumventing censorship, amplifying marginalized voices, and challenging existing power dynamics.

Structure of the Book

This book is organized in three parts. "Part I: An Oral History of Post-Soviet Graffiti" provides the reader with a roadmap of graffiti and street art in the post-Soviet region. This part describes the major players in the history of graffiti, how the practice spread geographically, and when it became politicized. Building on original fieldwork and interviews with the most well-known artists and crews in contemporary Russia – including Misha Most, Kirill Kto, Basket, Partizaning, P183, and ZUKCLUB – this text offers the first historical compilation of post-Soviet graffiti and street art since John Bushnell's *Moscow Graffiti*, published in 1990.

Part I includes three chapters. "Chapter Two: The Origins of Soviet and Post-Soviet Public Art" provides background information as well as newly collected materials about the history of graffiti in the region. Again, drawing heavily from artist interviews, I describe here the cultural transmission of Western breakdance, rap, and graffiti to Soviet cities such as Riga and Saint Petersburg. The chapter tells the story of largely apolitical graffiti, written to advertise a service, communicate ownership, or beautify a space from the time of the Rurik Dynasty (founded in Novgorod around the year 862 AD) to shortly after the fall of the Soviet Union in 1991. This chapter touches on examples, such as the early tags of the late 1960s and 1970s in New York City, writing on Tsoi Wall in Moscow, and the colorful murals of the Berlin Wall.

In "Chapter Three: Painting for the Highest Bidder," I write about international, corporate, and early government efforts to co-opt graffiti and graffiti artists in the 1990s and 2000s. In particular, I discuss the graffiti festivals first instituted by Nescafe and Nike and introduce the concept of a legal festival as a predatory form of top-down control and co-optation in the early capitalist years of the post-Soviet era. This is an important juncture as it demonstrates an external validation of a previously believed-to-be subversive and illegal communication platform. In this chapter, I also draw from original interviews to bring in the second wave of graffiti artists, introduce the government-directed graffiti festivals, and discuss examples of how graffiti has been leveraged for the purpose of advertising products and ideas.

Having established in Chapter Three that graffiti carries external legitimacy and value, "Chapter Four: Art Against the Machine" integrates my interviews to narrate the transition of graffiti from a late-Soviet, aesthetically motivated cultural movement to a twenty-first century mouthpiece of political and social critique. Here, with examples ranging from street artists such as Misha Most and Radya to performance artists like Voina and Anton Litvin, I illustrate how political groups and activists have reclaimed graffiti in recent history to communicate discontent, share private information or opinions, and circumvent top-down censorship.

"Part II: Fundamental Questions about Post-Soviet Graffiti" serves as a theoretical primer for studying graffiti within the established disciplines of political science, cultural studies, or urban studies. The chapters in this part are particularly focused on protest, authoritarianism, and the theory of political graffiti. While Part I focuses on graffiti and street art predominantly in the case of Russia, Parts II and III expand these frameworks beyond Russia to the rest of the region.

"Chapter Five: Why the Public Space is Conducive to Political Graffiti" provides a theoretical underpinning for the relationship between public space and political action or protest. This chapter draws largely from postmodernist and post-positivist scholarship on space, while also pointing to literature on the unique quality of public space under authoritarianism. I also discuss how the placement and local context of graffiti matters in its capacity to communicate information or opinion, drawing on examples from my fieldwork across the region, from Budapest (Hungary) to Riga (Latvia) to Łódź (Poland) and Minsk (Belarus). This is a vital aspect in thinking about why graffiti has value and the degree to which this value is related to graffiti's inherently public nature.

"Chapter Six: Signs and Symbols as a Form of Political Expression" applies lenses of semiotic theory and communication literature to images, interpreting them as texts and symbols that can be leveraged for political expression and action. In this chapter, I reference graffitied signs and symbols that signal meaning because of their historical or cultural significance, such as the Pahonia in Minsk, the stenciled face of a presidential candidate in Tbilisi, or the swastika more broadly in a post-1945 world.

"Chapter Seven: Street Art as Text" is the theoretical center of this book. It explains that graffiti does not exist in a vacuum; rather, it can (and should) be read as a text or as a narrative about a place, the people that live there, and the things that matter to them. This chapter draws on the work of Russian literary theorist Mikhail Mikhailovich Bakhtin and his ideas about dialogism and the chronotope. I argue that graffiti is not a one-way monologue but instead part of a multi-way, or dialogical, conversation among writers, buffers (wall cleaners), passersby, and the physical environment surrounding each work. I illustrate the variation among the chronotopes of "Midnight Graffiti," "Corporate Graffiti," and "Co-opted Graffiti" with a story about a late-night painting outing with Basket in Moscow in 2011.

In "Part III: Interpreting Graffiti," I conduct a multi-state comparative analysis of thematic trends across the region. "Chapter Eight: The Political" examines how artists critique leaders, parties, and policies across the spectrum of regime types. To illustrate these themes, I reference graffiti about political figures in Tartu and Tallinn (Estonia), about corruption in Kyiv and Vladivostok, about political repression in Saint Petersburg and Minsk, and about foreign control in Prague (Czech Republic) and Sofia (Bulgaria).

Following the logic that one must change society to change the way it votes or demands action, "Chapter Nine: The Social" highlights topics ranging from feminism to environmentalism and from ethnic tolerance to inequality. In this chapter, I reference a wide range of eco-conscious works of public art, from Anton Cheremnikh's 2018 "Lungs of the City" in Perm, Russia, and ROA's murals of deconstructed animals in Berlin, to calls for veganism in Vilnius, Lithuania. I also use this chapter to discuss the anti-nuclear graffiti of Chernobyl, Ukraine, a mural about the rights of indigenous people in Russia's remote Taz Peninsula, references to the COVID-19 pandemic from Novosibirsk, Russia, to Brest, Belarus, and works advocating for LGBTQIA+ rights by Yav Crew in Saint Petersburg. Additionally, in this chapter I discuss the work of Kormfox from Budapest, Mikaela from Moscow, the DOXA crew from Bishkek (Kyrgyzstan), and the New Rhythm crew from Osh (Kyrgyzstan), all of whom paint on topics like feminism, women's rights, and domestic violence. Finally, given that graffiti is a public discourse available to all those who wish to participate, I also discuss in this chapter how graffiti can be used to promote less palatable narratives such as the hate speech that favors one racial, ethnic, or national group over another.

"Chapter Ten: Who Controls Discourse?" unearths the multiple layers of agency, discourse, and the shaping of outward-facing narratives within the realm of graffiti and street art. This chapter compares the antisemitic and xenophobic graffiti cataloged on fieldwork trips across Eastern and Central Europe with that of the nationalist, pro-state murals appearing under authoritarian leadership across Russia and Kazakhstan. I open with an anecdote about the graffiti of a six-pointed Jewish star that was etched onto my grandfather's home after he and his family were forced to flee their home in then Munkács, Hungary (now Mukachevo, Ukraine), to seek refuge from genocide in 1944.

Why Does Graffiti Matter?

In *Post-Soviet Graffiti*, I aimed to produce a manuscript both rigorous and expansive in terms of both geography and discipline. My goal regarding the audience of this book is that it is situated within the scholarly conversations happening in the social sciences around comparative authoritarianism, protest politics, and state–society relations, but also, in light of the current events, that it remains accessible for non-academic audiences and the policy community.

My intentions for conducting this research are threefold. First and most simply, I seek to fill an academic gap with my historical and analytic summary of a contemporary counterculture. The existing literature on the topic is somewhat outdated. John Bushnell's notable *Moscow Graffiti* provides a good assessment of the Soviet countercultural progression and outlines thoroughly how each movement (hippies, pacifists, rockers, sports fans, and so forth) used graffiti to share their ideology, but his analysis stops with the end of the Soviet Union. Based on my interviews and fieldwork in the region, I build on Bushnell's historical perspective by adding an updated and detailed account of the art form's progression from 1985 through the present day.

Second, I want this project to encourage domestic and foreign journalists, scholars, and political analysts to consider the street narrative when offering their assessments of public sentiment in authoritarian states. When formal surveys are unavailable, recording the street narrative is an adequate method for developing one's understanding about the aims of a particular movement or the trends in popular opinion. After all, many stencils clearly state a movement's goals and often include a web link where interested individuals can learn more about a particular issue or viewpoint.

Third, I hope this book inspires individuals to recognize the political and cultural value of street art. Any person can walk down the street – from New York City to Tbilisi – and read the street narrative as it is painted on a city's walls. To me, this is the best way to explore a new place and to understand the nuances of its problems. Consider, for example, in the United States, the Anti-Eviction Mapping Project of San Francisco's historic Mission District, which seeks to educate passersby about the city's alleged more than 12,000 no-fault evictions and 33,000 displacements from 1997 to 2016 under the Ellis Act. A reaction to Silicon Valley's booming growth and subsequent gentrification, the mural project both educates and provides a peaceable outlet for those who feel disempowered. This street art initiative is successful in maintaining the popular relevance of local voices regarding marginalization, addiction, and displacement. Indeed, each citizen who wishes to influence the social discourse of their community need only to pick up a can of spray paint. The tool and medium of street art is accessible, affordable, and effective.

I wrote *Post-Soviet Graffiti* to reveal that street art does not exist in a vacuum; rather, it can be read as a narrative about a place, the people who live there, and the things that matter to them. This book is the result of a decade of fieldwork – of combing through alleyways, underpasses, and public squares of cities once under communist rule, from Berlin, Germany, in the west to Vladivostok, Russia, in the east, recording thousands of cases of critical and satirical political street art, and cataloging these artworks linguistically and thematically across space and time. During those years, I also conducted interviews with leading artists, activists, and politicians from across the region. The result is a book that provides evidence for free speech under authoritarian rule, theoretical reflection on public space as a site for political action, a semiotic reading of signs and symbols, and a call to consider street art as a form of discursive text.

To view more images in full resolution, visit www.PostSovietGraffiti .com.

PART I

An Oral History of Post-Soviet Graffiti

The first chapters of this book draw on original interviews with regional artists and present their perspectives on the history of street art in the Soviet and post-Soviet regions and eras. These chapters outline the origins of graffiti and street art, major players, and the trajectory of this art form from antiquity through the early twenty-first century.

"Chapter Two: The Origins of Soviet and Post-Soviet Public Art" provides a brief global context – early wall scribblings in Argentina and the lost city of Pompeii, New York City tags – before tracing graffiti's trajectory in what is now Russia from the ninth-century Rurik Dynasty through the Soviet era. As a popular mode of expression among sports fans and hippies, street art painted in Soviet times was largely morally and politically neutral, and dissident graffiti was rare. This avoidance of overtly political topics allowed graffiti writers some degree of plausible deniability.

"Chapter Three: Painting for the Highest Bidder" shows how a variety of actors – from international corporations like Nike and Nescafé to political institutions such as the US Consulate in Saint Petersburg and the Government of the City of Moscow – attempted (and sometimes succeeded) to co-opt this art form, as well as its creators and the public spaces in which it exists. This chapter demonstrates the value that corporate and government actors perceive in street art, introduces the concept of the legal festival as a form of twenty-first century creative control, and makes the case for street art as a valuable avenue of communication.

"Chapter Four: Art Against the Machine" shows how Russian artists leveraged street art specifically for political communication. My interviewees narrate how they used graffiti in post-Soviet times to express explicit political sentiment: to challenge political leaders, to criticize controversial political decisions, and to mobilize for political causes.

Chapter Two

The Origins of Soviet and Post-Soviet Public Art

Humans have used graffiti, or wall markings, to communicate for millennia. Among the earliest known examples of graffiti are the prehistoric rock art of *Cueva de las Manos* (the Cave of Hands) in Santa Cruz, Argentina (made between 9,500 and 13,000 years ago), the lewd sexual advertisements of Pompeii (buried by Mount Vesuvius' eruption in 79 CE), Rome (200 CE), and Ephesus, and a collection of "subtle human touches" – a drawing of a woman or a fish – left on a door jamb in the Palace of Merenptah (dating believed to be sometime between 1213 and 1204 BCE) (Wegner 2011). A sort of graffiti even appears in the Bible. Prior to receiving their freedom from slavery, the Israelites smear the blood of a sacrificial lamb on the doorposts of their homes to signal their identity. In the region that later became Russia, graffiti originated around the time of the ninth-century Rurik Dynasty, when it largely served a labeling or basic advertising function (Bushnell 1990, 8).

The graffiti that we are most familiar with today is the twentieth-century variety – tagged monikers and bright blasts of color on subway trains and highway underpasses: words that seem to jump off the walls of a city's back alleys and bar bathrooms written by people who are desperate to be heard or in search of glory. Such graffiti became so popular in New York City in the early 1970s that mayor John Lindsay slapped back with an expensive "war" on graffiti in 1972 (Schumach 1973).

In the United States, graffiti artists splatter city walls with one goal in mind: to achieve fame. At least this is the understanding that graffiti artist Roger Gastman, a participant in the early Washington, DC, graffiti scene and an expert on the history of graffiti in the United States, shared in February 2011. Gastman insisted that credibility among American graffiti artists was more about the frequency of their tag than the quality of their work: "The more your name is written across the city, the more famous you become. Quantity is the only goal" (2011).

This quantity-based mindset is reflected in the lexicon developed in New York City, in which artists that dominated a space became known as "kings"; writers that were seen as weak or inadequate became known as "toys."

This spray-can art form spread throughout the late twentieth and early twenty-first centuries across the walls of the Americas and Europe. For example, in Washington, DC, in the 1960s, writers marked black-owned businesses with "Soul Brotha" to protect them during mass protests (Gastman 2011), and in Osh, Kyrgyzstan, phrases such as "Kyrgyz Zone" or the anti-Uzbek slur "Sart!" were painted on buildings and roadblocks to signal the boundaries of ethnic communities (Wooden 2011). After Hurricane Katrina devastated New Orleans, in 2005, residents used graffiti to protect themselves from looters, writing phrases like, "I am here. I have a gun." or "Don't try. I am sleeping inside with a big dog." Post-Katrina search and rescue teams used graffiti to mark which homes had been searched and indicate whether those houses were empty.

In Europe, the Berlin Wall that was designed to separate communist and democratic Germany became a central hub for West Berlin graffiti artists, including French writer Thierry Noir and American artist Keith Haring, both of whom saw the wall as a symbol of oppression and divisiveness (Noir 2014). Meanwhile, until the mid-1980s, many living east of the Berlin Wall remained ignorant about graffiti, aside from its capacity as a tool for advertising a product or making a lewd sexual reference. After all, during the Soviet era, the state tried to hold a monopoly over expression on buildings and public transportation.

Those artists that *did* paint illicit works left largely unremarkable and politically neutral art, a decision that nods to the state-sanctioned Socialist Realist movement that preceded it. Socialist Realism was the official creative doctrine of the USSR since the early 1930s. Socialist Realist art was tightly curated by the state to celebrate the proletariat, Marxist-Leninist philosophy, Soviet leadership, and everyday life in the Soviet Union. As a result, artists who wanted to create subversive works had to do so in an exceedingly nuanced and subtle manner. The avoidance of overtly political topics allowed those artists some degree of plausible deniability (Bown 1998; Gutkin 1999; Clark 2002). By burying political messages in allegory, metaphor, and symbolism, or claiming that paintings were merely "art for art's sake"[1] – as opposed to verbally assaulting or taunting political elites directly – artists can distance themselves from contentious and punishable political expression, which has especially severe consequences in the authoritarian context.

This art world trend also continued into the late 1960s through the 1980s in the Soviet Union when Socialist Realism intersected with the style of Western pop art to produce the Sots Art movement. Sots Art artists repeatedly denied the overtly political messaging of their work despite intuitively critical political themes and subjects. Sots Art artists, as well as the contemporary artists inspired by them, achieved this plausible deniability by leaning heavily on humor and satire. For example, the obtrusive red stripe in Erik Bulatov's 1971-72 Red Horizon mirrored a Soviet citizen's inability to escape the Party's presence, and the Siberian Blue Noses Group painted a boxer-clad Putin in bed with former American president George Bush and al-Qaeda leader Osama bin Laden, poking fun at geopolitics through the lens of satirized masculinity, sexuality, and conservatism.

This aversion to political themes in creative content is also common among late-Soviet graffiti artists. Explicitly dissident graffiti was rare in this period. Instead, artists buried their political messages in socially critical or merely aesthetic casings. During this time, graffiti in the Soviet Union was largely limited to a select number of societal groups: *fanaty*, punks, hippies, and rockers (Bushnell 1990). The first group, *fanaty* (football fans in English), broadcast their allegiance to a particular club – FC Spartak Moscow, FC Dinamo Moscow, or CSKA (in Russian, *TsSKA Moskva*), for example – by painting the team's name or the team captain's name on the walls of Moscow's residential outskirts (Bushnell 1990). Fan graffiti quickly devolved to reflect the belligerence of its artists' raucous, boyish, and instigative behavior, such as stencils that encourage fans to "Fight for Zenith," a football club in Saint Petersburg. While fan graffiti continued to avoid political targets, their messaging and casings developed over time to reflect more extreme gang lifestyles, excessively vulgar speech, and violent expressions of both pride and contempt. At the same time, punk groups, ideologically opposed to figures of authority, also began to systematically tattoo the Soviet streets with their chosen badge – the anarchist symbol. This symbol, a capital letter A inside of a circle, was intended to critique the political system without targeting individual politicians, policies, or institutions, which might attract the state's attention and beget a negative response.

Deviating from the plausible deniability of fan and punk graffiti, hippie youth used the walls to openly promote pacifism. For example, groups such as the Free Initiative drew peace signs and wrote absurdist slogans to promote lovingkindness, such as "Make Hair Everywhere," and "Long Live Butterflies" (Bushnell 1990, 14).[2] While state threats of detention and arrest frequently derailed their demonstrative efforts, pacifists remained undeterred to speak out against the wars that they opposed, and graffiti proved to be an available medium for expressing these political concerns. Alienated from the censored Soviet press and public sphere,

Soviet antiwar demonstrators used graffiti to publicize their opposition to the Soviet Union's 1979 invasion of Afghanistan, the United States' imperial expansion, and the heightened threat posed by Cold War nuclear power, using slogans such as "End the Shameful War in Afghanistan," "Out of Afghanistan," "Gorbachev – Murderer of Afghan Children," and "Russian Children's Skin is Just as Sensitive to Napalm as Afghan Skin" (Bushnell 1990, 15). This form of communication remained so unusual that political graffiti often set off KGB investigations and sometimes political trials (Bushnell 1990, 113).

Rock-and-roll enthusiasts took to graffiti and street art somewhat later than their sports fan, punk, and hippie peers, after Soviet leadership softened its stance toward Soviet-born rock-and-roll artists in the late 1970s. Through regional tours and relatable lyrics, Soviet rock musicians began to develop domestic fan bases. Rock devotees began dedicating graffiti to their favorite singers, painting the words to popular songs on public walls. State and public support for foreign artists soon followed: in early 1979, American blues artist B.B. King played "22 sold-out gigs in five cities: Moscow, Saint Petersburg (then Leningrad), Baku, Yerevan, and Tbilisi" (Baker 2015), and in May of the same year, British crooner Elton John played an eight-concert tour across the Soviet Union. By 1983, graffiti writers used their platform to laud foreign rockers, from the Beatles and AC/DC to the Sex Pistols and Led Zeppelin.

Then, in June 1983, minister of ideology Konstantin Chernenko proclaimed to the Communist Party Central Committee that the rockers were causing ideological and aesthetic harm to Soviet youth. Soviet leadership responded swiftly by canceling rock-and-roll performances, censoring lyrics, and requiring the dissolution of many non-conformist musical groups. Those in the domestic rock-and-roll community reacted with a wave of creative changes: Musicians reworked band names to sever their future projects from their former identities (now deemed un-Soviet by the authorities); the black market capitalized on selling outlawed tapes; and thousands of performers simply declined to register themselves with state officials, further enhancing their authenticity as subversive and counterculture (Bushnell 1990, 12). In 1985, a little over a year later, Mikhail Gorbachev took over as general secretary of the Communist Party of the Soviet Union and promoted the policies of *perestroika* and *glasnost. Perestroika,* loosely translated into English as "restructuring," introduced pseudo-market economic reforms to the Communist model, and *glasnost* (in English, openness) established a more transparent government and encouraged free debate. The latter policy resulted in a substantial loosening of media censorship and increased individual speech freedoms. In tandem with the opening created by these top-down reforms, the Soviet rock-and-roll subculture made a state-supported comeback.

Figure 2.1. "Tsoi Zhiv." Thirty years after Tsoi's death, fans continue to use street art to memorialize Kino's fallen frontman as a symbol of peace, youth, and independence. Here, Tsoi's face is shown alongside the words "Tsoi Lives." August 2011. Tsoi Wall, Old Arbat, Moscow, Russia. (Photo: Alexis Lerner)

Through 1988, the amount of graffiti about rock-and-roll continued to increase, centered primarily within permitted graffiti spaces known as "fan walls." Viktor Tsoi, the frontman of celebrated Leningrad rock group Kino, inspired late-Soviet Muscovite youth through his many albums, allegedly wholesome lifestyle, and well-crafted lyrics. Many of Kino's albums were *samizdat* (self-produced and self-distributed), as the band lacked state support. The authorities marked Kino's frontman as an undesirable figure on account of his anti-establishment and antiwar themes. In 1990, Tsoi died tragically in a (sober) car accident. Brokenhearted followers mourned Tsoi's death by memorializing his life through street art. Along the Old Arbat in downtown Moscow and throughout the streets of Russia's urban centers, fans still pay their respects by dedicating ritualistic street art to their beloved hero (Zimberg

Figure 2.2. The stylized SS is a symbol for the Schutzstaffel, the institution responsible for surveillance and genocidal terror during Nazi rule. More generally, it is used as a symbol of support for Nazi ideology regarding Aryan racial purity. This SS lightning bolt is located on the heavily trafficked bridge that adjoins mainland Saint Petersburg and Vasilievskii Island. July 2011. Saint Petersburg, Russia. (Photo: Alexis Lerner)

2012). Even today, Tsoi Wall remains a sacred, dynamic, and unbuffed fan wall (Figure 2.1).

Street art can reflect *all* marginalized voices, regardless of perceived moral standing. As such, the fascist revival of the early 1970s and its impact on the Soviet street narrative cannot be ignored. Graffitied far-right, white supremacist, and xenophobic slogans such as "Russia for Russians," "Heil Hitler," and "14/88" began to appear frequently in urban centers by the early 1980s. Seeking maximum exposure in the public consciousness, the leather-jacketed youth became active graffiti writers, especially outside of Moscow's urban center (Bushnell 1990, 17). Fascist graffiti – swastikas, the lightning-bolted SS insignia, and antisemitic slurs – long outlasted the Soviet Union, and slogans such as "Love Your Own Race" continue to permeate the public spaces across the contemporary post-Soviet sphere (Figure 2.2).

The graffiti written by skinhead youth does not exist in a vacuum. In response, an anti-fascist revivalist counterculture – reminiscent of the punk

Figure 2.3. "Smash Fascism." 2011. Budapest, Hungary. (Photo: Alexis Lerner)

Figure 2.4. "Good Night White Pride." 2011. Prague, Czech Republic.
(Photo: Alexis Lerner)

writers active a decade prior – took to Russian streets as early as 1983 to demand a political existence void of fascism and fascists. Anti-fascist writers engaged their counterparts in discourse by crossing out fascist symbols or dwarfing them with peace signs. Today, anti-fascist activists, commonly referred to as members of the European Antifa movement, paint graffiti about life sans extreme nationalism. Intolerant and Antifa graffiti, alike, can be seen today across the region, from Berlin and Budapest to Saint Petersburg and Minsk, with slogans such as "Russia without Fascism," "Smash Fascism" (Figure 2.3), "Art Without Fascism," "Yellow, Red, White, Black, We Are All the Same," and "Good Night White Pride" (Figure 2.4).

In the twenty-first century, the graffiti counterculture is no longer limited to a community of hippies or punks who also happen to write. Indeed, contemporary graffiti artists use large-scale murals, complex stencils, and multicolored freehand to challenge national narratives, to take sides on political issues, and to mobilize otherwise isolated actors to support political causes. For example, in Misha Most's Kremlin-adjacent wall painting (used as the first anecdote of this book), Most makes public the constitutional right of free speech in Russia, suggesting that citizens have lived under authoritarian rule for so long that they have become complacent and have forgotten their civic rights. Most's contemporary, Kirill Kto,[3] suggests that political advocacy graffiti like Most's are not only a civic duty, but also a moral duty. Kto is a second-wave artist known for his combative social commentary and aversion to co-opted or commissioned work.

In a 2011 conversation, Kto said, "The general right to expression in the street on any theme is fiction and voluntarism. You should be reliable for a place, and you should write there impudently." This begs the question: how did the Soviet Union's graffiti-writing communities become the politically conscious and countercultural movement that exists today?

In interviews across the post-Soviet and post-communist European region, the graffiti and street art community's present-day leaders unanimously credit a small group of breakdancers as having inspired the counterculture movement. Colloquially known as breakers, these dancers served not only as cultural transmitters of street art from the West to the Soviet Union in the late 1980s, but also as transporters of the art form from the Soviet to the post-Soviet period.

Breakers entered the Soviet counterculture mix around 1985, when they began to meet at schools, at *sportzaly* (Soviet-style sport centers), and at informal breakdancing festivals. By 1986, officials noticed the growing dance trend and elected to sponsor more serious, cross-Soviet competitions, choosing cities like Kaliningrad, Donetsk, Moscow, and Saint Petersburg to host the large events (Bushnell 1990, 18). Party organizers identified talented breakers from across the Soviet Union and invited them to participate in the festivals, paying for their transportation, food, and local housing as incentives.

Despite government efforts to expand a subculture that they viewed as positive, the original breaker community in Saint Petersburg, Russia, remained close-knit and insular. The scene was still small enough that the breakers could meet to dance, undisturbed, in two or three secluded spots across the city. In an interview, Basket – an early proponent of Saint Petersburg's breaker culture – shared his narrative of the moment amid Gorbachev's reforms when the medium shifted from breaking to writing graffiti. "One of my friends told me that they wanted to show me something special. They told me that it was a secret and not to tell anyone." Basket continued (2011):

> I had no VHS player, nor did any of my friends. In Russia, only politicians had VHS players – we didn't have them. In Saint Petersburg, there was one coffee shop – a cafe – near Petrogradskaia metro station. It was very small... just three tables. And in this coffee shop there was a VHS player and a TV.

There, they had three videotapes – only three videotapes. There were only three of us there because we were about to see some secret information. We didn't have any money – only enough for a cup of tea or coffee. So we would sit and wait, and started watching while drinking a cup of coffee.

The movie that Basket watched was *Beat Street.* Produced in the United States in 1984, it tells the inspirational story of three young men – a hip-hop artist, a breaker, and a graffiti writer – who try to achieve success from the socio-economic depths of the Bronx slums. In the Saint Petersburg cafe, the breakers studied the film's novel dance styles and breaking techniques. Feeling like they had come across something momentous and exciting, they also became inspired to create graffiti that emulated the New York City breakers in its attention to color and style. Ponosov (2018) suggests that Basket knew about graffiti prior to watching *Beat Street.* He adds that Basket accompanied his father on a business trip to Amsterdam as a young teen, where he met up – and was arrested – with a group of Dutch graffiti writers.)

At this time in Saint Petersburg, there were a limited number of shops – reportedly no more than five – where one could buy spray paint. Even then, the only colors available in these shops were neutral tones, such as yellow, white, and gray. Determined to experiment with color and texture, Basket and his friends knew that they needed to find more paint. Riga, at the time was at the forefront of various creative movements and an intuitive place to travel to acquire a wider variety of paint colors. Basket said in 2011:

> The only paint factory for the whole Soviet Union was in Riga. So I took money from two or three friends and went to Riga where the factory was. In this shop, I bought all the colors. It wasn't like it is now, of course, but you could get, maybe, twenty or twenty-five colors. One can cost two rubles then.

Lacking tutorials and teachers, the Soviet breakers resorted to trial and error with the basic tools available to them. At first, Soviet artists stuck to simple tagging, the practice of writing one's name either in unadorned freehand or layered bubble letters. Like artists around the globe, Soviet writers developed tags, or stylized signatures of self-assigned pseudonyms, by which they were called for the remainder of their careers as graffiti artists. (One artist who goes by the pseudonym Make jokes that his son did not inherit a patronymic from his father's given name but instead from his graffiti name – Makovich (Polskaya 2012).) The act of tagging served to signal ownership, to communicate that one was the dominant actor in a neighborhood, and/or to achieve notoriety (Gastman 2011). In many cases, the tag became more famous and more dominating than the artist who created it, an idea that I expand upon in Chapter Six.

At first, there were only a few known graffiti writers in the USSR: Basket from Saint Petersburg, Vadim Krys (*Krysa* is the Russian word for rat) from Riga, and Maks Navigator from Kaliningrad. In these early years, the ramifications for destroying – or improving, depending on one's perception of the practice – private property remained unclear. This uncertainty of consequence often drove artists to react to police presence in a suspicion-inducing manner.

On a clear afternoon in 1988, for example, the aforementioned trio of graffiti artists dropped their spray cans and broke into a sprint when a squad car unexpectedly rolled past. Terrified, they ducked into a Soviet-style courtyard and realized that the enclosed area had only one exit, which was now blocked by the officer and his squad car. When the officer probed into what the breakers had done wrong to warrant such fear, they explained that their act was not criminal, and in fact, that they were only painting. Per the police officer's request, the group agreed to bring him to their mural to show him. To the trio's surprise, the officer did not punish the writers for vandalism, nor did he demand a monetary exchange for his silence on their assumed crime, but instead complimented them on their artistic skills.

This vignette illustrates the lack of precedent for graffiti dealings in the late Soviet Union days; at the time, there existed no legal ruling or cultural norm that deemed graffiti a criminal, destructive, or morally problematic action. According to Basket, some *babushki* (elderly Russian women or grandmothers) supported the artists because their pieces brought beauty and color to their otherwise dull, cement-lined apartment complexes. In a 2013 interview at a vegan cafe in an affluent residential area of downtown Moscow, artist Anton Litvin reflected on his own public works in the late 1980s, stating, "Today, we realize that at that time, our actions faced zero resistance. Neither television nor the police stood in our way" (Litvin 2013).

As the Soviet Union teetered on the precipice of collapse in 1990, Moscow-based artist Dmitri Vrubel brought graffiti to the previously inaccessible east side of the Berlin Wall. In "My God, Help Me to Survive This Deadly Love," which is a depiction of an actual photograph, communist leaders Leonid Brezhnev of the Soviet Union and Erich Honecker of East Germany are shown locked in a kiss (Figure 2.5).

With the fall of the Berlin Wall, information about Western culture flowed rapidly into the fifteen newly formed post-Soviet states as well

Figure 2.5. "My God, Help Me to Survive This Deadly Love" by Dmitri Vrubel. In an interview with Andrei Borzenko in Kommersant (2014), Vrubel said that the painting was about "total love" and unity – the opposite of the Berlin Wall, which was designed to "separate two worlds." Vrubel painted the original mural in 1990 and restored the work in 2009. This photograph is of the restoration. 2013. East Side Gallery. Berlin, Germany. (Photo: Alexis Lerner)

as into Soviet satellite states across post-communist Europe. Hip-hop music, break dancing, and graffiti gained widespread popularity, and local artists began relying on Western magazines and videos to learn new techniques. In Moscow, members of break dance team and hip-hop association Da Boogie Crew, who often appeared on television and radio promoting hip-hop and graffiti culture, "opened a special shop dedicated exclusively to [selling] graffiti products" and hosting educational and social programs (Ponosov 2018, 37).

Basket also capitalized on graffiti's increased popularity. Not only did he help create *Hip-Hop Info*, the first Russian magazine devoted to the graffiti and hip-hop counterculture, but he also began to run a school for artists in Saint Petersburg. Under the guidance of Basket and his friends, students familiarized themselves with the history and social norms of graffiti while also perfecting their painting techniques. Many students participated in Basket's program with the wide-eyed hope that it would help them to become famous. In a 2011 interview, Basket said that the schools were often more about making money than inspiring the next generation. He joked that he and friends taught "a lot of children of rich people who wanted to be cool, but who did not actually feel passionate about learning to do graffiti." Cynicism aside, the 1990s were a politically tumultuous time when many young people found themselves involved with organized crime and drugs, and the graffiti community provided a safe and supportive outlet – a respite, even – for this demographic (Partizaning 2012; Most, 2011; Ponosov 2018, 38).

Having originated in proclamations about flower power and football fanaticism, Soviet and post-Soviet graffiti had a popular explosion in the late 1980s and early post-Soviet period. In the 1970s and 1980s, graffiti was gently subversive and mildly countercultural in that its content was, in select examples, pacifist or anti-fascist. Each graffito was unremarkable; these works were not designed to stand out. Even graffiti with a semi-political theme – an international symbol of peace or the lyrics to beloved Kino songs about dysfunction and change – were only that: emblems propagated transnationally or lyrics to a song that someone else once sang. And while signs and symbols surely carry meaning beyond the overt, this careful concealment of political content in socially relevant or aesthetically pleasing casings allowed artists (and their readers) to feign political disinterest, an act that would safeguard them – for the time being – from political targeting and intimidation.

Chapter Three

Painting for the Highest Bidder

The graffiti craze was growing quickly in the former Soviet states, and everyone wanted to take advantage of the hype. At home, Basket, Vadim Krys, and Maks Navigator – the *grandfathers of graffiti,* as other writers affectionately call them (Basket 2020) – opened the informal graffiti schools discussed in Chapter Two. Meanwhile, Western actors and organizations entered the post-Soviet market to capitalize on untapped talent and youth in search of trends to adopt. At first, this transmission of Western culture happened informally, through television shows and print magazines that promoted Western brands and styles. In particular, the advent of MTV (Music Television) east of the now-defunct Berlin Wall amplified the artform to resemble the American style more closely as it became an international trend.

The MTV channel was first launched in the United States in 1981. The wildly popular channel initially operated as a continuously streaming platform for showcasing music videos by stars such as Michael Jackson and Madonna, with interludes by five so-called video jockeys, or VJs (Marks and Tannenbaum 2012). Over the subsequent decade, the channel's following grew, not only defining American youth culture but also reflecting it. By the time MTV reached the collapsing Soviet Union on March 8, 1991, the network was in its prime (Shogren 1991a).

MTV – and specifically its London-based affiliate, MTV Europe – broadcasted popular music videos "24 hours a day over Leningrad Cable Television ... [to] about half a million viewers" (Shogren 1991b). This steady stream of videos – including scenes featuring hip-hop, breakdancing, and graffiti writing – aided the global transmission of American and European popular culture directly into some 140,000 Soviet households (Shogren 1991b). Televised depictions of graffiti culture in the early- to mid-1990s were reinforced by the cross-border influx of Western graffiti magazines, such as Norway's *Fat Cap,* the United States' *Under Cover,*

Crazy Kings, and *Can Control*, Australia's *Hype*, and the United Kingdom's *Graphotism*.

So-called first-wave artists in the post-Soviet region worshipped and emulated what they saw in these television shows and magazines, following suit by covering train cars with complex tags that referenced self-designated pseudonyms, whether individual or for a crew (e.g., Rus crew, BfG, and Zachem). For these artists, the illegal act of creating graffiti was fundamental to the artform and, in turn, to the counterculture. Describing the quality of illegal graffiti, Jennifer Baird and Claire Taylor put it best when they said that graffiti images, such as the tags used in the first wave, were intended to kick "against authority with what they say or depict," and that "their primary and defining characteristic is spatial insubordination, that is, appearing on surfaces where they have no right to be" (2010, 74).

Corporate Sponsorship of Legal Festivals

At this point, Western corporations – interested in appealing to young creatives – began to participate – formally and directly – in the spread of graffiti culture within the post-Soviet region. These major corporations – Nescafé, Nike, and Monster, for example – began to sponsor large festivals throughout the newly accessible post-Soviet region. These festivals, known among artist communities as graffiti festivals or graffiti jams, sponsored graffiti-writing competitions that were lucrative in prizes and/ or renown. These major festivals were, in part, inspired by small, neighborhood festivals organized in the mid-1990s by local community centers that were interested in engaging local youth and directing them away from the drug and gang culture that was prevalent in the early-to-mid-1990s (Basket 2012). The first corporate sponsor of a regional graffiti festival was Nescafé, an instant coffee manufacturer operating under the umbrella of the Swiss-based food conglomerate Nestlé. Nescafé – the product – formally entered the post-Soviet market in 1995, and the company sponsored its first festival, also called a graffiti jam, in 1999 (Ponosov 2018, 88).

Along with other winter activities, such as competitive snowboarding, the Nescafé festival sponsored a graffiti competition, inviting young artists to drink its coffee and compete with one another. In these competitions, artists painted centrally located, large-scale murals on intentionally uncontroversial topics. Nescafé hired Basket, who had already established himself as a top artist of the first wave, as an expert judge who adjudicated on the applicants' proposed projects. Basket reflected on this experience in a 2011 interview:

Every day, there was a theme, or a challenge, that each artist had to accomplish. The applicants brought me about thirty or forty sketches. I took their sketches into the tent, where there was alcohol and some food, and went through them. I chose the ten best sketches and announced to the artists, "Okay, you paint here, you paint here, and you paint there." There were ten guys, all Russians from Moscow. These ten guys were freezing while they were drawing.

Cold weather aside, there were many benefits to artists for participating in graffiti festivals. First, newer artists developed actual and potential partnerships and collaborations with leading graffiti artists and major international corporations. Writers coveted an association with or, even better, a sponsorship from a counterculture clothier or a popular brand-name paint company, such as Rush, Arton, or Trane. Even if festivals did not lead to any major formal collaborations, novice artists hoped that their participation inspired spin-off financial and professional benefits – for example, painting the façade of a local restaurant, representing a smaller paint or clothing company, and/or being invited to other competitions, including more prestigious competitions domestically or abroad.

The second benefit to artists was durability, as participation in the sanctioned festivals meant that artists got to paint in prime locations, unencumbered by the usual threats of interference, legal repercussions, and post-production buffers. Graffiti festivals protected artists' work both from traditional forms of interference, such as police officers and community watch networks, as well as from other artists who might otherwise paint over their work (the ultimate insult among graffiti artists). Because festivals are widely attended, crowds may prevent other artists from painting illegally over a festival work, and their intrinsic state approval increases the likelihood that a work is along a major road and/or is protected by some form of security. Additionally, works painted during graffiti competitions tend to be expansive and intricate, and as a result, they physically dwarfed post-hoc writing on or near festival paintings.

Artists at festivals can also paint without legal repercussions, such as those outlined in the amendments to the Criminal Code of the Russian Federation for destructive behavior or those imposed by the Criminal Code of Ukraine for hooliganism in 2001. This gives their work another form of durability. Without exception, each of my interviewees recalled a past run-in with local authorities.[1] One spoke about a night when the police determined that their painting on a bridge was a threat to national security; another reminisced coyly about the multiple times that she was stopped by the police but released without demerit on account of her gender; and another shared the story of the time when she and some friends were apprehended by the authorities for writing graffiti, only to be invited to paint a colorful mural in the police headquarters in exchange for a speedy and paperwork-free release. Older writers explained how, over time, they simply learned how to avoid spots frequented by the police. Legal graffiti festivals provided an opportunity for artists to paint without having to engage in such cat-and-mouse evasion.

Further, graffiti festivals provide durability in the form of protection from state-funded buffers, those who local authorities hire indirectly or directly to remove, powerwash, or paint over existing graffiti. Buffing has two motivations: to establish the reputation of a place as "clean," "sterile," or otherwise "appropriately respectful" and to enforce censorship.[2] Government-led buffing began in the mid-1990s in Russia in response to the heightened visible presence of street art and graffiti. A buffed painting implies that it was a controversial, vulgar, undesirable, and, most of all, unsanctioned message.

In an August 2011 interview, a Saint Petersburg graffiti writer who goes by the name Light Graffiti shared an anecdote about a writer in Moscow who waged a personal war with these seemingly tireless street buffers. On a given night, the friend would paint an extravagant and detailed mural on a quiet side street only to have the buffers arrive in the morning to clear the wall. The friend would return the following night to replicate their piece and, again, the buffers would return the next day. No longer was the battle directly between the writers and the police, or the writers and the political authorities, but rather it became a matter of situational absurdity between two parties – the writers and the buffers.[3] Participating in graffiti festivals alleviates these pressures for artists. No longer do they need to worry about state-sanctioned buffers removing or covering their work – or even other artists painting over their work – which results in more opportunities for their art to be seen by passersby.

The third benefit for participating artists was payment. Of course, there were prizes for the best pieces at some of the festivals, as well as the possibility of getting noticed and hired for other paid contracts. But much of the compensation was non-monetary. During the long, cold festival days, artistic labor was rewarded with food, alcohol, coffee, and paint in excess (Most 2011; ZUKCLUB 2012).

The Nescafé festival recurred annually, with other organizations following suit (such as the Realisation graffiti jam of 2003), and artists reportedly anticipated these festivals eagerly. Ponosov (2018, 40) explained that "It was the perfect time to meet people in person, exchange views, and communicate a common interest." Basket (2011) remembers, "... a couple guys who later joined my crew [participated in the early graffiti festivals]. I remember Misha Most was there, too. This festival really showed everyone in the second wave how to do graffiti. After this

Figure 3.1. Prostitutes. Painted by C215. Photographed in November 2018. ArtPlay, Moscow, Russia. (Photo: Alexis Lerner)

festival, the normal tagging and the crews really started." Indeed, the camaraderie these festivals fostered led to what artists call the *second wave* of Russian graffiti writers.

This second wave was "younger, larger, and cooler," joked Basket in 2011. This generation of writers did not need to create the artform from scratch – literally searching for the last vestiges of paint in a crumbling Soviet Union. Instead, second wave writers were able to look to existing institutions – MTV, Western graffiti magazines and films, and writers from the first wave – to acquire new skills, techniques, and methods of practice. Many prominent contemporary street artists, such as Most, Kto, and Make, emerged during the second wave (Basket 2012; Ponosov 2018).

Second-wave artists were eager to establish their own innovative styles. Soon, everyone writing both illegally and legally had a logo, somewhat like their own unique, personal watermark. For example, at the ArtPlay outdoor art gallery in Moscow, French graffiti artist C215 places a stencil of his logo next to a painting of two alleged prostitutes – societal outsiders (Figure 3.1). Some second-wave artists went beyond the streets, for example creating *samizdat* publications[4] about post-Soviet counter-cultural trends, such as Make's *Outline* magazine. "For most artists in the 90s, street art was less about politics and more like lots of advertisements. You can tell how graffiti became more of an industry [during the second wave]." Most lamented in 2011, reflecting upon the decade:

> You can buy the caps, the gloves. It's like coming to a shop to become a fisherman. You buy these things, the camouflage. You put the things in the pockets. You say that you want to be a graffiti artist. You buy two videos, a couple magazines, ten different cans of spray paint specifically designed for graffiti. It's really less interesting from certain points of view. I remember the old times, when we used to mix the paint ourselves. You feel the process more. You make the cap yourself; you make the color yourself. It's a bit different.[5] You learn from the photos of your friends, not from magazines or on the internet. It's a different thing now. Graffiti has become an industry where any businessman can put his money into it.

Most recalls the graffiti jams of the late twentieth century and early twenty-first century with disdain. In the same interview, he reflected upon that first festival in 1999:

> I saw all of it – the legal parts, the legal jams run by Nescafé coffee. Only in Russia can this happen. They put up a big wall of this shitty material – pressed wood or something. Basket was the judge and the organizer. It was always during the winter, so it was –10, –15 degrees [Celsius], and there were snowboarders, and everybody was drinking this coffee and doing graffiti. I didn't like it at all. I went one time and spray-painted colorful blasts all over the wall and wrote: "Graffiti Should Be Without Frames." The authorities and the media heavily influenced everyone [to create in a legally sanctioned place and manner] because the stuff that we saw at legal festivals was really all that we knew.

Most continued his lament, critiquing what he saw as a popular acceptance of legal graffiti writing,[6] at a cost to traditionally subversive graffiti-writing culture:

> Nobody was thinking [about the festival], "Oh, this is nice, painting on the wall." They were saying, "Oh these guys want to make the city better, they want to make it beautiful." The graffiti scene in the 1990s was pretty romanticized. A lot of guys started their careers at these legal jams and then went on to work as legal writers. Not a lot of illegal writing came out of this.

People who like to do something beautiful, they are usually less destructive. This is why legal and illegal writers belong to separate categories. There was an outline at the beginning [explaining how to do graffiti], but we started to break the rules; I started using roller paint, working with the environment, and other methods that were different from standard graffiti writing.

Artists like Most critique legal festivals as undermining many of graffiti's fundamental qualities – opposition to authority, anonymity, and subversiveness – thereby robbing graffiti of its ability to circumvent censorship and offer genuine critique. When graffiti is illegal, works are painted anonymously in the shadows of dark back alleys. But through jams, the mainstream culture welcomes graffiti artists and provides them with what they need to paint on private property in broad daylight.[7] In the latter context, communities welcome otherwise outlawed graffiti artists back into the social fold. As such, the celebration of legal graffiti ostracizes illegal writers, who pride themselves on their ability and unspoken mandate to express some form of Truth (Kto 2012). Kirill Kto ruminated about this obligation that graffiti artists express Truth in February 2012:

> There is a tacit consent among writers that we have all the tools, and therefore the responsibility, to tell something as it truly is. Still, most continue to write their names, which – to me – only confirms their social lethargy and indifference to political change. To me, name graffiti and loyalty to the existing regime are one and the same. If you are quietly engaged in your own business and do not react in any way to an event in society, then you agree with the current political and social course of your society.

When integrated into legal festivals, graffiti artists are no longer able to express some kind of Truth but rather are limited by the political and aesthetic preferences of the festival organizers, sponsors, and judges. Whereas illegal graffiti might critique the legitimacy of a president by, for example, painting their head on the body of a cartoon character, festival art would not show subversive works like this. If a political leader is shown at all, they will be shown as strong and virtuous – in military dress, for example – and decorated with patriotic symbols such as national flags and bold diagonal lines (pointing upward toward a brilliant future, à la Malevich and the early twentieth-century Suprematists). A legal mural is more likely to show cultural or literary figures, societal heroes that symbolize values like unity and nationalism, often depicted in front of historically or culturally relevant backgrounds. So-called legal graffiti is no longer a nuisance but rather a prized tangible, which external actors can possess, sell, dominate, and control. The veil is lifted and the artist – no longer anonymous – steps through to the venerating corporate world, simultaneously losing legitimacy within the graffiti realm (McDonald 2001, 169).

Not only did festivals co-opt illegal graffiti and promote a self-censored version of public art, but they also provided opportunities for novice writers to create art that international corporations, such as Nike, used to sell their products. Again, I define co-optation as when a previously critical individual or group of individuals publicly trades loyalty for provisions (Lerner 2020, 5).

Most critiqued this practice in 2011, calling it vandalism:

> For example, Nike organized a jam. They gave graffiti artists a white shoe and had an exhibition to show it and reproduce it and don't pay you or anything. Vandalism meets consumerism when artists are exploited to create a consumer product. It's free advertising, and they make the young kids do it. There are also skateboard jams here where graffiti artists paint skateboards for corporate sponsors. I have mine here though. I broke it and put a cast on it. But the young kids made these beautiful skateboards so that the companies can hang in the shops. I consider it a bad thing when graffiti artists are used to design a product for free.

Graffiti jams occurred beyond Russia and throughout the post-Soviet and post-communist European region in the early twenty-first century – in places like Łódź in 2002, Almaty, Kazakhstan, in 2003, Kyiv in 2003, Wroclaw, Poland, in 2010, and in Minsk in 2018 (Parfan 2010, 42). Exactly like in Moscow, these festivals were frequently sponsored by domestic companies like Belgazprombank in Belarus or international corporations such as Mars (the parent company behind the Snickers chocolate bar) in the case of Almaty and Kyiv. Efforts to commodify graffiti also took place outside of Eastern and Central Europe and Eurasia.

Consider Bristol (England)-based graffiti artist Banksy, for example, who in the late twentieth and early twenty-first century became one of the world's most famous public artists for his anti-war, anti-capitalist, and anti-establishment art. Banksy's stenciled political satire is frequently chiseled out of surrounding brick and thrown into museums or sold in galleries with exorbitant price tags (Trickey 2015; Ellsworth-Jones 2013). Artists in these situations rarely, if ever, benefit financially from these sales of their non-commissioned works (perhaps explaining why Banksy designed his 2006 "Girl With Balloon" framed painting on canvas to self-destruct after selling for $1.4 million at a Sotheby's auction. See Reyburn 2018 and Banksy 2018). By presenting subversive, transient,

Figure 3.2. Poster for GraffFest, a legal festival sponsored by major Russian corporations, magazines, local galleries, the City of Saint Petersburg, and the United States Department of State. August 2011. Saint Petersburg, Russia. (Photo: Alexis Lerner)

and anonymous graffiti and street art as *lasting* and *collectible*, corporations commodify the previously public work and undermine the artform.

Foreign Entities and Graffiti Jams

This "counterculture" framing was used to sell not only material goods – skateboards and high-priced, Western sneakers – but also to sell ideas, such as patriotism and nationalism. This explains why, as early as 2011, governmental institutions began sponsoring their own graffiti festivals in Russia. For example, the Government of Saint Petersburg partnered with the United States Consulate General in Saint Petersburg – along with about eighteen different sponsors, including magazine outlets, television channels, and technology companies interested in attracting counterculture youth – to co-sponsor *GraffFest* (see its flyer in Figure 3.2). The six-day festival in August 2011 was specifically designed to attract the top trendsetters in their mid-to-late twenties. ·

In an interview at the time, the GraffFest director, Nick Hopp, said that proposed murals with political, social, or religious sentiment were not chosen for inclusion in the festival (Hopp 2011). This tendency to avoid contentious themes through pre-censorship is not uncommon for legal festival planning committees, who must gain funding and permission for these events. According to Hopp, the goal of the festival was not to comment on policy or ideology but rather to beautify the city.

The US Consulate's Public Diplomacy Desk Officer for Russia, Ray Castillo, said in an unclassified email that the Embassy co-sponsored the festival as one facet of a year-long effort, called "American Seasons," to introduce the Russian public to contemporary US artists (Embassy Moscow Official 2011). He went on to say:

> As part of the "reset" in relations between the United States and Russia, the US Embassy in Moscow has launched an ambitious, year-long cultural program entitled "American Seasons." The name "American Seasons" is homage to Sergei Diaghilev and his efforts at the beginning of the last century to introduce Russian culture to Europe. "American Seasons" is designed to bring a similarly wide spectrum of cultural offerings to the Russian public in order to introduce them to contemporary artists from the United States. The program started with a tour by a troupe whose name has become synonymous with contemporary American dance, the Alvin Ailey American Dance Theater, and will run through the spring with performances of the Chicago Symphony Orchestra in April 2012.
>
> In Saint Petersburg, we were approached by an NGO partner, CEC Artslink, about supporting the participation of an American graffiti artist in the

festival. The Consulate co-sponsored the artist as part of the larger American Seasons goal of bringing a broad range of contemporary American artists to Russia. We have supported a wide variety of artists, from contemporary plastic and performance artists who took part in the "New York Minute" exhibition at the Garage Center for Contemporary Culture, through a diverse collection of musical groups representing genres of American music that are little-known to Russian audiences, to well-established and internationally renowned visual artists such as Annie Leibovitz, whose work is currently displayed at the Pushkin Museum of Fine Arts in Moscow. As for the graffiti artist, the medium and the festival also served our larger objective of youth outreach in Russia, reaching younger audiences and getting them interested in America and American Culture.

At GraffFest, graffiti was commodified not for money, as it was with Nike's jam, or for social capital, as with Nescafe's festivals; rather, in this case, two major governmental bodies representing the United States and the Russian Federation commodified graffiti in the name of ideology and cultural diplomacy.[8] This phenomenon of foreign entities – individual nations or international organizations – interfering with domestic politics by pushing forward a particular (often Western) political or social agenda through graffiti jams is not limited to this example. In 2019, the EU partnered with other diplomatic groups operating in Azerbaijan to host the "Maiden Tower. To Be a Woman." festival in Baku, Azerbaijan.[9] In a residential district of the city, Swedish artist Carolina Falkholt painted a graphic mural of a transgender adult, displaying clearly both male and female sexual organs. Falkholt's work was received with community outrage, prompting the Baku City Executive Power to issue a formal statement demanding that foreign visitors and artists exercise respect for the local population and reiterating support for culturally appropriate public art (2019):

> Even if Azerbaijan is a multicultural country, it has its own national values and mental characteristics. The visiting guests should take into account that Azerbaijan is a Muslim country, … If within the framework of the festival, artists are allowed to paint graffiti on some building, it does not mean that they should promote values that are against our morals in Azerbaijan … It follows that visitors to Azerbaijan should be allowed to promote their sects as well; this is not the right approach. As for considering this as disrespect for art and craftsmanship, we strongly disagree with this idea. Today, there are buildings in Baku where graffiti has been painted. But our artists did it in such a professional way that we and the visiting guests enjoy [viewing] it.

In the case of both the Saint Petersburg and Baku festivals, foreign governmental entities were able to determine the degree to which local norms influence the rules of participation – a decision that highlights issues of both cultural sensitivity and sovereignty. While a graffiti festival can lead to meaningful cultural exchange, it can also lead to diplomatic tension. Whereas artists were heavily censored in the Saint Petersburg festival (an effort to deal gingerly with already tense US–Russia relations), artists in the Baku jam experienced the absence of such festival censorship, permitting them the freedom to paint against local norms if desired. Whatever other benefits that sponsors may receive, when corporate and government actors use graffiti to convey their chosen messages, they inherently acknowledge the value of the artform in communicating information, leveraging social leaders, and shaping public opinion.

Guerilla Ad Campaigns

Local businesses and schools also began to commodify graffiti in the early twenty-first century by commissioning artists to paint murals on the exterior walls of their buildings. These efforts had seemingly wholesome intentions of beautifying a neighborhood, bridging the gap between residents and the felonious art scene, deterring youths from engaging in illegal graffiti practice, and bringing communities together in the name of shared experience. For example, a Japanese restaurant/nightclub commissioned Basket to paint a blacklight mural near Moscow's Belorusskaia metro station. Such a commission might result in new customers for a business, as passersby might notice the colorful mural and decide to frequent the establishment as a result. In addition, this kind of co-optation can enhance a business's credibility as a fixture within a subset of city life. For example, a hardware shop with a mural of tools on a workbench might signal that the store is a durable, community-situated, and family-owned business worthy of repeat customers, whereas a nightclub might use a darker aesthetic to signal that it is a place for debauchery or countercultural expression.

Meanwhile, the general consumer was to some degree oblivious or apathetic to these arrangements between businesses and artists, and so the artform – at least aesthetically – retained its counterculture character. This allowed companies to use graffiti to signal a fresh, youthful, and urban style for whatever they were selling. For example, in Moscow, from late June 2011 to mid-August 2011 – a period of less than two months – the stenciled "flyers" for everything from car insurance to women's clothing and concert tickets (see Figure 3.3) doubled in frequency. Suddenly, from Red Square to the Old Arbat, the architectural grandeur of the

Figure 3.3. Guerrilla advertisements outside of the metro entrance. June 2011. Moscow, Russia. (Photo: Alexis Lerner)

Tsarist and Soviet eras were abruptly juxtaposed with a deluge of post-Soviet capitalist symbols.

A member of the urban art collective Partizaning and an art historian by trade, Igor Ponosov (2008) explains why businesses find guerrilla advertisements stylistically useful:

> Numerous corporations, recognizing street art messaging potential, promptly adopted its methods and employed them in marketing campaigns (spray, stickers, stencils, creative placement). As a result, advertising tried to mimic art, which originally used some of the advertising techniques (distributions, branding, and such). Urban dwellers have become unable to distinguish original art from commercial.

But, as we have seen earlier, not all second-wave artists appreciate the commodification of graffiti by corporations, governments, and local institutions. Kto (2012), for example, is a vehement opponent of the guerrilla-advertising trend:

> Is there anyone who likes the advertisements, which are everywhere? Or are they legitimized (or pseudo-legal; just because they are paid for does not

make them legitimate, I insist), protected by the fact that someone paid so much for them that it is shameful to tear them up in broad daylight in order to save people from obsessive appeals to buy another car or take a loan with covert conditions and crushing interest rates?

And yet legal works such as advertisements beget income for artists. Basket admits that, for the last ten years or so, he has painted primarily for money, income that supports his wife and children. He reminisces:

> Only in this century have we started to incorporate graffiti and airbrush [into advertisements]. There are many people that want to write only for art's sake but we, too, need money. For the last three or four years, I have only done contracted jobs and, of those, I only do airbrush work.[10] Nobody looks down on you for it. I can call up any graffiti-writing friends and say, "Hey I have twenty bucks if you come paint a wall." That's the human component. We are a part of a community that grew up together. Everybody needs money. Nobody looks down on you (2012).

While some artists, such as Most and Kto, do not agree with Basket's sentiment about the ubiquity and utility of painting contracted graffiti walls, it nevertheless remains true that many artists have benefited financially from the explosive popularity of the artform since the 1990s. In these years, writers have been able to influence youth fads, sell consumer products, and engage in debates surrounding public opinion (even in the United States, it was a graffiti artist – Shepard Fairey – who designed Obama's unofficial, iconic, and lucrative "Hope" campaign poster in 2008). In the twenty-first century, otherwise subversive artists have painted commissioned works for small businesses, international corporations, and nations (both foreign and domestic), whether directly through individual arrangements or indirectly through graffiti jams. By ways of co-optation, third-party commissioners turned a previously subversive tool and platform for communication into one that could be leveraged for persuasion.[11] This had a direct impact on the nature of political graffiti, how it was practiced, and its role in the public space (a phenomenon I discuss at length in Chapter Seven).

Whether it is a local business or the United States Department of State sponsoring a graffiti mural or festival, the co-optation of a previously subversive artform not only floods the public spaces where politically contentious graffiti might exist, but it also dilutes the artform as a communicative tool, as those familiar with the streets as a canvas for political dissent may begin to question the authenticity of a writer or the funding that influences a piece. As businesses and government officials designate prime locations for their own commissioned murals, graffiti writers interested in painting truly subversive works on controversial political topics must look for available space elsewhere. In practice, this often means these artists are forced to move from downtown to residential districts, into more traditional avenues such as galleries, or abroad.

Chapter Four

Art Against the Machine

If the symbol (the peace sign, the swastika) illustrates the graffiti mentality of the Soviet 1980s and the logo (a tag, an advertisement) corresponds to the post-Soviet 1990s, then the graffiti of the 2000s is about critical engagement. By the aughts, many second-wave artists had had enough of blending art and advertisement through commissioned works and legal festivals. Around this time, artists began to view graffiti's purpose as being larger than mere territory appropriation or the pursuit of fame. Second-wave writers began to actively engage their viewership through explicitly political themes, layered social critiques, intertextual references, and the sharing of otherwise censored information. Igor Ponosov (2008) explains:

> The art of the 2000s was a new form of backlash on gallery art and the total commercialization of every[day] life, both virtual and real. Artists turn streets into a battlefield where they fight against advertising for public attention. They mock ads, redefine them and, like pop-art artists, use their contents to create original art.

Indeed, there was a popular push to reclaim graffiti from those who had commodified it and return the artform to the illicit shadows. One such anti-corporate artist, Kto, uses buffing to censor hateful, unappealing, or poorly executed subculture or corporate graffiti, like that of the global name graffiti trend. As shown in Figure 4.1, Kto buffs out the graffiti works of other, usually less experienced, writers to criticize their unfounded attempts to dominate an area that does not "belong" to them; he sees himself as – and, in many ways, is – the social censor of the artist district in a modern-day graffiti turf war.

Kto also damages advertisements and corporate banners, including those that cover Moscow's skyscrapers under renovation, highlighting

Figure 4.1. Buffing. Kirill Kto paints construction-style bricks and hats over works that do not contribute to society, such as the tags that are semi-visible beneath his painted bricks. Pedestrian tunnel between Vinzavod Contemporary Art Center and the Kurskaia Metro Station. March 2012. Moscow, Russia. (Photo: Alexis Lerner)

their transience and societal irrelevance. "Advertisements are not usable," Kto told me in 2012, "so we damage them and harvest the parts to create something usable." For example, as shown in Figure 4.2, Kto cuts slits in heavy vinyl advertisements and repurposes the pieces of cut vinyl. The holes resemble eyes in the mask of a superhero (or supervillain!) – a fitting reference for a graffiti artist who imagines himself a vigilante – and remind onlookers to look beyond corporate interests.

Other second-wave artists joined crews, or groups of artists who painted together, such as ZUKCLUB, Zachem, No Future Forever, Search & Upgrade, and the Group of Change. These artists and groups understood and acknowledged the inherently contentious quality of public art and, by the mid-to-late-2000s, began to innovate in how placement, context, and aesthetics strengthened a message. While select artists experimented with the natural or manmade features of their "canvas" – a spigot, a stone archway, or a tree branch – others tried out new tools of public art, shooting paint from fire extinguishers and drones or replacing paint altogether with moss and yarn (see Figure 4.3).[1]

Figure 4.2. Kirill Kto demonstrates social responsibility by damaging advertisements in Moscow. November 2017. Moscow, Russia. (Photo: Alexis Lerner)

Figure 4.3. Yarn bombing. 2011. Riga, Latvia. (Photo: Alexis Lerner)

Artists especially embraced tools that let them produce at high volume in a brief time. These "fast art" tools included stencils, adopted by Blek le Rat as early as 1981 and popularized by Banksy in the early 2000s, stickers, banners, wheatpastes, and mailing labels. These tools accorded both functionality and ease: artists not only designed their works entirely from home but could also quickly repeat one message across a larger physical space, resulting in a more widely visible and uniform mark on the public sphere. "Stencils are number one in political graffiti," stated Most in a 2011 interview. "You don't have to have good handwriting; you just spray over a cut-out."

Noting the high visibility and practicality of "fast graffiti" tools, political parties have co-opted them to garner support for – or campaign against – their political rivals. Figures 4.4, 4.5, and 4.6 show how groups used stickers in the 2012 Russian presidential election.

Political stickers, stencils, and graffiti were so pervasive during the 2012 presidential election in Russia that some second-wave artists stepped away from the streets and retreated to their workshops. For example, in a March 2012 interview, a member of ZUKCLUB explained that while

Figure 4.4. "We Demand More." Oligarch Mikhail Prokhorov used stickers when he ran for president in 2012. March 2012. Moscow, Russia. (Photo: Alexis Lerner)

Figure 4.5. "Stop Stealing and Lying." Anti-Putin activists used stickers to campaign against the incumbent. March 2012. Moscow, Russia. (Photo: Alexis Lerner)

Figure 4.6. "Thief. In the Kremlin or in Prison? You decide on March 4
(election day)." 2012. Moscow, Russia. (Photo: Alexis Lerner)

his graffiti crew cartooned a banner depicting thievery and deception
for the "For Fair Elections" opposition gathering that took place on
December 24 the previous year, they intentionally avoided adding art
to the cluttered streets during the presidential election season of 2012.
They acknowledged that their viewers would be so inundated with visual
noise produced in the name of pseudo partisan politics that actual political sentiment might become overpowered and muted.

The mid-to-late-2000s were a turning point for post-Soviet graffiti
and a political awakening for second-wave writers, especially those
in Russia. The Putin administration entered its second term in 2004
and, shortly after, shifted its ideology toward "sovereign democracy,"
which was first coined by Kremlin aide Vladislav Surkov and rested on
two fundamental ideas: that Russia is democratic, and that any accusation otherwise would be regarded as "unfriendly and as meddling in
Russia's domestic affairs" (Lipman 2006). In practice, "sovereign democracy" meant the centralization of power, the destruction of private
financial institutions and the elites who ruled them, state control of the
media, and a general turn away from civil liberties and the rule of law
(Krastev 2006, 114).

Whether it was called hybrid authoritarianism, Putinism, or some form of populism, individual rights were being threatened, and Russians lacked platforms to freely discuss those threats. Those holding dissenting opinions about corruption, flawed elections, or undesirable political leaders could not broadcast their political discontent for fear of job loss, social alienation, or a response from intelligence or security forces. A hierarchy of topics prevailed: it permitted discussion of certain foreign relations (save Crimea and the conflict with Ukraine), some local authorities, and some police actions; it encouraged steering clear of Kremlin elites, corruption, and nepotism; and it entirely prohibited critique regarding strife in Chechnya, murdered journalists, and abused human rights activists.

Without a platform for free political speech, citizens were compelled to resort to alternative avenues of expression in which they could unabashedly express political critique. Several tertiary platforms for political expression appeared, including punk rock music, internet chat boards, town hall meetings, public marches, and, in the city of Barnaul in February 2012, mock protests attended (and policed) by Lego toys. Yet each of these avenues for political expression ran the risk of grave consequence.

Graffiti and street art remain one of the last-standing, truly free, and effective avenues for political expression. Their value as forms of unrestricted communication is largely due to their inherent characteristics of anonymity and accessibility, which allow artists to speak freely about their political and social discontent to a wide audience with a low risk of grave consequences (provided one is not caught). The platform's anonymous and illicit nature permits it to be effectively subversive and to engage in unbounded critical expression. Politicized writers and viewers can read the writing on the walls to access a public discourse that is notably absent from the mainstream media. While many graffiti artists continued bombing trains and using tags,[2] several twenty-first-century writers and crews established renown during this period for their politically critical work.

The art group Voina (War) created some notorious examples of shocking twenty-first-century political public art. The radical, political group never had a set list of members but rather a rotating stream of participating artists, which included leaders Vor (translated as Thief) Vorotnikov and his wife Natalia "Kozol" (in English, Little Female Goat) Sokol as well as Leonid "Lenya" Nikolaev (who died in 2015), Nadezhda "Nadya" Tolokonnikova (who later fronted the punk feminist collective Pussy Riot) and Tolokonnikova's husband, Pyotr Verzilov.

Voina persuasively combines art and activism, referenced in Russian as "actionism" (Platt 2017). While the group was primarily concerned with radical performance art – for example, throwing live cats at McDonald's employees in 2007 to interrupt the assumed monotony of labor – they have also engaged in large-scale graffiti projects. Voina is infamous for painting a 213-foot phallus on the Litenii Bridge in 2010. The bridge rises nightly to make way for passing ships, at which point the painted phallus points skyward, directly facing the Saint Petersburg headquarters of the Federal Security Service (FSB), the successor agency of the KGB.

Other artists, including Anton Litvin, Pyotr Pavlensky, and the performers of Pussy Riot, engaged in politicized and public performance art or nonconformist actionism. Litvin, who began his actionist career in the early 1990s, organized marches against the appointment of Sergei Sobianin as the mayor of Moscow in 2010 and against the imprisonment of protesters arrested during the Bolotnaia pro-democracy protests of 2011.[3]

In an interview, Litvin advocated for an explicit and intentional coming together of art and activism (2011):

> We must expand the artistic role in meetings.[4] We artists must have a more effective role. Right now, the main problem is that the primary [outlet for artistic discourse] is happening on Facebook and among designers but it's all sarcasm and jokes. We must seriously address the protests. And who if not us may – and should – participate in these meetings? The artist can do more than simply remain a spectator... Artists, we will be really relevant. Leave the galleries and go to the people.

In May 2012, using only white paint on a white canvas, Litvin and seventeen other artists gathered along the Sofia embankment to paint portraits of the Kremlin.[5] In this "Plein Air" action, white referred to the white clothes that protesters – demonstrating against fraudulent elections in Putin's Russia – wore as a symbol of purity and sincerity. The color also camouflaged and illustrated the absurdity of the act and thus the absurdity of the relationship between the people and their representative body. The action critiqued the government's reluctance to engage in dialogue with its citizens on political matters, as well as the political impotence of artists and average citizens against the centralized Russian government. While police quickly descended upon the artists, they did not arrest them as the political message remained veiled. Artists around the world mimicked the hour-long event to show support for the Russian movement, and the collaboration was nominated for the 2012 Kandinsky Prize.

Painting a fifteen-story phallus on a bridge or making the Kremlin symbolically invisible seems tame, however, when compared to Pavlensky's work. For example, the brutal actionist nailed his scrotum to Red Square in 2013 to draw attention to political indifference and symbolize a lack of agency for the people of Russia. He also set fire to the Lubyanka building – the Moscow headquarters of the FSB – in 2015 in support of jailed filmmaker Oleg Sentsov and sewed his mouth shut in Saint Petersburg in 2012 to protest the jailing of three members of Pussy Riot after their anti-Putin performance in Moscow's Christ the Savior Cathedral.

There is a way to build a new Moscow without resorting to the extreme acts of pseudo-martyrdom (Zimberg 2015, 101). Graffiti proves to be tamer than actionism like Pavlensky's and safer from prosecution than Vorotnikov's. Further, graffiti announcements proved well-suited for publicizing unsanctioned gatherings. Under the Putin administration, and later under the Medvedev administration, many groups were denied state approval for public gatherings: for example, in 2006, authorities rejected applications for Moscow Pride, anti-G8 demonstrations, and the first "March of the Discontented," set for December. By 2009, political activists affiliated with the opposition began to organize unsanctioned "Strategy-31" meetings, so named because they took place on the thirty-first day of each month containing thirty-one days. Announcements such as the sticker of Saint Peterburg's Bronze Horseman statue, a symbol of Russia's founding and of Saint Petersburg's collective identity, trampling the city's former mayor Valentina Matvienko – a political official viewed as firmly aligned with the Kremlin – clearly communicated the details and oppositional tone of these meetings in a public, yet anonymous, way (Figure 4.7).

Artëm Loskutov used art to circumvent restrictions on political gatherings. The art actionist from the Siberian city of Novosibirsk began to organize absurdist demonstrations, called "Monstrations," in 2004. At Loskutov's Monstrations, attendees shout nonsensical slogans and carry signs with absurdist phrases to make critical statements without explicitly attacking individuals or policies, thereby providing individual protesters with plausible deniability and protecting them from accusations of political extremism and related consequences. The Monstrations became increasingly popular across Russia. By 2009, Loskutov organized demonstrations in twenty different cities nationwide; that number increased to three dozen cities by 2020, when the Monstrations abruptly came to a halt because of the COVID-19 pandemic.[6] Threatened by Loskutov's mobilizational capacity, local authorities arrested the artist in 2009 and kept him in a Novosibirsk jail for three months. Stenciled graffiti that called for Loskutov's release, such as that shown in Figure 4.8, flared up in urban centers nationwide. Even after his release, Loskutov's defenders continued to use a stencil that read, "Freedom to the Artist Loskutov!

Figure 4.7. Sticker showing the Bronze Horseman – a symbol of Saint
Petersburg – trampling Saint Petersburg governor and Kremlin-insider
Valentina Matvienko and advertising a Strategy-31 meeting. 2011. Saint
Petersburg, Russia. (Photo: Alexis Lerner)

Figure 4.8. "Freedom to the Artist Loskutov! Art is not extremism!" 2009. Vasilievskii Island, Saint Petersburg, Russia. (Photo: Alexis Lerner)

Art is not extremism!" Monstrations continued to take place on May 1 each year across the country, in person until 2019 and virtually until 2020. After Russia invaded Ukraine for the second time in 2022, Loskutov emigrated and the Monstrations – now deemed illegal – ceased to take place (Loskutov 2024).

While Loskutov uses absurdism to sidestep politics, other art activists throw themselves into civic – rather than political – engagement. The members of Partizaning, for example, are a collective of former or marginally connected street artists who use public art to inspire average people to take responsibility for their local communities and to spread knowledge about urban design. Founded by Make and Igor Ponosov in November 2011, Partizaning uses guerilla street art to call attention to and repair various government inefficiencies related to pedestrian rights, public signage, and civic responsibility. Make and Ponosov, along with Sonya Polskaya, Shriya Malhotra, and Kirill Kto, produce a bilingual activism news site, *samizdat* publications, and public lectures about street art and urban activism. In the past, they also organized art-activism events at Vinzavod, a former wine factory in Moscow. (Similar art world events were occurring in Saint Petersburg at the Street Art Museum, which opened in a former plastics factory in 2012 and closed to the public in 2022 due to government pressure after Russia forcefully shut down domestic activism and free speech after the beginning of its war in Ukraine in February of that year.)

Partizaning's *samizdat* manifesto explains why street art is the best possible tool for inspiring community engagement and thus eliciting societal change (2012):

> Since the 1920s, radical artistic experiments have sought to destroy the boundaries between art and everyday life. Old industrial buildings, city streets, the internet and mass media are increasingly replacing museums and galleries as the ideal forums and exhibition venues for modern art. Today's activist urban residents do not think of art [as] a distinct system. They use the language of art as a tool to challenge and change their daily reality: from DIY [Do-It-Yourself] urban repair to struggling for new forms of state representation. Unsanctioned interventions and interactions in our urban environments, combined with mass media connectivity, have become effective transformative tactics for a new, alternative vision for the future.

In a March 2012 interview at Moscow's ArtPlay Design and Architecture Center, Sonya Polskaya emphasized the group's passion for inspiring others to realize their individual and civic agency:

> In Russia, many people think that they cannot do anything because they think that there's no solution for this country and for its problems... A street artist is responsible for activating, organizing, and communicating with their community, and therefore has the power to bring its problems to public attention and hopefully to their dissolve.

Partizaning relies on the principles and tools of graffiti in its "unsanctioned interventions" or "participatory urban planning" (Lerner 2015, 101). For example, in 2013, the group produced a true-to-scale map of the Moscow metro system, to which they added maps of trams, trains, and bike lanes. In small print on the poster, they added a list of tongue-and-cheek rules:

> It's prohibited in the metro to advertise cars, use bad materials to repair old stations, make bad navigation, yell at and kick passengers (even if they are trying to pass for free), to unreasonably check documents, steal money, etc (sic). We recommend using alternative transport systems, spend more time

in your neighborhood, walk and cycle, help people, [and] feel comfortable in public spaces.

Partizaning affixed this map on top of the existing Ministry of Transportation maps on Moscow metro train cars and shared the vector file online so it could be used and revised in an open access fashion. Maps are political, and the group's hostility toward bureaucratic institutions is also political.

As a prominent member of Partizaning, Kirill Kto creates public art that attacks political institutions and leaders, which is a contrast to his buffing of advertisements. For example, Kto makes fun of Nashi, a "government-organized non-governmental organization" (GONGO) that bused 30,000 youth – predominantly young men in leather jackets and black toques – from around the country into Moscow on Election Day.[7] He paints Nashi slogans on luxury cars as a way of highlighting the connection between money and power.[8]

Kto also writes mini manifestos on the walls of Moscow, which assail political apathy, private ownership of public property, and the graffiti artists who clutter the public sphere with empty words. He writes messages about United Russia that sarcastically glorify the far right. When those in power abruptly decided to replace the long-time Moscow mayor Yuri Luzhkov with Kremlin insider Sergei Sobianin in 2010, Kto used the city's walls to send the new mayor a message: "Sobianin, you're just a baby," he wrote on a wall near ArtPlay Design and Architecture Center. "Don't disappoint me."

Prior to Partizaning, Kto banded together with Misha Most in 2003 to form Moscow's first major graffiti crew – Zachem (in English, "for what?"). The group achieved national fame by covering Moscow with the word "Zachem," deliberately writing in Russian. Most expounded (2011):

Most of the guys blindly transmit what they see on the internet and in magazines into what they do [on the streets]. A lot of graffiti artists were writing English words and English letters, which encouraged me to write a meaningful Russian word with Russian letters.

In its early days, Zachem was composed of two conceptual artists and four bombers who would bomb as many times, in as many ways, and in as many creative places as physically possible to assert a dominating street presence. It was important to balance the crew with these two types of writers, told Most, because it ensured that a concept would be both interesting *and* widely distributed throughout the city.

Figure 4.9. "Zachem." 2011. Saint Petersburg, Russia. (Photo: Alexis Lerner)

Zachem's objective was to inspire Muscovites to confront uncomfortable questions and decisions – Why do this? What good does apathy bring? Further, the phrase was "specifically addressed to the viewer" so high visibility was important (Most 2011). Therefore, the crew placed the value-loaded word in high-traffic locations, such as in schoolyards, on highway overpasses, and atop corporate advertisements across Moscow. Viral internet photography, magazine interviews, and numerous art and music videos brought the crew international recognition and helped them to achieve what most graffiti artists consider a real sign of success – fame. "Zachem" references began to appear in popular books and high-production films, as the graffitied phrase became an emblematic detail of the illustrated post-Soviet Moscow.

Across the region, new graffiti gangs imitated Zachem's tags and murals. Before long, the word, shown in Figure 4.9, coated major Russian-speaking areas in Belarus, Poland, and Latvia. Zachem reproductions soon became more common than Zachem originals, and the movement's expansion became more important than its founders or individual writers.

In 2004 and 2005, its early years, the intention behind "Zachem" was ostensibly political. In the public sphere, however, the tag's overall projection lost its overt message and became susceptible to contextual

Figure 4.10. "No Future Forever." 2012. Moscow, Russia. (Photo: Alexis Lerner)

influences. By 2006, the crew moved on from simply writing "Zachem" and adopted the punk-inspired phrase "No Future Forever" (see Figure 4.10). The slogan originates from "No Future," a Sex Pistols lyric that the Soviet punks of the 1970s co-opted to complement their "live fast and die young" mantra. Feeling as though the entire world was living by this motto, the members of Zachem added the sarcastic "Forever," because "[this mentality] seems like it will last forever." The co-opted slogan is explicitly intended as a critique of the political apathy, social lethargy, and total ambivalence rampant in the artists' local communities.

After all, Most and Kto have experienced a lifetime of civic dissatisfaction, from former president Yeltsin's drunken leadership, the gang violence of the 1990s, and episodes of economic crisis, to specific events such as the Moscow apartment bombings in 1999, the Beslan School Attack in 2004, the Crocus City Hall attack in 2024, the targeted murders of Anna Politkovskaya in 2006, Boris Nemtsov in 2015, and Alexei Navalny in 2024, and cascading and devastating wars with Chechnya, Georgia, and Ukraine.

In the basement of the Stalinist skyscraper near Barrikadnaia metro station in 2014, Most tells me about Russia in the 1990s. His words come together excitedly in spurts, as though he is working out the ideas as he ejects them. The Soviet dissolution left behind a power vacuum, he says. A constitutional crisis erupted into an armed conflict. Organized crime quickly rose in the place of the Central Committee. As we talked about the people who died in Moscow's notorious decade of violent crime, he could not hide his disillusionment as he eulogized the casualties of change.

Most is in his 40s now and understands that mass chaos rarely ends well. He is skeptical of revolution everywhere, not just the Russian sort. He remembers too well the optimism of December 2011 and March 2012, moments in Russia's recent history when real change seemed possible. These political movements, while invigorating at the time, ultimately lacked viable leadership and permanent solutions. Over the years, Most has learned to channel these feelings of disappointment into his work through the use of sardonic stencils and colorful freehand.

In 2007, for example, he criticized the Orange Revolution in Ukraine by painting a mural of apathetic, faceless protesters accepting cash to demonstrate. In 2012, he sketched the outlines of a public rally on a wall in Warsaw, Poland, to indicate that revolution everywhere can be orchestrated to achieve nearly identical results. In 2013, he memorialized the chaos of October 1993 in a mural outside Moscow's Historical Museum. And, in a more recent series, *Collapse*, Most painted a pool of blood beneath rubble, a critique on the costs of ideology – the bricks that once housed power and authority can easily come tumbling down (Lerner 2014).

Most and Kto's cynicism and frustration do not leave them drawing alone in a vacuum. The upper echelon of Russian artists largely approaches the medium with more careful and sustained forethought than in previous decades. Most notable are Yekaterinburg's intellectual Radya, Moscow's fantastical ZUKCLUB, Saint Petersburg's stenciled Group of Change, and P(asha)183, who died in 2013 (Lerner 2013a). These groups and individuals are concise and assertive actors in defining the narrative of the public sphere with succinct, nuanced political critique and a clear, visible writing style.

Radya

On the eastern slopes of the Ural Mountains in Yekaterinburg, street artist Radya organizes works of high production value, which aim to criticize political deficiencies, intellectual bankruptcy, corporate dominance, and social misgivings. Radya recognizes that when artists release their work into the public space, meaning and interpretation fall to the viewer. For this reason, Radya sticks explicitly to simple designs and phrases to express simple critiques (a distinct shift from the text-saturated posters of the early Soviet period). Nevertheless, Radya is an intellectual and the layers of his projects reflect this. For example, in an August 2010 Yekaterinburg installation, Radya designed an intertextual "face book," a shrine to the poet Vladimir Mayakovsky, a literary hero of the Soviet era, whose later work expressed disillusionment with the Soviet regime despite earlier conviction for its ideals. This was also a period when the social media platform Facebook became the world leader in usage with approximately 350 registered accounts and a multi-billion-dollar valuation. In this project, Radya paints on actual books filled with Mayakovsky's poetry as his chosen medium, highlighting an abandoned trail of masterpieces unread by the society of the technological age. In "face book," Radya also sought to comment on the endurance of literature; engagement with literary themes and concepts remains ever-available, regardless of the passage of time.

In January 2011, the artist painted a giant red square on the empty lot of a demolished home in Yekaterinburg. Authorities permitted contractors to illegally raze the property to make way for the construction of an adjacent skyscraper. "[We painted while] it was dark," Radya writes on his website, "but as the sun rose, it turned out scary – [the paint] looked like blood." The glass-windowed skyscraper overlooked the painted red square in the now-vacant lot, a symbol of the government's insurmountable right to power over its citizens. "The new glass house on the blood of the old one," the artist adds (2011). Two months later, in March 2011, Radya installed a wooden desk halfway submerged beneath Yekaterinburg's flowing Iset River, surrounded by the poetry of Joseph Brodsky, another Soviet literary icon known for his implicitly politically critical work. Radya explained that in the artwork, the river eats away at the material objects just as time causes the form of man to erode and transform.

Autocratic states may host regular elections that purport to be competitive. However, in practice, opposition candidates are not true political opposition, but rather *systema* or members of the systemic opposition (Lerner 2020, 15–16; Wood and Lerner n.d.; Gel'man 2015, 4).[9] Radya uses public art to express his frustration at the flooding of a ballot with systemic candidates. In Yekaterinburg, street artist Radya responded to the controversies of the March 2012 presidential election when he wrote "Nothing New" as though it were the only name available for checking on an electoral ballot. This work was displayed on a billboard overlooking a major Ural thoroughfare, criticizing the empty promises of democracy.

Other works by the satirical street artist reference managed and fraudulent elections under authoritarian rule. Most notoriously perhaps, Radya criticized the Duma 2011 elections, which led to mass protests across Russia, with an official-looking billboard atop a nine-story apartment building in Yekaterinburg. On the billboard, Radya wrote "You've Been Cheated" next to a small red checked box drawn to resemble an election ballot (photos of the project circulated on social media once again during the March 2024 presidential elections in Russia, implying that the sentiment was as relevant as before).

ZUKCLUB

In Moscow in 2000, four neighborhood friends banded together to form ZUKCLUB, a group of artists that began as a simple graffiti crew but soon developed into a non-conformist and audacious street art unit. By 2005, the crew expanded. The members of ZUKCLUB were younger than Basket, Most, Ponosov, and Make, and they were motivated to dramatically alter the street art status quo, both aesthetically and in content.

Artistically, this was an intuitive shakeup for ZUKCLUB, as many of the crew's members studied visual art in school. Their classroom training allowed them to approach graffiti in a systematic yet novel way. In a 2012 interview in Moscow, Kirill Stefanov said, "We went from four people to a big crowd that really wanted to create something unique. We ignored the rules of art – the norms of color and composition – and started painting some psychedelic and shocking stuff."

The crew also sought to remodel the content of Russian graffiti with an explicit turn to political critique. The cohort – including Sergei Ovseikin, Kirill Stefanov, and Artem Stefanov, as well as scores of other artists involved on a rotating basis – spoke animatedly about the widespread opposition protests mobilizing in response to the Putin administration. While artists before them expressed political discontent in graffiti, ZUKCLUB's paintings proved more direct.

At the ZUKCLUB studio in 2012, Sergey Ovseikin shared a digitized catalog of the crew's recent projects, Artem Stefanov practiced painting the colorful gnomes that ZUKCLUB would become famous for, and Kirill gushed about his favorite art action of the last decade:

> It was during the time of the Georgian–Russian war three years ago. Russia broke all of its meeting points with Georgia, but in the meantime, we claimed that we were friends though it was clear that they were our biggest enemy. It was really strange for me because Georgia always seemed like a part of Russia, a part of the USSR. Of course it wasn't but that's what it seemed like. After the war, I was so amazed that we had so many enemies at our borders. [Because of Georgia's close relations with the United States] We drew a big work that depicted a Russian bear destroying the USA flag. The root of Medvedev's name is medved, which in English means bear.

ZUKCLUB is also affected by the overarching themes of apathy and action that plague Kto and Most, and they envision themselves as important actors in a relatively new movement for the free expression of political and social discontent. In addition to demonstrating against December 2011's fraudulent parliamentary elections and the informational void in the media, the leaders of ZUKCLUB expressed their belief that the most important tension in contemporary society is the battle that pits young people against the status quo. According to one ZUKCLUB leader, who wished to remain anonymous for their own safety, Russians have spent so many years in a "catatonic" state that most do not comprehend the power of free speech and collective protest. Sergei added (2012):

> It's a new trend for young people [to express their political sentiment publicly]. It's a new thing that you can talk to other people about politics. Two years ago, it was really strange, just you and the people around you. It was very personal. Now it's an all-society thing. It's not dangerous. It's the birth of something very good. If you want to burn some cars in the street [like Voina did on New Years' Eve 2012], of course it's very dangerous but if you want to make some posters in the streets or you want to paint a wall in a beautiful color, and not in the color of depression, that's cool and right now

Figure 4.11. "Modernization or Death. The Group of Change." 2011. Saint Petersburg, Russia. (Photo: Alexis Lerner)

that's what people are doing. This is my truth: to do something is better than doing nothing.

Group of Change

While ZUKCLUB, Most, and Kto were painting in Moscow, the Group of Change was painting 750 kilometers to the north in Saint Petersburg. The group predominantly relied on stencils because they can be used to express explicit calls to action clearly and uniformly, without increasing threat of consequence for an artist. The crew plastered its city with stencils that demanded an end to state-led censorship, the historical preservation of pre-revolutionary architecture, and mass mobilization for greater rights. Their pieces almost always incorporate URLs that led to their website, where viewers could learn practical details about upcoming events and public demonstrations. Other artists include web links to share their portfolios, for interested parties to sign petitions, or to share information, such as election statistics.

In downtown Saint Petersburg and Moscow, the group wheatpasted small comics that depicted Putin and Dostoevsky's philosophical musings during hypothetical, quotidian outings. En route to an August 2011 interview in Saint Petersburg, a young, female graffiti artist, Manu, commented on a Group of Change stencil that read "Modernization or Death," shown in Figure 4.11. As a friend of the crew, she explained that the Russian public wants greater rights and an end to corruption more than any wholesale abolition of the existing system built around Putin and United Russia (2011). She suggested that the goal of the Group of Change and the opposition movement in general is not so much to create a viable opposition candidate, but rather to demand a better life for the average Russian in the workplace, at school, and in their community. Other Group of Change stencils opposed construction in the city, which is a United Nations Educational, Scientific, and Cultural Organization (UNESCO) World Heritage Site, criticized media censorship, and invited observers to mobilize in protest.

P183

Finally, Pasha 183 (P183) was best known for his socially critical installations and gray-scale photorealist murals. He was a poet of the streets, lauded by both his peers and the world press that made him famous by nicknaming him "the Russian Banksy" in January 2012 (Lerner 2013a), although P183 did not see himself this way. In an interview in 2012, he confessed that he had no intention of emulating the British street artist. In fact, he had begun to hone his craft with the rest of the second-wave artists, years before Banksy reached the forefront of street art fetishism. On that day, P183 explained how he learned to draw in the dark with lights and to incorporate existing environmental aides, such as Moscow's waterways and concrete spaces. Later, illustrating a move away from political engagement, P183 became known for grandiose installations that beautified the urban environment by bringing gallery-quality aesthetics to the streets.

For example, a stretch of barbed wire near a mental hospital became a good place for a fictional young girl to hang Novii God (New Year's) decorations. In *True to the Truth: 19/08/91 Reminder*, the swinging doors of Krasnie Vorota metro station became the ideal location for life-sized stickers of riot police so that the lay person could let out their aggression on them – pushing them aside with great force – without repercussion. P183 viewed street art as a vital instrument for shaking the citizenry into reclaiming expression (Lerner 2013a).

The Power of Public Art

With its formative years balanced precariously between chaos and control, freedom and security, this generation of graffiti artists paints about political revolution and dissent from the perspective of distrust and disappointment. In their freehand paintings, stencils, and murals, they toy with themes of nihilism and cynicism while attacking their communities for expressing apathy.

From the mid-2000s, public art about political elites, fraudulent elections, and the policies of the Putin administration saturated the streets of Russia. For some, such as the artists of Voina or the unholy rock-and-roll group Pussy Riot, brutal and shocking actionism became synonymous with rebellion or, at the least, with "contentious performance" (Tilly 2008). For others, like Kto, Partizaning, and ZUKCLUB, writing support for, or against, a particular political figure is pointless. In contrast, these street artists felt that they had an implicit obligation to inspire civic engagement and deeper waves of social change.

While some artists only practice street art (such as Kto) or actionism (like Pavlensky), others like Partizaning and Voina have a more fluid creative identity and engage in both activities. Ultimately, art actionism is closely intertwined with performance, which intrinsically implies that the artist must be *visible* during the period of art. This is the dominant way in which graffiti differs from actionism, as visibility, for example, decreases the likelihood of anonymity and increases the possibility of getting arrested or imprisoned for the performance. In some scenarios, arrest, imprisonment, and even the subsequent trial are important parts of an action, as these public events connect the extreme performance with an individual artist and their values or the causes they support (Vor 2012). On occasion, the radical action and punitive response garner the attention of the international press, and the artist may eventually be released from jail or prison with increased international prominence (Lerner 2020).

Public art – whether in the form of nuanced graffiti or striking action-ism – is an effective way to challenge those in power and/or the narra-tives put forth by a centralized state. This effectiveness is evidenced by the degree to which artists are arrested, imprisoned, and abused by the authorities – for example, if Loskutov's message and his mobilizational capacity did not present a political threat to the regime, his imprison-ment in 2009 would have been unlikely. Subversive public art is also use-ful in challenging existing power structures and narratives because of its accessibility for the lay person.

Any member of society can pick up a spray can, a paint pen, or a per-manent marker and anonymously write their political discontents on a wall, thereby inserting their uncensored perspective into a public narra-tive. This is the power of public art: graffiti, street art, and art actionism are platforms that allow artists and activists to draw attention and critical analysis to issues that are unlikely to appear on the nightly news. By ex-tending political discourse beyond a small circle of elites to the public, this type of subversive art can connect otherwise informationally isolated citizens and introduce new perspectives (and challenges) to existing po-litical conversations.

PART II

Fundamental Questions about Post-Soviet Graffiti

Chapters Five through Seven explore how our knowledge of post-Soviet graffiti intersects with our theoretical and practical understanding of political protest, censorship, and authoritarianism. These chapters aim to spur conceptual and theoretical discussion around political graffiti as a tool for communication in censored states. One or all of these chapters would be especially well-suited to an undergraduate or graduate course on these topics.

"Chapter Five: Why the Public Space is Conducive to Political Graffiti" discusses the relationship between public space and political action or protest and provides the postmodernist and post-positivist theoretical framework to support this thinking. This chapter explains the relationship between some of the key features of public spaces – population density and geographic space, for example – and graffiti as a mode of political communication. When there are many people in a relatively compressed space, such as the contemporary city, graffiti becomes a particularly effective way to convey political messages.

"Chapter Six: Signs and Symbols as a Form of Political Expression" outlines how the image – a combination of texts and symbols – has been used over time in the public space as a form of political action and expression. This chapter discusses artistic intentionality in the language or cultural references used to express a particular sentiment. It draws from foundational theoretical scholarship on semiotics and political communication to examine the image as a series of texts and symbols that can be leveraged as tools for political expression and action.

"Chapter Seven: Street Art as Text" argues that graffiti does not exist in a vacuum. Rather graffiti can (and should) be read as a text or as a narrative about a place, the people who live there, and the things that matter to them. I leverage literary theory, in particular Russian literary theorist Mikhail Mikhailovich Bakhtin's ideas about dialogism and the chronotope, to argue that graffiti is not only a two-dimensional artform or monologue but rather a dynamic dialogue among writers, buffers, passersby, and the physical environment surrounding each work. This chapter demonstrates the value of graffiti as an alternative avenue of political communication, as it permits marginalized voices to share information and discuss otherwise forbidden topics.

Chapter Five

Why the Public Space is Conducive to Political Graffiti

To understand how graffiti functions in the public space, it is important to begin with a discussion of why the public space works for political action. Uncontrolled public spaces are inherently neutral, informal, voluntary, and inclusive levelers that are generally accessible to the public and lack exclusive membership requirements. The most cardinal and sustaining activity of the public space is communication. It is where private individuals gather to celebrate, grieve, and pass the time (Habermas 1991 [1962], 27).

In public spaces, such as a neighborhood bar, a public square, or a parade ground, people can gather together, share news, and engage in debate (Oldenburg 1989, 16). Oldenburg writes of the public space: "Conversation is more spirited, less inhibited, and more eagerly pursued. Compared to the speech in other realms, it is more dramatic and more often attended by laughter and the exercise of wit" (1989, 30). The discourse present in the public space is not limited to celebratory cheers and gossipy whispers; inhabitants also come together to share information on matters of public opinion (Habermas 1991 [1962], 27). In addition to drama and satire, public spaces are also places where individuals can use morality and reason to critique those in positions of political power (Habermas 1991, 90, 127). As an unobstructed and frequently satirical vehicle, graffiti is an intuitive tool for communicating critiques, victories, and hearsay in the public space.

Lefebvre suggests that this freedom of speech associated with the public space explains why mass revolutionary events generally take place in the streets. "Space holds the promise of liberation," Lefebvre explains. "Liberation from the tyranny of time apart from anything else, but also from social repression and exploitation, from self-imprisoning categories – [space builds] liberation into desire. Space is radically open... speech can become "savage" and, by escaping rules and institutions, inscribe itself on walls" (Lefebvre 1970, XIV, 19). Political leaders are uniquely aware of the potential for mass action, and the potential that it could result in their own unseating, and therefore tightly monitor informal gathering spaces (Lefebvre 1970, 70). Many contemporary political scientists have convincingly made similar arguments about the power of the people to mobilize against an autocrat (e.g., Bernhard 1993; Bunce and Wolchik 2011; and Balzer 2003). Fu 2017 and Scott 1985, in particular, stand out for their compelling arguments about how activists use "disguised" collective action or "everyday resistance," accordingly, to slowly and steadfastly chip away at the tolerance of an authoritarian state.

What *is* the Public Space?

The categorization of space is generally limited to two varieties: the private and the public. The former connotes domestic, often familial, spaces, while the latter generally implies trans-domestic spaces, such as public squares.[1] Oldenburg, in his book *The Good Great Place*, expands upon this dichotomy by dividing the private space into two distinct variants: the nurturing and private home versus the contained workplace, with a set of production-centric temporal and spatial values that differ from those of the home (Oldenburg 1989). Therefore, a non-workplace public space occupies a separate position, which Oldenburg suitably names the "third space" (Oldenburg 1989, 16).

Alternative to the news shared in a private and insular first space or in a hierarchical and constrictive second space, the third space offers the "opportunity to question, protest, sound out, supplement and form opinion locally and collectively," a necessary practice for any functioning participatory system (Oldenburg 1989, 70). The third place, or public space, is where a citizenry can form ideas about their government, their society, and their loyalties. In this sense, the public sphere is a symbol of freedom, which gains its legitimacy and strength by means of public participation (Habermas 1964, 50).

Who Participates in the Public Space?

To be sure, there are dominant societal norms that privilege the behaviors or characteristics of some individuals over others, thereby affecting which acts and bodies can inhabit public spaces (Butler 2015, 4). Precarious populations are often kept separate from the public sphere, whether by official decree, such as the criminalization of homelessness, or through informal avenues like racial profiling (Butler 2015, 33). Precarious populations that either feel unwelcome or are, in fact, unsafe in public spaces are often exploited or marginalized minorities, including but not limited to women, people of color, individuals who wear identifiable ethnic or religious clothing (a Sikh turban, a Jewish *kippah*, or an Islamic *hijab*, for example), the physically and mentally disabled, the very young, the elderly, and individuals with discernible and non-traditional sexual preferences (two men holding hands, for example). Their sense of insecurity may be the result of a heightened state presence through police forces, a militarized public through policies like "Open Carry" (an American law that allows registered gun owners in select states to openly carry their weapon in select public spaces, including restaurants, bars, and university lecture halls), or through a history of aggressive behaviors that one cultural or ethnic group expresses toward another (for example, Russian nationals physically assaulting Central Asian migrant workers on night buses following football tournaments in Saint Petersburg).

In autocratic and censored regimes, the individual "right" to enter and contribute within public spaces is further limited to those the state deems uncontentious (Lefebvre 1970, 70). Such governments are keenly aware of the power of communication outside of the mainstream media. They therefore tightly monitor or discourage the heated discourse and oppositional activity that incubates in these informal gathering spaces (Lefebvre, 1970, 70). As such, the simple act of existing in an otherwise restricted space is a political act that can beget serious repercussions. To avoid these negative consequences, individuals must use tools designed to circumvent citations and arrests.

Graffiti as a Tool for Political Communication

In pre-literate societies, the public square was often the largest and central-most structure in the village (Oldenburg 1989, 17). Individuals could not only gather and communicate in these public spaces but also demonstrate against political ills and challenge existing power structures. Yet, gathering is not the only way to show an unwillingness to accept the dominant order; writing in public spaces challenges precarity without the same exposure to vulnerability. Historical examples of political graffiti written in public squares are many: the scribbled campaigns of Gaius Julius Phillipus or Marcus Epidius Sabinus in Pompeii, the calls for revolutionary student action in Paris in 1968, and demands for racial justice on historic sites across the United States in the summer of 2020. The city, with its dense population, walkable avenues, and political activism, has long been the preferred locale for political graffiti.

Graffiti excels as a tool for communicating, monitoring, and measuring unrestricted expression in otherwise restrictive conditions. Due to its anonymous and subversive qualities, graffiti can effectively circumvent both censorship and societal gatekeeping, and thus allows even politically contentious populations to participate in otherwise exclusionary discourse and in the public deconstruction of political hierarchies. This capacity to gain and share information, and therefore to invert some power dynamics, is available to all members of society, regardless of one's socio-economic standing, title, or ethno-religious background. Consequences of getting caught aside, status does not dictate who may elect to speak via graffiti or when, about whom, and how much.

Graffiti can do more than just communicate information neutrally; it is also a vehicle for political action. This can occur both indirectly and directly. Graffiti can inspire action indirectly if it can motivate readers or viewers to change their thinking on a particular subject or act on private beliefs. But graffiti can also beget change directly when it shares mobilizational details, such as when and where to meet regarding a particular topic.

Examples from my archive demonstrate some of the ways in which graffiti facilitates discourse in the public space. In particular, I probe two aspects of the public space that are conducive to this form of political protest: population density (and with that, multiple layers of understanding) and spatial design. Such discourse, by nature of being truly reflective of a society's actual composition and divisions, is often crass, a fact that some of these photos will demonstrate.

Population Size and Density

Urban centers have a large number of individuals living within their boundaries. This means that streets are highly trafficked and, in turn, that many people can see and engage with writing on a wall. Even if authorities buff or erase a work of graffiti, many individuals will likely have read it prior to its covering or erasure. Nevertheless, the consequences of getting caught painting unsanctioned public art – political or not – can be as severe as jail time, expensive fines, and, under the strictest regimes, prohibitive restrictions on routine acts such as obtaining a driver's license or traveling internationally. Given these potential repercussions, artists can turn to "quick art," such as stickers, wheatpastes, or stencils, to repeat the same symbols and messages across a large geographic space. This provides a more widely visible and uniform mark on the public sphere. Inspired by the aforementioned British street artist Banksy, who pioneered a global quick art movement around 2005, these techniques are especially useful for artists operating in tightly controlled public spaces, as they can largely design their work from home and reinforce their anonymity.

Figure 5.1. "Protesting is Good. United Russia is very bad." Pre-made stickers allow an artist to spread a uniform image quickly across a large public space. Satirical stickers near Saint Petersburg State University share the specifics of the Strategy-31 assemblies. July 2011. Saint Petersburg, Russia. (Photo: Alexis Lerner)

Politically minded street artists use stickers and stencils to communicate their dissatisfaction in the public space. For example, satirical stickers near Saint Petersburg State University from 2011 share the specifics of the Strategy-31 assemblies – meetings on the thirty-first day of each month with thirty-one days, near the Gostinii Dvor mall and public square. The "31" also refers to Article 31 of the Russian constitution, the article that declares the civic freedom to assemble in the Russian Federation.[2] The meetings spread from Moscow to Saint Petersburg and then to other regions in the winter of 2010. In downtown Saint Petersburg, just off the central avenue – Nevskii Prospekt – two 2011 stickers illustrate a clear oppositional tone for these meetings. The sticker in Figure 5.1 identifies the Strategy-31 meetings as "good," especially when compared with Putin's "very bad" political party United Russia.

These messages, and others like them, can affect private opinions and reinforce mobilizational efforts. They are particularly useful when demonstration organizers are forced to pivot quickly to new locations or dates due to administrative restrictions such as a denied permit for assembly. Moreover, the people putting on the stickers can engage in proactive plausible deniability, as in the example of posted advertisements about DirectSPB's "Direct Participation" meetings, which clarified that the Palace Square gatherings would be free from politics, symbols, and agitation. DirectSPB, like other activist groups seeking to mobilize, include a web address on their posters, a practice I note in Chapter Eight.

Stickers and stencils also sometimes incorporate machine-readable optical labels, called QR codes, to link public signage – whether legal or illegal – to web-based material about a cause. This allows interested observers to learn where to find more information about whatever topic is depicted on the poster or sticker. The primary difference between web links and QR codes is the speed and ease affiliated with the latter, as one need not physically type a URL address into a web browser, but rather use the camera on their cell phone to redirect a browser directly to a static page. However, the internet is neither private nor secure, and domestic intelligence can easily navigate locked web portals and IP (internet protocol) addresses to determine the location and identity of those posting information online and visitors to certain sites. In contrast, graffiti can be a fully anonymous tool for information sharing.

The information that graffiti can share is not limited to its substantive content; it also includes intrinsic qualities such as its placement in the public sphere. For example, during a highly politicized election period in March 2012, two stencils appeared outside Kurskaia Metro in the center of Moscow. Instead of venting explicit criticisms, these stencils state their support for independent courts and free speech to spray the city with democratic values, or at least tongue-in-cheek sarcasm. One translates as "I love Independent Courts," and the other reads, "I love (the) Free Press" (see Figure 1.2 in Chapter One). The very placement of these works on a public wall implies that speech is not free and that one has to engage in illegal defacement to express a wish for truly free speech. When the disenfranchised lack access or equal representation to power vacuums – in this case, specifically the Russian media and the Russian judicial branch – the anonymous nature of graffiti provides a certain shared power to this otherwise voiceless societal group.

That these two stencils were placed immediately outside of one of Moscow's largest and busiest public transportation hubs adds to this inversion of power, increasing the number of people who will see it and possibly engage with it. While the message displayed in this example would be effective in a less-heavily trafficked area, the *urgency* of the artist is communicated by the location, as this individual took on additional risk to publicize their discontent. In both cases, an artist's use of graffiti as a medium to express discontent with repressive censorship or power barriers specifically illustrates the unrestricted quality of the public art form.

Inevitably, passersby in a highly trafficked area will see politically critical or mobilizational works like these and engage with them by taking a photograph or mentioning them to a companion. The public disclosure of private political opinions can result in a ripple effect of overt critique, a phenomenon that scholars have observed across history, from the collapse of the Soviet Union to the Iranian revolution (Scott 1985; Kuran 1997; Kuran 1991; Kurzman 2004). By exposing one individual's private sentiment in the public sphere, graffiti has the potential to inspire others to reflect and publicize their own opinions on a topic. When individual graffitied topics challenge existing systems of power, they may inspire others to voice critical dissent, thereby increasing the potential for cascading dissent and widespread protest.

Last, the large population that frequents a public space likely has great diversity in knowledge, hobbies, professions, and lifestyles. Murals that reference select songs and pop culture icons may resonate with youthful passersby, while other public art that refers to historical battle-sites and wartime leaders might resound for observers with a military background. Given that not everyone will understand every intertextual reference painted by an artist, it is safe to assume that a greater density of passersby will result in a larger number of individuals who *will* understand references to niche interests, cultural and literary references, and text, including those in other languages such as English.

Geographic Space

Public squares have multiple points of access, and main thoroughfares have numerous parallel passages and side streets. This density of alternative routes, combined with geographic sprawl, results in more places where graffiti can be placed and a lower capacity for monitoring and buffing. Consider the following examples from post-communist Europe, in which graffiti can express nuanced political discontent on the side streets of a downtown urban space.

On a trash canister in Budapest in 2011, a street artist uses the wheatpaste method to affix a painting. Referencing an alumina plant spill in fall 2010, the image reads, "Send More Red Mud. We are Still Alive" (Figure 5.2). In the disaster known as Red Sludge, the Danube poured approximately 184 million gallons of toxic sludge across the Hungarian countryside, forcing entire villages from their homes in the middle of the night and destroying innumerable crop fields. On a side street in Prague

Figure 5.2. "Send More Red Mud. We are Still Alive." A tongue-in-cheek reference to the devastating Red Sludge toxic spill of 2010 into the Danube. July 2011. Budapest, Hungary. (Photo: Alexis Lerner)

in 2011, graffiti reflects a residual anger toward the post-war Soviet occupation of Eastern Europe. On a wall in a quiet neighborhood by the Vltava River, shown in Figure 5.3, one artist drew Che Guevara wearing a Che Guevara t-shirt, a mocking depiction of how both Soviet and Western activists overhype his image. On the same wall, a second artist stenciled the helmeted head of Yuri Gagarin, the famed Soviet astronaut. Next to this stencil the artist wrote, "Yuri Says: Reach for the Stars!" In a third style of handwriting, a commenter added anonymously: "Russian Go Home." An interviewee in Budapest suggested that artists often use English because of the universality of the English language, which increases access to an international audience that might mobilize behind their cause, which explains why the words "Feel Our Life," located in an artist neighborhood of Minsk would be etched in English rather than in Belarusian or Russian (Kormfox 2011).

    While there are many places throughout a city where an artist might locate their work, choosing a particular urban center can speak volumes about political control there. For example, politically critical "quick art" can also be found in Minsk: a 2011 stencil along the Svislach River depicting poet Yanka Kupala, who exemplifies Belarusian national identity and relies heavily on the Belarusian, rather than the Russian, language.

Figure 5.3. Yuri Says Reach for the Stars // Che Guevara Wearing a Che Guevara T-Shirt // Russian Go Home. 2011. Prague, Czech Republic. (Photo: Alexis Lerner)

Figures 5.4–5.8. The first three images ("Luka[shenko] Sucks," "Freedom to the Anarchist Nikolai Dedka," and "Freedom to the Belarusian Anarchists and National [Illegible]") were all located downtown or on the banks of the Svislach River, whereas the latter images were located outside of the city center, either in a "student" district (near campus or student-frequented pubs and concert halls; in red, "Long Live Belarus") or outside the city center altogether ("We Will Have Freedom," at the bottom). July 2011. Minsk, Belarus. (Photo: Alexis Lerner)

Other pieces in Minsk include a freehand scribble "Luka(shenko) sucks" on the clear, glass wall of a downtown bus stop, and sprayed stencils alongside the Svislach River calling for the release of political prisoners. Symbols such as Belarusian national figures, the use of Belarusian instead of Russian, and pre-Soviet emblems like the Pahonia signify continued public rebellion against the Lukashenko administration and its forced Russification of Belarus(see Figures 5.4 through 5.8).

Politically critical works like these will not be found in downtown Minsk (Belarus), nor will complicated and aesthetically pleasing murals. They will not even be located in neighborhoods frequented by artists, as is the case in other cities, such as Moscow or Budapest (Lerner 2021). Instead, these political critiques can be found in dark alleys and in abandoned buildings, far away from the city center.

This location of political graffiti in Minsk is counterintuitive. Why would the most critical works be in places where they would not reach a broad possible audience? In Lukashenko's autocratic Belarus, the public space is tightly controlled. I witnessed this myself in 2011, when I observed the Minsk police patrolling a public square, searching for, and promptly carting off, potential protesters following the July clapping demonstrations. Therefore, painting in downtown spaces, which might be available in other cities like Prague and Budapest, is simply not possible unless one wishes to become a martyr. The consequences for anti-regime behavior go beyond fines and jail time; after arrest for various forms of protest, a young person may find that they are not able to acquire a driver's license, retain their employment or spot at a university, or obtain approval to travel abroad.[3]

But the police cannot be everywhere. In spaces where the police are absent, Belarusian citizens act as informal collaborators by monitoring their city's streets. This results in a three-pronged form of censorship: official censorship, community-driven censorship, and self-censorship. To avoid fines, arrests, and even jail time, most artists stick to freehand marking and quick stencils to hasten their practice without foregoing it altogether, or they paint where they will not be observed. As a result, in contemporary Belarus, many of the downtown public spaces contain graffiti reminiscent of the late-Soviet era – messages about countercultural movements, such as parkour, rock-and-roll, and pacifism scrawled onto a brick or scratched into a windowpane.

Further, the city provides many opportunities for an artist to engage with their surroundings, such as the muralist in Łódź who plays with light when commenting on ethnic minorities or the Moscow-based artist who turns tiny water spigots into friendly faces. Other artists, however, explicitly reference space and history in their work. Consider, for example, a 2011 wheatpaste photographed in Riga, shown in Figure 1.7 in

Figure 5.9. "Stop (the) G8!" 2011. Riga, Latvia. (Photo: Alexis Lerner)

Figure 5.10. The hero Lāčplēsis vomiting with alcohol bottles around his feet.
2011. Riga, Latvia. (Photo: Alexis Lerner)

Chapter One of this book, which depicts a female figure being inserted into – and coming out of – a meat grinder while holding stars above her head. The meaning of this wheatpaste is also influenced by its placement in and reference to Riga's urban core. The figure is not any female, but rather Latvia's Lady Freedom who stands atop the Freedom Monument in the city's center. The statue is meant to represent Latvia's freedom and sovereignty, initially from Russia and then as a symbol of preserved Latvian identity under Soviet occupation. Understanding the historical context of this figure makes its demolition via meat grinder all the more meaningful. Large pieces of meat enter a meat grinder and thin uniform tubes exit. This critique of Latvian national identity placed through a meat grinder mirrors the public narrative of Riga, which explicitly expresses fear about the country's accession to the EU and the concessions that Latvians must make to gain respect and dominance in this global community.

In addition to considering the local context and geographic placement of a work, it is also vital to understand the intersection of a work of art, the state that houses it, and the geopolitical and economic relationship between that state and the global system, as art is often a reflection of the political environment within which it exists. Indeed, Baltic fears about the political influence of foreign states are made explicit throughout Riga, such as in the examples of an anonymous downtown freehand piece that calls to "Stop (the) G8"[4] and in an Andrejsala Island mural of Lāčplēsis' demise (see Figure 5.9 and 5.10, accordingly). Lāčplēsis is a mythical Latvian figure – the Paul Bunyan of the Baltics – who stands high above our heads, wears skins and furs of his own making, and is the trusted friend to all of Europe's forest creatures. Known as the bear-slayer, Lāčplēsis leads his people into battle and wins the hearts of the most sought-after maidens in Riga. With alcoholism at a steady high for regional males, the vomiting folk hero in the mural criticizes the weakened and intoxicated Latvian national identity, a common critique in response to Latvia's constantly changing identity in response to foreign pressures.

In summary, the public space – and neither a government building nor a private apartment – is ripe for subversion and satire. The public streets and squares are the places where demonstrations occur and where revolutions pass their tipping points to incite comprehensive political change. Those changes would not be possible without the communication of hidden, censored, and provoking information. Graffiti and street art are uniquely positioned to share these kinds of information with an audience; the density of passersby, combined with purposeful geographic placement, makes the urban space especially effective for circumventing censorship and exposing privately held information and sentiment.

Chapter Six

Signs and Symbols as a Form of Political Expression

Signs and symbols are what make graffiti both visually appealing and persuasive as a form of communication. Intentionally or unintentionally, the artist integrates text and pictures into their artwork to generate intertextual and often multilingual meaning more effectively. Symbols also help artists use indirect, coded language to communicate subversive content, such as support for a particular cause or mobilizational details, thereby securing some plausible deniability for both themselves and for their followers while potentially misleading the authorities. Semiotics, literary theory, cultural sociology, and media theory all help us see how this meaning-making functions in graffiti.

Signs, Symbols, and Text: Signifying Meaning in Graffiti with Semiotics

Linguistics, the study of language, can explain a great deal about how sentient beings communicate with one another – for example, how humans form particular sounds, structure grammatical clauses, and adopt new jargon (Martinet 1964). Its philosophical subdiscipline, semiotics, considers non-linguistic systems of communications, such as signs and symbols, taking a taxonomical approach to the understanding of nuanced and non-linguistic communication (Peirce 1931-1935; Peirce 1958; Peirce 1991). While semiotics is concerned with "all sensory stimuli that could create another idea in the receiver's mind ... [such as] smoke [as] a sign of fire, or flowers [as] a sign of love," semiology is focused only on intentional acts of communication, such as speaking, writing, and gesture (Daylight 2012, 37). As such, semiology (from the Greek word for sign) is a helpful lens through which to analyze art.

Semiology draws heavily from psychology and therefore takes a social scientific approach to the study of communication. For instance, it assumes that there are certain laws governing communication. Within semiology, and semiotics more broadly, communication is organized into three nuanced categories: the symbol, the signal, and the sign.

Symbols are vehicles of communication used to represent an idea. For example, in Prague, a painting of a dove carrying an olive branch is a symbol of peace. Symbols can represent conventions, beliefs, and associations established in the natural world or created by humans. The meaning of a symbol can be constituted either individually or through cultural contexts.

Signals are distinct from symbols in their capacity to indicate direction or action. A signal not only conveys meaning; it also triggers some kind of reaction, whether inducing or modifying a viewer's behavior. Signals are simple and striking, such as the ringing noise that drives a listener to halt their current activities and race to the telephone (or to consciously ignore it).

Finally, a sign is the most basic unit of meaning in semiotics. Almost everything in everyday interactions can be interpreted as a sign, including the viewed, heard, seen, gestured, and spoken elements of daily life. Central to semiology is the conception that the sign is two-sided. The two sides, or components, of each sign are what Ferdinand de Saussure named *the signifier* and *the signified* (Saussure 1922). The signifier is the expression – literally the acoustic image – and the signified is the concept that this combination of acoustic images expresses. When the sign includes a word, for example, the signifier may be the word "STOP" whereas the signified is the actual halting order.

Given the assumption that graffiti is a text that can be read, each image, scrawl, or logo can be understood as a sign, with both a denotative (or literal) meaning as well as a connotative (or derived) meaning. This also applies to graffiti and street art that lack actual words. Just as, in the case of a formal school crossing sign, the line of children depicted does not represent an *actual* line of children, but rather the philosophical concept of children walking in a line, a drawing of a rainbow may represent optimism or one's identity in the LGBTQIA+ community rather than merely the phenomenon of a rainbow in nature.

In Russia, following the initiation of the Kremlin's war in Ukraine, coded symbols were used to mobilize by communicating the details of an opposition meeting. These subversive methods were necessary, as public antiwar expression, if prosecuted, could lead to severe punishments such as long jail sentences and large fines. For example, Ilya Krasilchik's February 24, 2022, social media post showed a sketch of Russian poet Alexander Pushkin, the number seven, and the repetitive icon of a walking man. The post does not explicitly share that the gathering is to be a march, parade, or demonstration. Rather, from this combination of symbols, the viewer understands that they are to meet at 7 p.m. in Push-kinskaia Square, a pedestrian space in Moscow, to "take a walk" together, assumedly to protest (Wood and Lerner 2022). This use of symbols to communicate the details of an opposition meeting is reminiscent of the tools used to indicate the details of the opposition's Strategy-31 meetings, such as the 2011 Saint Petersburg sticker of Peter the Great Trampling Valentina Matvienko alongside a time and place, as discussed in Chapter Four.

In Łódź – as in urban centers elsewhere across post-communist Eastern Europe, such as in Ukraine and Lithuania – graffiti regarding wartime collective memory and ethnic hatred are common. Despite a nearly non-existent Jewish population, the walls in Łódź are overloaded with antisemitic and pro-Nazi references in hundreds of different handwritings. Therefore, a scribbled "HEIL HITLER" near Manufaktura, a mid-city textile factory converted into a contemporary arts center and shopping mall, is not uncommon. The signifier in this case is the collection of letters that make up the words "Heil Hitler." Given the textual nature of this example, the signified is relatively clear: the artist supports, or wishes their viewer to support, Adolf Hitler, the German fuhrer and leader of the Nazi party responsible for a genocide and war that left upward of 20 million dead, including 6 million Jews.[1] This pro-Hitler sentiment is especially problematic in Łódź, given that an estimated 6 million Poles in particular died under Nazi occupation.

Five kilometers away, on the outskirts of town, graffiti demarcates the outline of the Łódź Ghetto – the second largest WWII-era Jewish ghetto – which was designed for the forced displacement of Jews from their homes and their isolation from the non-Jewish population (Figure 6.1). In this case, too, cultural context aids the transmission of information. While the signifier here shows the name and years of the Litzmannstadt (Łódź) Ghetto, the signified communicates that this graffiti marks the separation of physical space, like a symbol on a map, as well as the violence that occurred in this space. Such a graffitied demarcation has a different impact depending on the intentionality of the viewer: For a visitor who came to the former Łódź ghetto for some kind of closure, the exactness of this line serves at minimum as tacit acknowledgment and at most as evidence of the crimes that took place there, whereas for the wandering person who stumbles upon this boundary, the graffiti may shock them out of their ignorance. For both the planned and unplanned discovery of this graffiti, the painted designation acts as a memorial to, and even witness of, the inhuman acts that took place within this area of Łódź.

Figure 6.1. Graffiti demarcates the boundary of the Litzmannstadt Ghetto (1940–1944). August 2011. Łódź, Poland. (Photo: Alexis Lerner)

However, graffiti does not need text to communicate effectively. When Manufaktura was a textile factory in the early nineteenth century, many of its working-class employees lived in nearby apartment-style housing developments. Today, these developments are rundown and, in some cases, abandoned. The exterior walls are coated with layers of swastikas, representing ideological stances such as Aryan supremacy, Nazism, xenophobia, and antisemitism. Artists use graffitied swastikas to communicate hate and intolerance quickly to their community, but Jews and other minorities no longer live in this neighborhood of Łódź. Therefore, these swastikas may not only be painted to indicate hate *toward* minorities, but also to communicate insular membership in a skinhead gang. The latter meaning is reinforced by the location of these swastikas, as they are not located in tourist or commercial neighborhoods of Łódź, but rather on the walls of rundown, interwar housing developments, where these artists are likely to live or socialize.

These swastikas are juxtaposed – over and over again – with six-pointed stars (the Jewish Star of David) and phrases such as "Jews to the Gas" or "Anti-Jews," such as in the example shown in Figure 6.2, where the swastika in the lower left corner has since been refashioned as a shaded-in

Figure 6.2. Jewish stars etched into the wall of an industrial-era housing development. August 2011. Łódź, Poland. (Photo: Alexis Lerner)

square (a common solution for an etched swastika that cannot be buffed). This highlights, in true Saussurian style, the arbitrary and subjective quality of communication when it comes to signs that lack text. This is because "Jews" in this case may refer to the Cracovia football club that historically welcomed Jewish players and therefore was known as the Judes. Its competitor out of Wisla became known as the Anti-Judes. The nearness of these football references to swastikas and Hitler indicates a more nuanced and multifaceted meaning than the signifiers alone. This is one of the most intriguing transformations in my opinion, and one that I unpack at length in Chapter Ten of this book.

Not all post-Soviet signs and symbols are about Nazi ideology and ethnic politics. As I discuss in detail in Chapter Seven, graffiti is traditionally intended and received as subversive. The use of coded messages is inherent to that subversiveness as an artist who writes, "Down with the President!" may find themselves detained or jailed. This is doubly true if an artist includes their name or pseudonym next to blasphemous words. On the other hand, symbols can communicate messages without drawing attention to oneself from the authorities or one's community. They provide an artist with some plausible deniability, particularly when one's pseudonym is not drawn next to the symbol as their identity cannot be elucidated.

Consider, for example, a Saint Petersburg stencil of a double-headed eagle, the national symbol for Russia dating back to the Tsarist era, with what seems to be a bottle of vodka in its talons, criticizing the alcoholism understood to plague Russian men. (A similar stencil advising Russians to "Stop Drink and [Instead] Engage in Athletics" was among the first I observed during my fieldwork in Saint Petersburg in 2009.) In Figure 6.3, a Minsk-based artist painted a stencil that illustrates a knight on horseback, the "Pahonia" or, in English, chase.

Those with local historical knowledge understand the political meaning of the Pahonia, which was originally a symbol used during the Grand Duchy of Lithuania in the thirteenth century. In the eighteenth century, it appeared on the royal coat of arms of the unified Polish–Lithuanian Commonwealth and then on the imperial coat of arms of the Russian Empire. The Belarusian state adopted the Pahonia symbol in 1918, at which time it showed on the Belarusian Democratic Republic's coat of arms, but during the postwar Soviet period, the Pahonia became an outlawed symbol of Belarusian political identity. The independent Belarusian state co-opted it once again after the fall of the Soviet Union in 1991, but in 1995, soon after he came to power, Aleksandr Lukashenko banned the image from all aesthetic discourse. After this ban in 1995, the opposition adopted the symbol as representative of their desire for

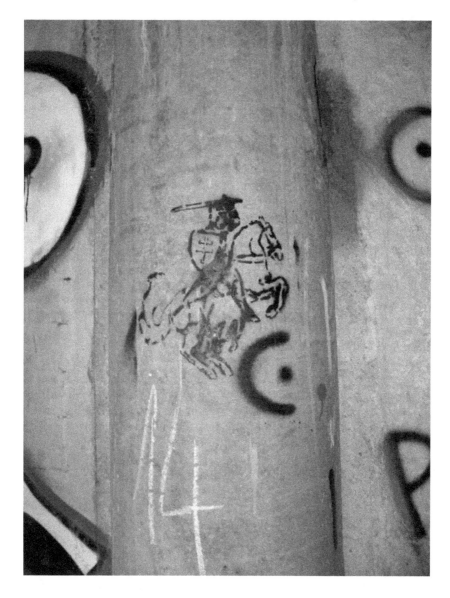

Figure 6.3. Pahonia stencils in an abandoned parking garage on the outskirts of the city. July 2011. Minsk, Belarus. (Photo: Alexis Lerner)

freedom, independence, and a unified opposition.[2] The images do not include explanatory text; however, their historical, political, and social associations make the meanings of these symbols clear.

Mirroring, Repetition, and Replication in Graffiti

The concept of mirroring, which I borrow from literary theory, can clarify how the stickers and stencils used in graffiti intrinsically reiterate one message over time and across space. Mirroring occurs in two ways: the repetition of one's own work and the replication of others' work. Through the act of repetition, an artist builds public recognition for their symbol and what it represents, even building meaning for images that had no previous contextual relevance (Bauman 1987). At first, an artist writes his name or message next to a symbol, and over time, the symbol speaks for itself, and the accompanying name or explanation will cease to appear.

An example is a simple wreath-like symbol. Alone, this has no explicit meaning, but if a viewer has lived in a city like Prague or Vladivostok for an extended period, they are likely to be aware that the symbol previously accompanied nationalist and xenophobic slogans like "Love Your Own Race," shown in Figure 6.4. Even without the text accompaniment, the wreath symbol maintains this association and therefore perpetuates its antagonistic capacity for those who recognize its historical relationship with a hateful phrase or a violent graffiti crew. Further, while local authorities may erase or quickly cover an explicitly xenophobic statement, a wreath with no accompanying hateful language may stay on a wall for a longer amount of time.

Replication applies to those artists who imitate another's work in a memetic manner. Each graffiti artist develops a unique style over their career, recognizable not only by their chosen tag but also by their preferred color scheme, placement, style, and size. Copying another artist's style or tag does still happen, despite being looked down upon. A suitable example of this is in the case of the Zachem crew and the eponymous tag it painted ubiquitously across Moscow in the early twenty-first century. At the height of Zachem's efforts, the phrase transitioned from being added to a space to being "part of nature there." This became apparent when Zachem graffiti began showing up in popular Russian films, as a visual representation of post-Soviet, late-capitalist ennui. After having surpassed a tipping point in popularity, copycat crews popped up around the city, imitating the original crew's style, lettering, colors, and placement.

The original Zachem crew found this meme-like propagation of their work without their consent frustrating (Most 2011). According to a 2011

Figure 6.4. "Love Your Own Race." 2009. Saint Petersburg, Russia. (Photo: Alexis Lerner)

interview with the group's leader, Misha Most, the sheer frequency of the imitations led the original members to perceive that their work would have less of an impact on their neighborhoods. The flooding of the public space with copycat graffiti resulted in Most's impression that some might view the originals as less unique and less groundbreaking. To some degree, Most was right; not only did this proliferation of imitations increase the public familiarity with and endearment for the *concept* of Zachem, but it also resulted in the artistic and social devaluation of the original Zachem crew outside of the graffiti-writing community.

The accuracy with which a reproduction mirrors an original is irrelevant. More important is how the reproduction impacts or affects the viewer. The concept of mirroring applies not only to repetition and replication *among* artists but also to the way graffiti writers mimic phenomena found in nature. French sociologist, philosopher, and cultural theorist Jean Baudrillard, in his text *Simulacra and Simulation*, attests that fabricated signs and symbols are often constructions and mirror-image simulations of the real (*real* here meaning that they are originally found in nature) (1994 [1981], 103). In this seminal work of postmodernist literary theory, Baudrillard uses the concepts of simulacra and simulation to illustrate the breakdown of truth and reality. Simulations are intended to reflect nature, however imperfectly, and simulacra are symbols that emerge fully from cultural and media representations of nature – that is, they do not reflect nature themselves – and proceed to construct human experience.

According to this lens, cultural and media representations of nature are both falsified and overproduced reflections. Even on an intuitive level, we know this to be true. For example, while a mirror image replicates an original with great accuracy, one cannot reach out and touch the face in the mirror in the same way that they can connect with the face in nature. The mirror also distorts the true image by flipping the original right to the mirrored left and vice versa. This may resonate in a late- or post-pandemic world, as we also consider the difference between face-to-face "in-person" interactions and virtual interactions that occur over digital video conferencing platforms. Digital displays of our conversational counterparts, while occurring in real time, are nevertheless incomplete, mirrored, and even retouched images of those with whom we are interacting.

This replication of reality can also be used when thinking about photographs, videos, and, yes, graffiti stencils and murals, of political and cultural leaders. For example, Russian president Vladimir Putin's face is constantly depicted on banners, in street art, and on television. The image of Putin is perpetuated so heavily throughout Russian society that the form gains a fictitious air. These generated copies of copies produce a collection of signs and symbols that represent a new truth, one that is ultimately fabricated, though authoritative, and dominant over nature.

The mass reproduction of symbols of "truth" and "reality" largely impact a breakdown of the distinction between the real and the reflection. Not only are mirror images and simulations flawed representations of the original object in nature, but reproductions of these mirror images in media and culture – simulacra – *replace* the original objects in nature in their capacity to shape society. Therefore, when the Russian president appears in his actual form before a crowd, it is not the poster that "feels" falsified, but the true self. The ability to mass-produce the replica but not the original empties the latter of its meaning and value. When the form is propagated, the real is devalued.

Through this form of mirroring, an artist creates a reputation for a symbol, building meaning into an image that previously had no contextual relevance.[3] Figures 6.5, 6.6, and 6.7 depict three prominent Russian or Soviet leaders. Starting at the top left and moving clockwise, Vladimir Putin is shown in Prague alongside the words "Putin Totality." In true satirical Gogolian style, the eminent leader is missing his nose, an orifice that symbolizes elitism and pretension in the Russian literary canon. To the right is the head of Tsar Nicholas II on the body of a mythical, bird-like, claw-footed creature, reflecting that, in Moscow, political leaders hold celebrity-like status, even long after their death. Two courtyards away, in a train yard underpass, a wheatpaste shows revolutionary icon Vladimir Lenin standing in Red Square and asking Vladimir Putin to lie with him in the immortal tomb.

An adherence to an authentic reality and therefore to the image in nature is not as important as the message expressed in the symbolic reproduction. This is because the latter allows subsequent discourse to evolve farther from its origins and potentially creates new ways of seeing and understanding the initial concepts.

By depicting the Russian autocrat as missing a nose or having feathers for fingers, the graffiti artist establishes a new truth. In nature, the so-called power vertical implies that authoritarian leaders maintain complete control over everything that occurs under their rule – including the ability to express political discontent. However, according to the new truth established over time through literature, media, and culture, the leader *can* be satirized, and the average person can regain their capacity to express themselves politically. Art – including graffiti – is fundamentally involved in this process of truth creation, in its ability to produce and perpetuate memetic narratives.

Figure 6.5. "Putin Totality." August 2011. Prague, Czech Republic.

Figure 6.6. The head of Tsar Nicholas Romanov II on the body of a mythical
bird. November 2016. Moscow, Russia.

Figure 6.7. Vladimir Lenin inviting Vladimir Putin to rest beside him in the Immortal Tomb. March 2012. Moscow, Russia. (All photos: Alexis Lerner)

Placing the Signs and Symbols of Graffiti into Context

Canadian critical theorist Marshall McLuhan's 1964 mantra "the medium is the message" helps us explore the environment in which signs and symbols exist, demonstrating how important the tools and methods used to produce the replication are in a message's construction and interpretation (also see McLuhan and Fiore 1967, as well as Berger 1972). For example, in Budapest, a downtown stencil shows a blindfolded person speaking into a radio microphone. Below the character is the word "Szólásszabadság" (in English, Freedom of Speech) (Figure 6.8). This image implies that those with access to the media are to speak with closed eyes – whether the result of state-led censorship or self-censorship – so that they only speak on government-approved topics and from government-approved perspectives.

The medium of this work – a stencil fashioned in a third location to be spray-painted illegally onto a crumbling wall – offers a meta-critique on Hungary as an unfree society. At the time that this stencil appeared, mass protests were taking place there in response to Hungary's so-called

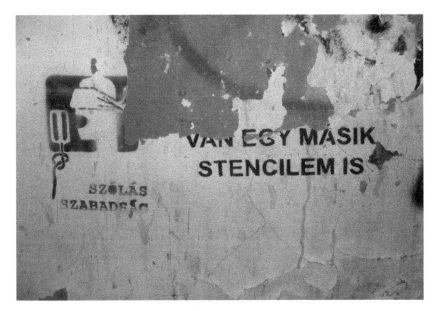

Figure 6.8. "Freedom of Speech." Stencil. July 23, 2011. Budapest, Hungary. (Photo: Alexis Lerner)

Media Law. Introduced by the Fidesz government in January 2011, the controversial law subjected all published material on the net and in print to government approval. If denizens were able to speak freely on traditional media channels, such as the nightly news or the daily digest, surely, they would not have to take to the streets to stencil tongue-in-cheek critiques about stifled media freedoms.

Chapter One discusses another example, the stencils that appeared outside Kurskaia Metro in Moscow saying in Russian, "I love Independent Courts" and "I love (the) Free Press" (Figure 1.2). Again, the very placement of such works on a public wall imply that speech is not free and that one has to engage in illegal defacement to express a wish for truly free speech. When the disenfranchised lack access or equal representation, the anonymous nature of graffiti provides an otherwise voiceless societal group a certain shared power. Indeed, an artist's use of graffiti as a medium to express discontent with repressive censorship or power barriers illustrates the unrestricted quality of the public art form.

Graffiti as Confrontation

Signs and symbols do not need text to communicate information, but words have a particular capacity to perform intent or to call listeners to action. This assumption that language serves a greater purpose than the sharing of factual data is captured by John Landshaw Austin's speech act theory (1962 [1955]), later developed further by John Searle (1969). Austin categorizes types of text or speech into three categories of analysis: locutionary acts, defined as the utterance itself; illocutionary acts that refer to the meaning packaged within the locutionary act; and perlocutionary acts, which reference the effect of the former two types of text on the observer (1962 [1955]). Analyzing text as locutionary/illocutionary acts can be thought of as conceptually parallel to analyzing signs and symbols in terms of signifier/signified and can similarly be used to unpack the references and meaning in graffitied communication (though the theoretical frameworks used in speech act theory differ somewhat from those used in semiotics).

For example, the artist Radya created a four-story mural on a parking garage at an arts compound in Vladivostok, which reads, "эй ты люби меня" (in English, "Hey, you love me") (Figure 6.9). While this is one of the Yekaterinburg-based artist's less political works, it nevertheless

Figure 6.9. "Hey, You Will Love Me. Radya." November 2018. Vladivostok, Russia. (Photo: Alexis Lerner)

demands an action of the observer. The locutionary or signifier in this example is in the unpunctuated utterance written in a neutral font, while the illocutionary or signifier is in Radya's instruction for those living in the Far East to love the artist and his unique approach to street art. However, in past interviews, Radya has mentioned that he has ideas for graffiti based on things that he has read or overheard, implying that the statement could be reminiscent of song lyrics or serve as a private "Overheard in Vladivostok"-type anecdote made public, in which case the perlocutionary effect would be to bring forth a memory of a beloved song lyric or to stimulate feelings of judgment from the observer toward the person who uttered the abrasive or overly proud statement to another person.[4]

In Tbilisi, an anonymous stencil depicts Georgian president and public figure Mikheil Saakashvili alongside the words "I Bet You'll Vote Next Time, Hippie" (Figure 6.10). The text is a play on a phrase often used to mock the Bush administration's hawklike approach to foreign policy and its involvement in wars in Iraq and Afghanistan. Despite successfully reducing corruption, strengthening ties with the West, and improving business conditions, Saakashvili's administration is nonetheless viewed by many Georgians as rife with state repression, human rights abuses, and responsibility for a five-day war with Russia in 2008.

This Old Tbilisi stencil is not so much telling the viewer to behave in a certain way but rather establishing a particular mood of combativeness. Saakashvili's hands, shown holding up two fingers in a V-shape, add another layer of intertextuality as a symbol for peace. Yet, the peace sign, combined with a smirk and the word "bet," could be interpreted as pugnacious, as though the figure shown in the stencil were looking to start an argument for the sake of arguing. Perhaps whoever attempted to scratch away the character's face – something we know to have occurred after the creation of the stencil because of the absence of black paint – agreed that the character, or its creator, was "behaving" impudently. In this case, the text challenges the observer to a confrontation.

To conclude, an interdisciplinary theoretical framework illuminates numerous aspects of how graffiti – and signs and symbols more generally – generate meaning. The content or neutral envelope by which information is presented can be noteworthy, as can the memetic influences and intertextual references that give that information meaning. Theoretical approaches including semiology, literary theory, and media and communication studies alert us to the rhetorical devices that graffiti and street art can leverage. Through these disciplines, we come to understand, for example, how repetition can either increase the visibility of a symbol, thereby improving its communicative effectiveness (as in the case of the

Figure 6.10. "I Bet You'll Vote Next Time Hippie." January 2017. Tbilisi, Georgia. (Photo: Alexis Lerner)

nationalist wreath) or devalue a sign's meaning through over-propaga-
tion (as happened with Zachem). Further, these approaches encourage
us to consider the placement of a work, as well as the accompanying
text, and how these features are designed to affect an observer's mood
or encourage their action. They help us understand that the way the
contemporary artist uses graffiti as a medium to express discontent with
repressive censorship or power barriers reflects precisely the free and
effective nature of the public art form.

Chapter Seven

Street Art as Text

Graffiti's discursive power and potential strengthen its role as a form of public political participation. Artists and activists who write in the public sphere are in constant conversation with the subjects of their works, the funders of those works, local authorities, passersby, as well as one another. No sign or symbol exists in isolation; understanding the context of each work illustrates how a particular piece responds and contributes to a greater political discourse.

An incident during my fieldwork made this clear to me:

In the winter of 2012, Basket, the grandfather of Russian graffiti, invited a friend and me to join him for a night of mural painting. As an ethnographer of political graffiti, I all but jumped at the opportunity to observe this instrumental figure in the history of post-Soviet public art while he created new works. After midnight, we met deep underneath the city on one of Moscow's striking and monumental metro platforms. My anticipation grew as we crossed the city by train, switching lines and pausing our expedition to buy beers and snacks at a corner store.

We exited the metro and trekked by foot to Flacon, a Soviet-era crystal material industrial complex refashioned as a hipster shopping and arts district around 2009. Flacon rents its enormous warehouses, open-style lofts, and divided stalls to entrepreneurs and artisans. One such vendor was a third-party computer sales and repair shop. This was our final stop for the night, as Basket had been hired to paint a mural of an apple on the interior wall of the repair shop.

Our destination on this outing took me by surprise, but it should not have. In an interview a few days earlier, Basket explained that he had begun to paint these commissioned works because they provided a creative outlet as well as a generous paycheck. He insisted that known artists commonly performed commissioned works and that painting on assignment was not looked down upon by others in these social groups.[1]

Observing Basket, a graffiti legend, in action remained meaningful for me. Nevertheless, the commodification of his talent, knowledge, and tag in the hyper-capitalized twenty-first century post-Soviet space struck me as symbolic. Experiences like this occurred time and time again over my fieldwork trips, which led me to theorize about the boundary between classical and co-opted graffiti, or between what graffiti once represented and what I saw it becoming. To me, the commodification of graffiti not only co-opts both the artform and the artist, but also inverts the characteristic of graffiti from subversive to sanctioned.

Graffiti is an ever-evolving form of communication that engages passersby, fellow artists, and the environment in which it is painted. Graffiti in this sense shares characteristics with the novel, as it can be read as a *dynamic and dialogic* text about the world that exists around it. It is through this lens that we can apply Mikhail Mikhailovich Bakhtin's concepts of the *chronotope* and the carnivalesque. The Bakhtinian chronotope (literally *chronos-topos,* or "time-space") represents "the intrinsic connectedness of temporal and spatial relationships that [is] artistically expressed in literature" (Bakhtin 1937 [Holquist, ed, 1981], 84). In this chapter, I outline three such *chronotopes* as they relate to the practice and art of graffiti: what I call "Midnight Graffiti" chronotope, or the classical communicative artform; the "Corporate World" chronotope, which stands in opposition to the Midnight Graffiti chronotope; and the co-opted or commissioned version of the communicative artform, which I call the "Co-opted Graffiti" chronotope.

Graffiti Must be Read as a Text

The public space fosters a communicative and narrative art, which, though not published within two book covers, transforms a city's walls into a discursive text. Graffiti artists use this artform to bring underlying themes of human existence into the public space for all to see, highlighting conversations that typically occur behind closed doors – for example, identifying the targets of xenophobic violence, broadcasting the identities of corrupt elites, critiquing policies that undermine societal equality, and promoting contested versions of history.

Not only does graffiti anonymously publicize the content of private monologues, but artists also engage with each other dialogically. Dialogism reflects a pluralism in opinion among societal or geographically organized groups (Hodge and Kress 1997, 49-50; Hodge and Kress 1988). After all, societies (even fully insular communities) are not uniform or monotonous, and neither are the artists or the art that imitate a society.

Instead, each neighborhood projects a multitude of contradictory voices, and hence, each mural contains multiple layers of negotiation and inter-textuality from among those voices.

The discursive nature of this artform is observable. With each new day, new images and messages are added to, and used to cover, old im-ages and messages. This dialogue occurs among writers as well between said artists and the state. Local authorities engage with graffitied public sentiment by sending teams of cleaners to buff content perceived to be unacceptable. In some cases, authorities will hire artists to paint state-curated messages on behalf of the powers that be (Lerner 2021). This is especially true when public sentiment is otherwise controlled by author-itative bodies, as graffiti has the capacity to share censored or private information.

Further, state engagement with political graffiti proves to be dispro-portionate. Select pieces elicit a larger response than others, and certain artists are silenced more often than their peers. This disproportionate engagement indicates that certain narratives (for example, those works that critique gentrifying and elite-led construction projects) are "intoler-able," while others remain in the public space for years on end (for ex-ample, the phrase "Jews are Vermin," which lasted unbuffed from 2009 to 2011 on the same block as Budapest's Great Synagogue on Dohány Utca, or Dohany Street in English).

What is the Chronotope?

Because we must read graffiti as a text, as an artform, and as an aesthetic that, like a literary work, responds to its context, I suggest that scholars and observers of graffiti integrate existing literary techniques and tropes into our analysis of the dialogic nature of graffiti and public art. As afore-mentioned, Bakhtin's *chronotope* is a literary tool useful in categorizing and understanding the temporal–spatial plane upon which an event, or a series of events, takes place as well as the viewer's interaction with that temporal–spatial intersection.

Bakhtin provides many examples of how the chronotope aids our reading of literature. In the Greek Romance, for example, he shows us that both time and space are abstract, boundless, and simultaneously suspended in a state of "at just that moment" (Bakhtin 1937 [Holquist, ed, 1981], 92). As a result, even if the observer (the reader) resumes reading the Greek Romance after a twenty-year hiatus, the protagonists remain equally youthful, brave, courageous, and physically able to rise to the challenges separating themselves from their lovers. By entering and exiting the chronotopic realm as one chooses, the reader interprets a narrative according to their own contextual understanding (through a lens of a risk-taking youth, inspired to find adventure, for example, or through the rose-tinted nostalgia of old age), engaging in discourse with and therefore legitimizing the constructed reality of the narrative (Lotman 1984, 72).

If a literary trope is crafted correctly and expressively, the reader will inevitably draw aspects of the chronotopic reality from within the binding into his own, non-literary, quotidian version of existence. Consider, for example, the chronotope of the road in Viktor Nabokov's *Lolita* or in Cormac McCarthy's 2006 post-apocalyptic novel *The Road*. In both stories, time slows and geographic space spreads while the characters are on the road; at the same time, this period is fleeting, as we know the end of the road and its consequences lay ahead. Temporally and spatially, reality is no longer "concentrated in the spaces of rooms where private family life goes on, rather [it] unfolds under the open sky, in movement around the earth. It must spread out as far and wide as possible" (Lotman 1984, 167).

The Midnight Graffiti Chronotope

The *topos* of the chronotope I call Midnight Graffiti is a clandestine realm where events take place in the depths of shadowed dark alleys and separated from the workers and families slogging through their responsibilities. With regard to *chronos*, this kind of art is always created late at night, or at least in darkness, and it exists with fluidity from night to night. This is because Midnight Graffiti transcends contemporary, results-driven, and measurable time; instead, it follows a time cycle that more closely reflects pre-industrial notions of time that revolved around sunrise and sunset. When created within the Midnight Graffiti chronotope, illegality and trespassing make even seemingly apolitical work subversive (such as that shown in Figure 7.1).

The Midnight Graffiti chronotope resembles to some degree that which Bakhtin identifies as the Rabelais or the literary carnivalesque. The foremost devices of this chronotope encourage licensed misrule, or a controlled kind of chaos, in which the balance of power and social hierarchy are temporarily inverted. This disruption not only "destroy[s] traditional connections and abolish[es] idealized strata; it also brings out the crude, unmediated connections between things that people otherwise seek to keep separate, in pharisaical error" (Bakhtin 1937 [Holquist, ed, 1981], 170).

Figure 7.1. Graffiti created after midnight. Alexis Lerner and Misha Most. 2015. Moscow, Russia. (Photo: Alexis Lerner).

Bakhtin writes:

> The ancient matrices are re-established here on a new and loftier base. They are freed from all that had disunited and distorted them in the old world. They are freed from all otherworldly explanations, sublimations, [and] interdicts. These new realities are purged through laughter, taken out of the high contexts that had disunited them, distorted their nature, and are brought into the real context of a freely developing human life. These realities are present in a world of freely realized human possibilities. There is nothing to limit this potential. This is the most fundamental distinguishing feature of Rabelais' work. All historical limits are, as it were, destroyed and swept away by laughter. The field remains open to human nature, to a free unfolding of all the possibilities inherent in man. In this respect Rabelais' world is diametrically opposed to the limited locale of the tiny idyllic world ... All limitations are bequeathed to the dying world, now in the process of being laughed out of existence (1937, 270).

In the carnivalesque ritual of reversal, the king is demoted to a joker and the joker promoted to a position of power. Bakhtin specifically writes

Figure 7.2. Viktor Orban as Mickey Mouse. 2011. Budapest, Hungary. (Photo: Alexis Lerner)

that the carnivalesque occurs where the "footlights are turned off," or in those public places where the division between spectator and performer have been removed (Marjanovic-Shane & White, 2014).[2] The notion of a public space without footlights also brings to mind the dialogic and uncontrolled nature of communication typically associated with private spaces.

The literary devices that facilitate these instances of destruction, inversion, and exposure – humor, vulgarity, irony, and parody – are also used discursively in the graffiti realm, a plane that certainly qualifies as "the real context of a freely developing human life." Within the Midnight Graffiti chronotope, artists use these techniques to poke fun at political leaders and their policy decisions. For example, in Budapest, the sticker shown in Figure 7.2 depicts Viktor Orban wearing Mickey Mouse ears. Below the character, the sticker reads "Viki Mouse," a feminization of the prime minister's first name. In another stencil, fashioned to appear like a cigarette package label, a Saint Petersburg artist wrote, "The Party United Russia May Be the Cause of Impotence," referring to the Russian

Figure 7.3. "The Party United Russia May be the Cause of Impotence." August 2011. Saint Petersburg, Russia. (Photo: Alexis Lerner)

president's own political party (Figure 7.3). By painting messages like these on a city's public space, the artist gains some control over the public reception of a political leader, thereby elevating their own power as the keeper of the information.

Of course, this acquired power and control depends on the visibility of the piece and its reception. Bakhtin scholar Sue Vice writes, "the whole point of the carnivalesque, and equally dialogism, is that the viewer is also a participant" (1997, 18). By nature of being truly reflective of the society's actual composition and divisions, said discourse is often crass.

This crass language – derogatory slurs and swear words – allows for writers in the Midnight Graffiti chronotope to express their discontent with particular emphasis. On a trash canister in Budapest, shown in Figure 7.4, one artist wrote "F*ck Jobbik" (a far-right political party with just under 20% of the country's parliamentary seats); another artist wrote "Cigány (a derogatory term for Roma);" a third wrote, "666" (a universal sign of the devil); a fourth, a cross; and a fifth, an anarchist symbol (2011).

Figure 7.4. Pluralistic graffiti discourse. 2011. Budapest, Hungary. (Photo: Alexis Lerner)

This variation in perspective reflects many different political camps in contemporary Hungary, from xenophobic populists to devil worshippers, anarchists, and Jobbik opponents. This dialogical graffiti not only highlights the diversity of political perspectives held by the Hungarian population but also that these coexist with each other in one small rectangle of space. None of the artists tried to buff or cover the statements of their colleagues, regardless of whether they agreed with the latter's sentiment. When reading a wall – or a trash can – for a city's narrative, it is important to consider the competing voices, contexts, and interests. All sides of a political conversation or negotiation can engage in the discourse of the streets.

The types of viewers that a work will engage is determined by the dynamics of a particular neighborhood, its inhabitants, and its societally attributed value (Logan and Molotch 1987, 18). Midnight Graffiti artists pick up on this attributed value of place and act accordingly. In general, places that are more valuable in the corporate world (in dollars) are also more valuable in the graffiti world (in social currency). Social constructions, such as proximity to pedestrian districts or public transit, make X a better place to tag than Y. For example, critiques of political leaders, parties, and policies may be most effective when painted in wealthy or high-traffic neighborhoods, where its readership is likely to be more closely linked to political, financial, or social elites. Further, given that graffiti is used to deconstruct the status quo by vandalizing (private) property, the artist can temporarily dominate a high-value public space by covering it with his own symbol of ownership (usually their name).

The Corporate World Chronotope

The Midnight Graffiti chronotope exists in contrast to what I call the Corporate World chronotope. Communication in the corporate world is generally monologic and filtered through official channels prior to utterance. The key characteristic of the corporate world is human domination over both the temporal and spatial planes. In the Corporate World chronotope, time is on a strictly cyclical schedule, measured in production, coffee breaks, paid time off, and contract lengths. If one needs to move more quickly toward the future, that time can be purchased as time is a commodity that can be bought and sold. When citizens do not possess the hard currency necessary to buy time (for example, by hiring help or investing in time-saving tools), they may risk their equity in the form of personal sacrifice of well-being, savings, or stability (Harvey 1985, 80). Likewise, space in the Corporate World chronotope is divided up into tradable portions and the system is, according to Luhmann, "operatively closed on the basis of communication" (2000, 30-31).

The tools of technology and industry allow humans to run the contemporary corporate world with greater efficiency than ever before. The advertisements, marketing campaigns, and symbols of the corporate world – however transient – carry a sense of permanence and authority, as if these completed products and ideologies have always existed. The physical manifestation of this aesthetic – the shopping mall – exists as an allegory to this presentation as symbols are delivered in a suspended state for public viewership and consumption.

While the inhabitants of the Midnight Graffiti and the Corporate World chronotopes exist on different temporal planes and rarely (if ever) cross paths in person, the two groups still exist in the same physical, geographic place. One might imagine, for example, a group of wayward Muscovite teens, armed with spray cans, illegally "bombing," or painting their personal tag, on subway trains and Moscow businesses at 2 a.m. The rest of the city – the corporate world – wakes up the next morning to pass the new works on the same streets along their commute. The Midnight Graffiti realm, inhabited by a group of people who take over a space and propagate it with stolen supplies and clandestine operations, is a completely separate world that intrudes into the Corporate World's regimented existence through signs left on the walls. The presence of each group is only discernible to the other by what they leave behind. For the Midnight Graffiti painters, that is their completed works of public art.

The social hierarchy of the corporate world is clearly defined, and the methods of climbing the corporate ladder are based on having a shrewd ability to produce, dominate, and successfully consolidate power. In the corporate world, the elites determine which events are newsworthy and how news is communicated to the public. In this realm of ownership and consumption, average citizens earn relative obscurity beneath the domination of their masters (Luhmann 2000 [1996], 30-31). Yet in the graffiti world – and in the Rabelais for that matter – social constructions and corporate ladders are deconstructed and devalued. In the graffiti realm, a determination of what information is newsworthy depends on the individual with the spray can.

An Attempt to Bridge these Worlds with Co-opted Graffiti

> If graffiti merely consisted of empty signifiers that 'have no content and express no message,' rather than signs that were charged with multiple meanings far beyond those intended by their makers, the corporate world under the conditions of the 'new spirit of capitalism' would hardly have shown such interest in this type of aesthetic. (Beyes, Krempl, and Deuflhard, eds., 2009, np)

The Midnight Graffiti and Corporate World chronotopes link together through the Co-opted Graffiti chronotope.[3] Central to this third chronotope is the phenomenon of legal or sanctioned graffiti, where the tools of the people are leveraged to benefit the capitalist marketplace. Legal writing specifically indicates a commissioned graffiti job, in which a business or local institution contracts with the artist to market a product or a brand through a mural. As I have argued earlier, legal work – commissioned street art and corporation-sponsored graffiti festivals – undermines the artform's inherent opposition to authority and robs it of its ability to offer genuine critique.

Financial sponsors and businesses secure prime locations for these public artworks. These placements frequently guarantee the artists high visibility in addition to a stipend, reimbursement for paint, and a per diem in exchange for co-optation of their artform and the commodification of their work. A business that can contract an artist known for their subversive work is likely to further popularize their own brand because of the social capital it would provide. In some cases, businesses may donate their exterior walls to create a forum for non-commodified and non-state-sponsored artistic work, such as in the case of the Audubon

Society's Harlem 115 murals about 155 different species of birds negatively impacted by climate change.[4] In either case, commissioning provides artists with the privilege to create slowly, casually, and in broad
daylight if they so choose.

While Co-opted Graffiti *appears* similar to Midnight Graffiti and is often created by artists who otherwise paint subversive works, it is created
on a unique temporal–spatial plane. As previously discussed, street artists and their audiences exist on separate chronotopic planes, particularly when street art is created within the Midnight Graffiti chronotope.
Rarely, if ever, should the temporal and spatial (at the moment of creation) existences of the viewer and artist collide. And yet, this collision
is the precise intention of a commissioned work, as it is with the legal
festivals discussed at length in Part I of this book.

The problem with legalized graffiti is that the artform – the Midnight
Graffiti type – is inherently anti-authority (MacDonald 2001, 172). The
chronotopic realm of Midnight Graffiti wages war on private property
and mainstream media censorship. In their book *Ancient Graffiti in Context*, Jennifer Baird and Claire Taylor explain that while graffiti images
sometimes kick "against authority with *what* they say or depict, their primary and defining characteristic is spatial insubordination, that is appearing on surfaces where they have no right to be" (Baird and Taylor
2011, 110; 174). The corporate realm moves pieces from unsanctioned
to sanctioned physical and temporal spaces, which are shared by artist,
commissioner, and audience, thereby commodifying the image. This
serves to undermine both the nature and purpose of graffiti.

Legalizing the practice – changing both the place and the time of
graffiti – pits artists willing to create murals for payment against those
who create for non-commercial purposes. When graffiti is legalized, stencils no longer need to hide in the shadows of dark back alleys; rather the
corporate world welcomes graffiti artists to paint on private property in
broad daylight. Communities welcome previously outlawed graffiti artists back into the social fold. Yet the practice of legal graffiti in fact ostracizes illegal writers and those that refuse to participate in commissioned
or curated projects, who believe themselves – according to an important
aspect of the chronotope of the carnivalesque – to be expressing a Truth.

The graffiti, when legalized, is no longer a nuisance but rather a prized
tangible that humans can possess, sell, dominate, and control. The veil is
lifted and the artist – no longer anonymous or untouchable in a separate
time and space – steps through to the venerating corporate world, which
is generally seen as occurring simultaneously with the loss of social credibility within the graffiti realm (MacDonald 2001, 169). The basic characteristics of the Midnight Graffiti chronotope – laughter, crude vulgarity,

and the deconstruction of social hierarchy – disappear to some degree with the legalization of the artform. Legal graffiti does not deconstruct the existing social hierarchy but rather joins it.

I suggest that this commodification is the result of legal festivals and gallery attention to graffiti. The very boundaries of a legal festival contradict the essence of the carnivalesque and midnight graffiti chronotopes, spatial–temporal realities that are supposed to have unlimited time and space in which to grow and expand. The festival is organized around a predetermined time, location, and participatory setlist, therefore dominating the carnivalesque temporal–spatial reality with that of the corporate world. Through the legal festival and across all regime types, artists have quite literally come out of the shadows to register with the state so that they may paint on the state's behalf (Lerner 2021).

Moreover gallery attention to graffiti artists has skyrocketed in the past decade and graffiti artists can now make a living through their paintings, if they know how to market them correctly. Bristol (England)-based artist Banksy paints political stencils around the world such as the child portrayed in the ruins of Detroit's Packard Plant, accompanied by the words, "I remember when this was all trees." Yet, Banksy's works are so often chiseled out of surrounding brick and thrown into museums or sold in galleries with exorbitant price tags. Banksy retains his artistic independence – in some cases, such as his grotesque Holocaust references in the context of a faux-hotel in East Jerusalem, to a fault. In fact, it is precisely his shocking viewpoints through which Banksy is able to draw his loyal fan base. By presenting works like Banksy's as edgy products in demand, the Western gallery market has commodified the previously anonymous and illegal art of graffiti and thereby undermined the artform.

In the Midnight Graffiti chronotope, the art of graffiti purges the corporate world of its inauthentic men and deities, restoring the authenticity of the corporate world by sharing with its citizens a liberating truth. If uncontrolled and dialogical conversation is nearing its death in the pre-determined and contained temporal–spatial reality of the corporate world, then the narrative in the Midnight Graffiti realm at the intersection of two boundless planes is only just unfolding. The social capital artists accrue by engaging in these subversive and destructive acts is then bought and neutralized through the process of co-optation. As a result, the Co-opted Graffiti chronotope not only puts forth a message pre-approved by local government or business but also capitalizes on the social capital held by the artist who painted the commissioned work. The co-opted work harnesses the Midnight Graffiti chronotope's echo of subversion and chaos and brings it *into the light*, thereby establishing a completely new temporal–spatial plane of creation.

PART III

Interpreting Graffiti

Chapters Eight through Ten shift the conversation about graffiti and street art from the theoretical to the applied. In this section, I unpack three of the most common themes found in graffiti and street art. I also trace how depictions of these themes vary across the region and over time. For a description of how I tracked these themes, see the Note on Methods in the frontmatter of this book.

"Chapter Eight: The Political" explores public art with current political content. This includes references to contemporary political parties, leaders, candidates, state policies on issues related to foreign policy or war, as well as political institutions. These references span the entire spectrum of regime type, from consolidated authoritarian to fully democratic. However, certain policy issues are deemed contentious in authoritarian regimes. As a result, the targets of political street art in these states tend to be top leadership, the leading party, and the political institutions that prop them up. As states lean more democratic, the targets of political critique become corrupt local leaders, the agents of gentrification, and the economic concerns of a society.

"Chapter Nine: The Social" evaluates the social content of public art, including references to musical groups, drug and alcohol culture, contemporary national identity issues, and calls for social reform. By definition, more liberal and democratic states allow for basic critique of the regime and its leadership. As a result, social critique – works about LGBTQ+ rights, equality among the sexes, environmental concerns, and the like – often flourishes in these environments. Therefore, much of the social critiques found in Chapter Nine justifiably represent the region's democracies.

Lastly, "Chapter Ten: Who Controls Discourse?" looks closely at themes of political nostalgia and nationalism in public art. In this chapter, I focus on how graffiti expresses and promotes sentiment regarding World

War Two, the Holocaust, xenophobia, minority relations, and identity politics across the region. This chapter addresses the question of agency and why authorities permit some content (e.g., discriminatory slurs) but not other (e.g., critiques of corruption or war). I argue that this decision of which voices to tolerate, and even bolster, can tell us a great deal about the character of the state, its tolerance for pluralism, and of those that lead.

Chapter Eight

The Political

Most graffiti and street art address current political themes, which may entail explicit attacks on political leaders, political parties, and the integrity of various political institutions, such as elections or courts. Political thematic content may also reference the status of individual freedoms, such as freedom of speech or of assembly, through images that allude to human rights abuses, including the repression of opposition leaders, journalists, and activists. But political thematic art is different in authoritarian states like Belarus and Russia than in liberal democratic states such as Latvia or the Czech Republic. This chapter traces these differences, using photographs and anecdotes from my personal fieldwork archive.

Attacks on Leadership

Graffiti often pokes fun at leaders to diminish their legitimacy or reveals otherwise concealed information. Such is the case throughout the post-Soviet and post-communist European regions. This occurs in two ways: as critique of one's own leader or as critique of another state's leader.

In post-Soviet states, residents might use graffiti to critique their own leadership. They might mount a direct attack, such as the post-2018 slogan in Russia "Putin Must Go," or satirically undermine a leader by combining their appearance with a cartoon or imaginary figure. Consider, for example, a Moscow mural of Tsar Nicholas II's head on the body of a mythical bird (discussed in Chapter Six), or the aforementioned Budapest stencil of Hungarian prime minister Viktor Orban's head with Mickey Mouse ears and the label "Viki Mouse," a feminization of the leader's name (see Figure 7.2 in Chapter Seven). We can see similar satirical word play as a tool of delegitimization in a stencil of Kremlin insider and ideologist Vladislav Surkov. In Russian, the word Surkov doubles as a

Figure 8.1. "Surkov, Look For Other Marmots" (a play on the name Surkov). 2012. Moscow, Russia. (Photo: Alexis Lerner)

plural noun for marmots, a type of burrowing rodent. Therefore, when one Moscow-based artist decided to make fun of the politician in 2012, they wrote in Russian "Surkov, look for another Surkov," also interpreted as "Marmots, look for another Marmot," implying the rodent-like quality of Putin's top strategist (Figure 8.1). When an artist critiques a domestic leader using subversive, anonymous tools, their act indicates that they lacked alternative platforms for publicizing their discontent.

Such satirical representation of political leaders is common outside of Russia as well. During the Euromaidan protests across Ukraine in 2014, numerous murals and stencils explicitly attacked then-president Viktor Yanukovych. Some showed his face with a Hitler-like mustache, implying that his leadership resembled that of dictatorial Nazi Germany, while others depicted the incumbent behind bars with the dehumanizing sexual taunt "Pederast," used to accuse the former president of being a homosexual, sexual predator, or possibly engaging in sexual activity with prepubescent boys. In Prague, in 2011, left-wing political posters showed the faces of political candidates with phrases such as: "They are gambling with our lives" and "They tell me to adapt. What should I adapt to? Their shopping? Their careers? Their slavery?" In Budapest, activists targeted elected officials indirectly, such as in the sticker reading, "Policymakers are paid whores" and a freehand piece reading "Every four years, a monkey takes his throne." Writing graffitied critique of political officials is a way for residents to express their discontent in a public manner.

In Estonia, Edward von Lõngus (EvL) covers the country with Banksy-style stencils. For example, in 2013, EvL painted a piece titled "Oligarch," which showed Vladimir Lenin in a full-length fur coat with several thick, gold chains around his neck, a tongue-and-cheek reference to the inevitable, ego-based transition of political leaders to corrupt plutocrats. In Tallinn Old Town, in 2015, he created the "Naked Emperor," a piece that shows a proud political leader in the nude while carrying a briefcase full of cash, intended as a critique on the parliamentary elections taking place at the time (he has since replicated the work across Europe, from Brussels (Belgium) in 2017 to Aberdeen (Scotland) in 2023) (Rahman 2021; @edwardvonlongus). In 2018, in Tartu, EvL painted a play on Andy Warhol's Campbell's Soup piece, showing spoofs of World War Two-era president Konstantin Päts, a controversial and antidemocratic figure in Estonian history. In the mural, the artist lays nine side-by-side stylized versions of Päts, including Päts dressed as Batman, Päts dressed as David Bowie, Päts dressed as Captain Jack Sparrow, and Päts as Smeagol from *The Hobbit* and *The Lord of the Rings* trilogy, undermining the leader's credibility by fashioning him as a series of over-the-top popular culture characters.

Artists can also use graffiti to critique incumbents of states where political competition is non-existent, such as in the long-time authoritarian state of Belarus. In Minsk, authorities and the citizenry monitor downtown streets together; this high level of alert and scrutiny means that painting a political mural in a public space could land a writer in jail. As a result, to hasten their practice without foregoing it altogether, critical Belarusian artists often scrawl freehand with marker on a brick or scratch into a windowpane. For example, one artist quickly scribbled "Luka(shenko) sucks" on the clear, glass wall of a downtown bus stop in July 2011. Nevertheless, in the clean downtown district, the occasional piece of public political critique is immediately perceptible and buffed, as was the case with this work. Indeed, in authoritarian Minsk, the most critical words and symbols must exist out of sight, below eye level, and in its darkest corners.

Writers can also use graffiti and street art to critique the leader of some other nation. This is more commonly seen in liberal democratic states. For example, in Vilnius, Lithuania, Mindaugas Bonanu painted a mural of former United States president Donald Trump lip-locked with Russian president Vladimir Putin. A play on the famous Berlin Wall painting of Soviet leader Leonid Brezhnev kissing the German Democratic Republic leader Erich Honecker, the painting of Trump and Putin critiqued the mutual adoration of the two leaders and their oversized egos (Johnston 2016). A stencil in Prague critiqued the masculinity of former leader of the Soviet Union, Joseph Stalin, through a classical regional trope by depicting his face without its nose. Another Prague stencil called attention to then-Iranian president Mahmoud Ahmadinejad for arresting and imprisoning one of his critics without due process of law.

In my experience, critical graffiti directed at foreign leaders is almost exclusively written in the English language. Not only does the act of writing critical sentiment in a communal space publicize a particular issue but doing so in English further expands the potential international reach of a message when it is, for example, photographed and shared by passersby on social media or in a foreign publication.

Attacks on Parties

Artists use political graffiti to not only critique political leaders but also confront political parties, which play different roles under different regime conditions. Contemporary democratic states host multiple political parties, each designed to represent the interests of some subset of society. While some parties are dominant over others, in that they mobilize more voters or put forth more successful candidates during an election year, many small and niche political parties give voice to otherwise marginalized perspectives.

Alternatively, many autocratic states, especially those within the post-Soviet region, operate as single-party regimes, where there is one, or one dominant, party that effectively controls political life. In hybrid authoritarian states, some semblance of political competition exists in the form of multiple parties, regularly occurring elections, and public debates. Despite these performed rituals of political pluralism, these states experience little electoral uncertainty due to what Levitsky and Way (2010; 2002) call an uneven playing field. That is, candidates *can* compete, but certain candidates have an advantage over others due to their access to state resources, such as security and intelligence forces, which can both propel their own campaign forward and impede or halt the campaigns of their rivals.

Street art and graffiti often mention political parties in conjunction with elections, for example in the numerous references to Jobbik and Fidesz (two dominant political parties) that covered downtown Budapest in late spring 2010 during a parliamentary election. The phrases in these freehand scribbles, stickers, and stencils provide a directive – "Vote for Jobbik!" "Victory to Fidesz!" – or an accusatory tone, such as in one freehand piece, reading: "Jobbik are Fascists." However, not all references to political parties appeared during election cycles, such as one stencil on Vasilievskii Island in Saint Petersburg that poked fun at Putin's party more generally. Shown in Figure 7.3 and mentioned briefly in Chapter Seven as an example of graffitied political satire, the artist of this work criticized Putin's ruling political party with a lewd play on the Russian cigarette label, reading: "The Party United Russia May Be the Cause of Impotence."

Artists in Budapest, also use graffiti to call attention to the pseudo-political movement called the Two-Tailed Dog Party. Founded out of a frustration with a lack of viable political options, the Two-Tailed Dog Party established itself as an officially registered "Joke Party," running on platforms of eternal life, a never-ending supply of cold beer, and other promises intended to poke fun at the average candidates' unrealistic campaign vows. A mouthpiece for freedom of speech and the deconstruction of power hierarchies, the political party's principal avenue of information sharing is pretend campaign posters, which they wheatpaste liberally across Budapest. Most posters feature an upside-down illustration of their foremost "political candidate," Istvan Nagy (the Hungarian naming equivalent of John Smith), a small dog that is "too cute to steal." While many of the Two-Tailed Dog Party's posters are nonsensical, some address serious issues, mostly regarding an unsanctioned political

Figure 8.2. "I Must Stop these Parliamentarian Antics. Two-Tailed Dog Party."
2011. Budapest, Hungary. (Photo: Alexis Lerner)

invasion of the public space, as shown in Figure 8.2, with the words "I
must stop these parliamentarian antics…" atop an inverted parliament
building. They play on Hungarian xenophobia with a faux commemo-
rative plaque that marks the place where aliens will arrive several thousand years in the future, a satirical confrontation with the government's
decision to remove all World War Two-related plaques from the former
Jewish Ghetto. The Two-Tailed Dog Party may run on sarcasm, but the
pseudo-political party's mock campaigning offers a justifiable critique
regarding the emptiness of politicking and the way that it clutters the
public space by degrading the quality of the visual public discourse.

Indeed, graffiti and street art critique parties as vessels of political
power that must be challenged. This is a common practice in any situation where the group in power marginalizes and/or silences one or more
parties. It can occur in democratic societies, for example in the ubiquitous graffitied references to Antifa (anti-fascist political groups and
movements) across Berlin or wheatpasted critiques of corrupt politics in
Prague. Due to the pervasiveness of censorship in authoritarian states,

graffiti as an anonymous tool for political expression becomes doubly effective there. Consider, for example, initiatives such as the Polish Orange Alternative in the 1980s. In places where the communist Polish regime had buffed over or censored anti-state graffiti, Orange Alternative mobilized artists to draw dwarves on top of these buffed squares of neutral-colored paint. This initiative began in 1982 in Wroclaw and soon spread to other cities across Poland, eventually inspiring similar movements across post-communist Europe.

On occasion, political graffiti and street art support a particular opposition candidate. In Kyiv for example, many murals appeared in the wake of the 2014 protests in support of then-jailed politician Yulia Tymoshenko, recognizable by her unique golden braids (Szopiński 2014). In Saint Petersburg, in 2021, a mural of then-poisoned and imprisoned opposition leader Alexei Navalny appeared next to the words "A Hero for a New Time" before the authorities buffed it away (Reuters Staff 2021).

Graffiti and street art can also be leveraged to support candidates from the systemic, or managed, opposition. An autocratic incumbent commonly establishes a systemic opposition, or *sistema*, to flood a ballot with a curated list of challengers and establish a façade of political pluralism (Lerner 2020, 47). While these systemic opposition candidates may not be running with the goal of winning an election, they have many incentives to run, including attention to their brand or business, ego-driven fame, or a heightened awareness for a particular policy, such as unemployment benefits or pension reform. Such candidates also appear occasionally in political graffiti, such as in the example of stickers across Moscow, introduced in Chapter Four, proclaiming support for the candidacy of systemic opposition candidate and billionaire businessman Mikhail Prokhorov in 2011 (though it is likely that these stickers are funded by Prokhorov himself).

Attacks on Institutions

Political graffiti and street art often target institutions, the systems of rules or norms that govern human behavior and serve as the fundamental pillars of any society. Whether organizational, such as the supreme court, or process related, such as elections, institutions provide a nation with guidelines on which actions are acceptable. In democratic states, they provide structure for everything from economic transactions to individual freedoms to life or liberty. As such, institutions under these conditions can prevent various forms of corruption, theft, and, to some degree, inequity. Institutions must maintain some degree of independence. For example, if a judge is appointed by a political leader without the protection of tenure, that judge could be terminated for ruling against the political leader's interests. As a result, the judge is likely to determine rulings according to the political leader's preferences. In this situation, the institution of the judiciary is not independent and cannot be relied upon to rule on cases objectively and fairly.

The most popular institution to target, however, is elections. Consider the Tbilisi stencil mentioned in Chapter Six, showing the face of Georgian president Mikheil Saakashvili with the words "I bet you'll vote next time, hippie," a dig at Georgians that chose not to vote in the 2008 election when the center-right and reputedly autocratic incumbent won with only 54.73 percent of the popular vote. At Saint Petersburg's Pushkinskaia 10 urban artist colony, a satirical stencil of a Soviet-era-style Winnie the Pooh asks, "Were there elections?" – also translated as "Was there a choice?" – sarcastically hinting at Russia's corrupt democratic system and dearth of truly competitive elections (Figure 8.3). Street artist Radya responded to the controversies of the 2012 presidential election with a Yekaterinburg billboard that offered "Nothing New" as though it were the only name available for checking on an electoral ballot (see Chapter Four).

Figure 8.3. "Was there a choice/election?" 2011. Saint Petersburg, Russia. (Photo: Alexis Lerner)

In the days leading up to the 2012 Russian presidential election – the heyday of political street art in Russia – stickers calling for the end of Putin's time in office littered Moscow's metro stations and underpasses. As mentioned earlier in this book, stickers allow an artist or activist to quickly dominate a sizable space with a consistent message and minimal threat. Hence, they are an effective medium for political expression. For example, one sticker located on a set of swinging glass doors in the Okhotnii Riad Metro Station read "1999-2012: The Time has Come," a hopeful reference to an end date to Putin's era in office. (By election day, however, most anti-Putin stickers such as this one had largely disappeared. That night, Putin and Medvedev took the stage in Manezhnaia Square just meters above the spot where this critique formerly stuck.)

Other artists engaged each other in dialogue about the election. For example, on a busy street corner in Moscow's central artist district in 2012, a pro-Putin stencil appeared by the Sunday before election day. The stencil showed Vladimir Putin holding a pair of scissors, cutting the "R" off of the word "Revolution" to produce the word "Evolution," a nod at a tightly controlled and purportedly "evolved" Russian state where political dissent remained unwelcome. It disappeared behind a buff on Monday, and by Tuesday, someone wrote "Sorry" in English in its place. This transition is illustrated by Figures 8.4 and 8.5.

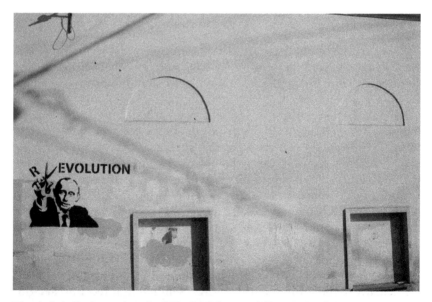

Figure 8.4. Putin cutting the "R" off of the word "Revolution" to spell "Evolution." March 2012. Moscow, Russia. (Photo: Alexis Lerner)

Figure 8.5. The buffing of Figure 8.4 with the word Sorry written in English. March 2012. Moscow, Russia. (Photo: Alexis Lerner)

Other artists use graffiti to attack domestic police and security services. For example, in Saint Petersburg, in 2009, one artist shared a degrading stencil of a police officer depicted as a pig, a common slur used to attack the police. In Moscow, in 2016, shown in Figure 8.6, an artist portrayed three police officers with the heads of birds, a device used to attack the legitimacy and credibility of the institution of the police. In Budapest, in 2011, an individual wrote on a poster "Hey, Fascist, the police don't see you," indirectly accusing the police of permitting intolerant and hate-driven violent acts to occur within their jurisdiction, whether due to negligence or tacit approval. In Minsk, in 2011, shown in Figure 8.7, artists painting in an abandoned parking garage on the outskirts of town draw the outline of a police officer and a civilian engaged in combat, with the phrase, "The 15th of March is a day to fight against police brutality."[1]

Street artists and activists also use graffiti to attack international institutions and actors. While this does appear in authoritarian states, particularly in the form of anti-American sentiment in recent years, this focus on outside influences is especially common in states with stronger representative democratic systems. For example, in Sofia, Bulgaria, artists painted soldiers on a Soviet war monument as superheroes and pop

Figure 8.6. Three police officers with bird heads. 2016. Moscow, Russia. (Photo: Alexis Lerner)

Figure 8.7. "The 15th of March is a Day to Combat Police Brutality." 2011. Minsk, Belarus. (Photo: Alexis Lerner)

culture icons; in Prague, one stencil comments on human rights abuses related to the Beijing Olympics; and in Tbilisi, an artist depicts a television news show, narrating the crash of democracy in Greece.

Attacks on National Identity

Artists also use graffiti to comment on their own national history. For example, in Budapest, one can observe multiple references to the Treaty of Trianon written on the city's walls; see, for example, Figures 8.8 and 8.9. The Treaty of Trianon is a 1920 post-war peace agreement that redefined Hungary's borders, resulting in a loss of approximately 70 per cent of its territory (including five major cities and its seaport) and about 60 per cent of its population to neighboring Austria, Croatia, Czechoslovakia, Ukraine, and Romania. Wheatpasted maps of pre-Treaty of Trianon Hungary with the word "GULAG" (pointing to the repressiveness of the Treaty that took away Hungary's port cities) and freehand scribbles of "Get Lost Trianon" reflect rhetoric that the Jobbik far-right political party has effectively co-opted.

Figure 8.8. A map of pre-treaty Trianon, Hungary, with the word Gulag. 2011. Budapest, Hungary. (Photo: Alexis Lerner)

Figure 8.9. The words "Down with Trianon" scrawled near Filatorigát Station. 2011. Budapest, Hungary. (Photo: Alexis Lerner)

This aversion to foreign influence and its perceived negative impact on national identity also appears in the Czech Republic, where a residual anger toward the post-war Soviet occupation remains central to the Czech narrative. The topic appears frequently in the streets of Prague. Chapter Five discussed an anonymous stencil of Che Guevara wearing a Che Guevara t-shirt, beside which another artist stenciled Soviet astronaut Yuri Gagarin and the English-language phrase "Yuri Says: Reach for the Stars!" to which an anonymous commenter added the words (also in English), "Russian Go Home!!!" (see Figure 5.3). The graffiti of Prague, reflecting the open nature of the national and independent media, was explicitly critical of different political candidates, shared rumors of corruption, and frequently stenciled calls to "Stop the Reforms." The latter referencing the austerity-driven social initiatives that negatively impact women, workers, and families (Figure 8.10).

Georgia, too, has graffiti criticizing the twentieth-century period of Soviet rule. In Tbilisi, in 2017, stencils near the Old Town showed the pig Napoleon from George Orwell's *Animal Farm*, along with the quote

Figure 8.10. "Stop the Reforms!" 2011. Prague, Czech Republic. (Photo: Alexis Lerner)

"Some animals are more equal than others." Napoleon is believed to represent Joseph Stalin – a Georgia native – and the book *Animal Farm* presents a critique on the totalitarian policies of the Soviet Union under Stalin's leadership (Orwell 2014 [1946]).

War

Graffiti is an effective tool for expressing political sentiment, even – and especially – during wartime, when authoritarian incumbents are known to silence antiwar critics to create the façade of unified popular support. For example, as bombing flared up at the tail end of the Chechen insurgency in August 2008, Radya launched a project titled "On the Other Hand" that criticized the Russian government's actions in Grozni, the capital city of Chechnya, a republic of Russia located in the North Caucasus, during the 1999 Second Chechen War. Radya's work also critiqued the former party's unwillingness to accept responsibility for the bloody ramifications that continued in Russia for the next decade and beyond.

During the Kremlin's 2022 invasion of Ukraine, for example, the Russian state arrested upward of 15,000 peaceful protesters in 30 days, shuttered independent media outlets like Dozhd' (in English, TV Rain), closed the Saint Petersburg Museum of Graffiti (a host for frequent events and exhibitions for the public arts community), and introduced two new draconian laws designed to criminalize antiwar speech with long jail sentences and large fines (OVD-Info 2022). Given – or despite – these restrictions, activists and artists turn toward more subtle and subversive tools for political expression: graffiti.[2]

Spray-painted tags with a simple message – "No to War!" – appeared as early as February 25, even before the first major antiwar demonstration in Moscow. This message was often small and scribbled, a reminder of the severe punishments promised by the Kremlin and its enforcement agents if one is caught painting this very message. However, on occasion, this message appears elaborately, as in the case of Saint Petersburg artist MV, who fashioned the word "No" out of red, smeared handprints, designed to imitate bloody prints, with human bodies (and human body parts) spelling out the word "War," a comment on the human cost of Putin's so-called "Special Operation." This phrase has also appeared in smaller cities across Russia, such as Lipetsk, Irkutsk, Samara, and Tomsk. In one case, in Krasnoyarsk, activist Vera Kotova etched the phrase in a pile of snow gathered at the base of a Vladimir Lenin statue, an action for which she was arrested and charged (Army of Discreditation 2022).

Other artists use graffiti to target Putin and the Kremlin directly. In Moscow, for example, one anonymous artist used a stencil to write "You're carrying us to hell" in Russian, implying that the Kremlin is dragging the country into an undesirable conflict and, subsequently, unwanted hardship for attacked Ukrainians and sanctioned Russians. Other anonymous works read, "Putin is an aggressor," and "Kremlin thieves need the war, but not me or you." The latter implies that the Kremlin could benefit from the war through the capture of warm water ports on the Black Sea, the installation of a pro-Russia puppet government in Kyiv or by pocketing profits from military contracts (Grozev 2022). Many of these works were documented and shared among artists and activists through private channels on the Telegram messaging app, particularly after the Kremlin's closure of Western social media platforms such as Facebook and Instagram.

During the 2022 war, global audiences experienced powerlessness as they watched the Russian onslaught in Ukraine. Most onlookers were not able to stop the Russian advance, nor were they able to prevent deaths. One tool that did remain available to the average person was that their voice and graffitied support for the Ukrainian people and state could be observed globally during this war. In Poznan, Poland, artist Kawu painted a mural of celebrated Ukrainian president Volodymyr Zelensky as Harry Potter in front of the Ukrainian flag and the words "Free Ukraine." Kawu also painted a second mural of President Putin as a stylized Voldemort, Harry Potter's known enemy in the popular book series. A stencil of Zelensky's face, as well as the face of Kyiv mayor Vitali Klitschko, appeared in March in Montenegro, and the words "Stop Put-ler," a play on words that combines the names Putin and Hitler, next to a drawing of Hitler's face above the words "Adolf Putin." In Hungary, the opposition affixed a poster to a light pole in March 2022, criticizing Orban's support of Putin and suggesting that this support comes at the cost of Hungary's ties with the rest of Europe. This support also reaches beyond Europe: in Tel Aviv in March 2022, a member of ZUKCLUB painted about Russians that needed to use a virtual private network (VPN) to access independent media after it was blocked, and in New York City, a sticker shows the Ukrainian flag with the words: "Stop Putin. Arm Ukraine."

Many of the subversive tactics used by Russian artists in the winter of 2022 mirror those employed in 2011 and 2012, when Russia's activist circles and political opposition lacked centralized leadership. For example, in Saint Petersburg, in 2022, artist Leonid Skaletskii and colleagues gathered in a public square to paint abstract works on canvases, using the blue and yellow colors of the Ukrainian flag. Skaletskii's initiative harkens back to Muscovite Anton Litvin's Plein Air project of December 2011, where Litvin and fellow artists stood on the Kremlin embankment, using white paint on white canvases to paint the Kremlin and Red Square, symbols of Russia's political power (discussed in Chapter Four). Also in Saint Petersburg, an anonymous "lost dog" sign appeared in the metro, describing a search for a pet named "Peace." The sign reads, "On February 24, an unpleasant man with hints of Botox stole our Peace!" and uses a QR code to link passengers to a petition on Change.org demanding an end to the war in Ukraine.

Not all wartime graffiti is used to protest the state. Pro-Kremlin activists also use stickers and spray paint to indicate the home of antiwar activists. For example, in Kaliningrad, Russia, targeted participants at antiwar rallies in early 2022 returned home to find a sticker on their door reading, "A Traitor Lives Here," with an emphasis on the Cyrillic letters Z and V, symbols used during Russia's war in Ukraine to represent support for Russia's military and the righteousness of its efforts. Nevertheless, these cases of graffiti as an instrument for targeted intimidation are isolated.

Corruption

Artists and activists in several locations use graffiti to target corruption. Corruption occurs when someone in a position of power engages in fraudulent conduct by accepting bribes, hiring only their friends and family, and generally hiding misconduct and crime from the public to ensure the durability of their rule. In Russia, much of (since murdered) opposition leader Alexei Navalny's political activism centered around accusations of corruption. For example, on Christmas Eve 2011, Navalny mobilized 80,000 demonstrators on Moscow's Sakharov Avenue to protest government corruption and electoral fraud related to the December 2011 parliamentary elections. Parallel to the protests that occurred from December through March of the following year were stickers and stencils that critiqued the Russian political elite as a gang of criminals.

Graffitied accusations of political corruption are not limited to autocratic climates; for example, in 2011, an artist used wheatpastes in Prague to accuse politicians of specific acts of corruption, and in 2012, Roman Smetana defaced thirty campaign posters with various attacks, such as "Corruptioneers" and "Prostitutes" (Kirchick 2012). The accusation that corrupt politicians are "for sale' to those willing to pay also appeared in 2011 in Budapest ("Policymakers are Whores"). In the city's District VII, artists become more specific with their allegations of corruption, relating it to money or policy. For example, one artist wrote, "Banks = Treasonous Pig-Thief Fidesz Mafiosos," commenting negatively on Orban's political party, and in Deak Square, another artist wrote "No Tax Evasion [sic.]," an attack often used to target the homeless community that congregate there. In a 2007 mural, Misha Most responded to allegations that Kyiv's 2004 Orange Revolution demonstrations were populated with paid protesters. In the mural, Most shows empty orange banners held by faceless characters. In the corner sits a pile of foreign dollars, stacked higher than the revolutionaries themselves (Lerner 2014). He painted similar faceless protesters in downtown Warsaw in 2014.

In December 2018, I observed one of my favorite examples of how graffiti points to corruption in Vladivostok. On a large half-completed construction site in the center of the city, an anonymous artist writes the phrase "No to Corruption," with the year "2013." The eastern port city's former mayor Igor Pushkarëv was sentenced to 15 years in a maximum-security prison for construction-related corruption in 2016 (RFE/RL 2016). These freehand scribbles are powerful because they provide both explicit and implicit commentary on corruption in Vladivostok. Explicitly, they take an anti-corruption stance, implying that the funds supporting the construction project did not go toward the completion of the project. However, the works also carry an implicit message in the date "2013," indicating that five years have passed without progress on the now abandoned construction site.

The prevalence of corruption in Vladivostok is immediately perceivable to the visitor. The casual observer will see city buses driving at night without working headlights, and sidewalks completely covered with ice for weeks at a time in the city's downtown area. (Those familiar with everyday life in urban Russia will know that seasonal workers clearing sidewalks from blocks of ice with sharp tools are common features of the post-Soviet wintertime experience, making their absence keenly perceived).

In regional cities saturated with history, it is not surprising that much graffiti addresses corruption in real estate and as it relates to construction sites. This is especially true as so many regional cities are so saturated with historically significant buildings and public spaces. For example, in Budapest, an artist feverishly scribbled, "No to Corruption" on the exterior wall of a politically contested construction site, due to its location in a historic district of Hungary (Figure 8.11). Another Hungarian mural,

Figure 8.11. "No to Corruption," painted on a Budapest construction site. June 2011. Budapest, Hungary. (Photo: Alexis Lerner)

Figure 8.12. Mural of the costs of modernity. June 2011. Budapest, Hungary. (Photo: Alexis Lerner)

located on the outskirts of Budapest near Filatorigát Station, shown in Figure 8.12, portrays the glory of modern development – military strength combined with cultural tradition and urban growth – on a sea of bodies, highlighting the collective and frequently deleterious cost of modernity. Likewise, in Saint Petersburg, the Group of Change also used stencils with phraseology such as "The City as It Is" to oppose construction in the historic center of the city, particularly as the area is supposed to be a protected UNESCO World Heritage Site.

The Group of Change is unique because it uses the graffiti platform not only to scribble accusations and share information about corruption and historical preservation but also to mobilize for these causes. The Group of Change's stencils often include both a call to action (such as "On the 11th of March – and Write it Down – We Will Be Together") as well as a web address where passersby can go to learn more or get involved in their movement (see Figure 8.13). Likewise, their website shares images of their street art, building a mutually reinforced message. In the internet age, activist and artist crews like the Group of Change

Figure 8.13. Mobilizational tools used by the Group of Change. June 2011. Saint Petersburg, Russia. (Photo: Alexis Lerner)

understand and embrace the value in maintaining an accessible internet portal. However, they also acknowledge that the internet is oversaturated with threatening hacker groups, a sea of unsupported claims, and a good deal of pro-state basement activism. In turn, political movements must primarily engage with the streets to build legitimacy and to contribute to a more tangible aspect of street discourse and public opinion.

Individual Freedoms

Some political graffiti explicitly discusses opposition figures who were jailed or murdered. This is the avenue through which I first became interested in graffiti as a mouthpiece for political expression in censored states in 2009. Walking up and down Saint Petersburg's central thoroughfare, Nevskii Prospekt, every morning and evening, I became accustomed to reading the walls and store advertisements as I passed them. That spring, I noticed stencils calling for the release of opposition activist and artist Artëm Loskutov. Loskutov organized the nationwide absurdist Monstration demonstrations, largely understood as satirical and anti-state actions (discussed further in Chapter Four).

As I traveled from city to city, I noticed that jailed societal leaders commonly appeared in stencils and stickers. In Saint Petersburg, artist Vladimir Abikh affixed a wheatpaste of activist Pyotr Pavlensky carrying a gas can next to what appears to be a burned doorway, a reference to the artist's repeated arson attacks on perceived centers of power: first on the door to the Federal Security Service (FSB) of the Russian Federation in 2015 and then on a Paris bank as an expression of anti-capitalist frustration in 2017. In Moscow, Russian nationalists used graffiti stencils to demand justice for journalist Yuri Volkov, whose 2010 murder in Moscow is believed to be enmeshed in Russian–Chechen conflict. And in 2021, artists in Moscow used graffiti to challenge the imprisonment of Alexei Navalny on political charges.

This use of public art as a tool for demanding justice is also seen in other states. In Minsk in 2011, an anonymous artist used graffiti to call for freedom for jailed Belarusian anarchist and dissident Nikolai Dedka, shown in Chapter Five, and in Kyiv, the Embassy of Portugal commissioned graffiti artist Vhils (Alexandre Farto) to paint a large mural of Serhiy Nigoyan, an Armenian–Ukrainian activist who was killed by police while protesting during the Euromaidan civil unrest in 2014.

On many occasions, graffiti is used to highlight national political figures and symbols that represent the opposition. In Chapters Five and Six, I discuss examples of nationalist graffiti in Minsk, including stencils of the national poet Yanka Kupala and the Pahonia symbol for the opposition.

In the fall of 2020, Minsk activists painted (and repainted) a mural of two disco jockeys (DJs) – Vladislav Sokolovsky and Kirill Galanov – holding up their fists, a symbol of defiance under Lukashenko's autocratic regime (Topol 2022). In recent years, in Warsaw, multiple artists have painted photorealistic murals of Ukrainian poets and dissident activists, such as Vasyl Stus and Taras Shevchenko.[3] And in Estonia, the artist EvL (Edward von Longos) painted a series of stencils of national cultural figures, such as writer Anton Hansen Tammsaare, alongside a sign that reads "Redundant."

Concluding Thoughts: Co-opting Rebellion and Resorting to the Basics of Dissent

By 2015, autocratic leaders across the region showed interest in graffiti as a tool for expressing political sentiment, for mobilizing the public, and for signaling the unity among the inhabitants of a place. In Moscow, the Putin administration co-opted this form of low-level and public dissent in three ways (Lerner 2021). First, it incentivized previously critical artists, such as the members of ZUKCLUB, to shift from creating independent to state-sponsored projects. Second, the subject matter of graffiti shifted from attacks on Russian leaders and policy to pro-Kremlin narratives. Third, the Kremlin-sponsored works began to occupy downtown spaces, flooding unsanctioned art out of central areas and into the city's residential districts. The mechanism for this co-optation was the graffiti festival (see Chapter Three), in which previously anonymous and subversive artists agree to paint on Kremlin-approved themes in exchange for money, durability, and prime "real estate."

The effect of this phenomenon in Moscow was immediate and observable. Not only does Putin use graffiti festivals to promote a sanctioned narrative, but by permitting a limited and curated amount of political speech, the state establishes a facade of political pluralism to demonstrate insincere compliance with international norms (Lerner 2021; Hyde 2015a; Hyde 2015b). This tactic appeared in Kazakhstan around 2015, where sanctioned graffiti festivals resulted in multi-story murals of heroes, such as photorealistic paintings by Tigrohaud Crew of Kazakh poet Abai Kunanbaiuly, Kazakh politician during the Soviet era Dinmukhamed "Dimash" Kunaev, Kazakh painter Abilkhan Kasteev, Kazakh Islamic philosopher Al-Farabi, cosmonaut Aidyn Aimbetov, labor leader Kamshat Donenbaeva, and Kazakh composer Qurmangazy Sagyrbaiuly.

When these national heroes become the cultural symbols of statehood, rather than oppositional sentiment, the opposition must resort to the basics: calls for freedom and independence. These general symbols and vague statements are prevalent across the region, from photorealistic murals of peace-bringing doves in Prague and Riga to the actual word "Freedom" across student neighborhoods and artist districts in Minsk. At times, the words or symbols stand alone, with little apparent contextual relevance, such as the small pen-inked, English-language call for freedom behind the then-haven for intellectuals and activists, Cafe Moloko, and the adjacent Gallery Y, long since shut down. On other occasions, such as in spring 2014, in Kyiv, near Petrivka Station, the words "Freedom is Victory" are emphasized by their surroundings. These words, and others like them, were painted onto a monument celebrating Soviet military action in the Great Patriotic War (World War Two), indicating that true triumph is sustainable freedom from political oppression, rather than just a wartime victory against an enemy.

Chapter Nine

The Social

Graffiti is an effective tool for circumventing censorship, disclosing injustices, and even mitigating inequality through the dissemination of concealed truths. By publicizing otherwise censored information, artists and activists can deconstruct existing power dynamics and, on occasion, inspire societal change. Across the post-Soviet and post-communist European states, graffiti commonly engages the same tropes – satire, subversiveness, anonymity – to target not only political leaders and parties but also societal norms. Graffiti and street art with social themes can commonly be seen across the region. Such graffiti covers topics ranging from feminism to environmentalism and from ethnic tolerance to inequality. While some of these topics have been codified into policy, the graffiti about these issues largely aims to shake up or invert societal conventions more broadly.

I separate thematically political (see Chapter Eight) and social graffiti for several reasons. First, the targets of political and social art are different; while the former is directed at political leaders, their parties, and the institutions that fortify their rule, the latter targets societal norms and social change. This separation between the political and the social has precedent in the autocratic or Soviet context. Even though social change can evolve into mass dissatisfaction that incites either electoral or revolutionary upheaval, an artist who creates work about a social issue is generally safer and more secure than one who is explicitly political. This is why a Moscow-based mural attacking Putin's 2022 war in Ukraine or supporting an opposition leader such as Navalny or Nemtsov will be buffed more quickly than, for example, a stencil about migrant workers or gentrification. Painting about social issues rather than explicit political issues provides artists with some degree of plausible deniability. Moreover, thematically social content *can* lead to change if it can influence public opinion about or popular support for the desirability of the status quo.

Love, Sex, and Gender

Most of the region's graffiti artists are male (Zimberg 2012a, 108). But in recent years, women have begun to enter the practice at higher rates. In Budapest, for example, a woman draws sharp-edged, triangular foxes under the pseudonym Kormfox.[1] She uses stickers, wheatpastes, and freehand drawings of the foxes as a tag, inserting herself pointedly into what is a male-dominated public and creative sphere. Sometimes the foxes are shown practicing civic responsibility by demonstrating how to recycle glass bottles, and other times the foxes are hiding behind signs or poles from the unrelenting closed-circuit television (CCTV) cameras that watch over the streets of Budapest.[2]

In a 2011 interview, she told me about her experience as one of the few female artists painting in Hungary in the early twenty-first century. The public does not expect to see female graffiti artists, she explained over coffee in Budapest. As a result, while Kormfox paints in dark and abandoned houses and warehouses, she can also leverage her invisibility by painting in broad daylight and in highly trafficked areas, such as a metro entrance, while attracting limited attention or interference by passersby or the police. On the occasion that she did encounter the authorities, Kormfox recalls coyly, she was let off without demerit because of her gender.

In Russia, a female artist who writes under the pseudonym Manu[3] often paints large animals – birds, killer whales, tigers. (Her May 2012 Moscow wheatpaste of an oversized cat included the words, translated into English, "Is this enough to express my political opinion?"[4]) In an August 2011 interview on the outskirts of Saint Petersburg, Manu spoke about her craft, her community, and her experience as a female artist. Like Kormfox, Manu spoke of receiving "special treatment" by the police as a woman, recalling one night in 2010 when she was arrested for writing graffiti only to be released speedily after painting a colorful mural in the police headquarters. The mural portrayed a large bear with a small head and a fox drinking tea together, a commentary on the peaceful union that formed that night between a fox and the authorities that previously pursued her.[5]

Further south, in Moscow, the street artist who uses the pseudonym Mikaela paints about issues that plague contemporary women, such as sexual abuse and prostitution. In her most well-known series, she painted stencils of nineteenth-century Russian female revolutionaries, such as Vera Figner, Vera Zasulich, and Sofia Perovskaia. These women met and became politicized while in school in Switzerland, where they shared a dormitory under the tutelage of Frau Frichi (Zimberg 2009).

They returned to Russia in the early 1870s as the Frichi Circle, an all-female activist network organized around populist ideology, "enlighten-ing" those living in the Russian countryside, and education as a vehicle for social change. The Frichi Circle inspired several short-lived organiza-tions adhering to parallel agendas, including the People's Will (*Narodnaia Volia*), which collapsed after the assassination of Tsar Aleksandr II in March of 1881 (Zimberg 2009). Under each revolutionary's face, Mikaela paints the details of their sentencing.

This structure – a stencil of a prisoner's face above their sentencing or fate – imitates how graffiti artists paint about contemporary political prisoners across the region today, from Berlin to Minsk to Vladivostok. This practice reinforces beliefs about the effectiveness of so-called "arm-chair activism," or that idea that by spreading information or awareness about injustice, said injustice is somehow alleviated. Further, given the substantial institutional and social revolutionary impact of the Frichi Circle on the history of Russian politics, Mikaela's works have an im-portant educational purpose. They remind passersby that the Russian revolution was not only about its eventual champion, Vladimir Lenin, but also about the (female) revolutionaries that predated his rise and their attempts to elicit change for decades before Lenin ever returned to Russia.

Graffiti lauding feminist icons looks not only to the past. Much street art across the region exists as a tribute to contemporary feminist art col-lectives, such as Pussy Riot and FEMEN. Graffiti of balaclavas behind bars and scribbled calls to "Free Pussy Riot" appeared across Russia, from Moscow to Vladivostok, as well as around the world, from Tehran (Iran) to New York City, after the collective's attempted punk show denouncing the role of the church in Russia's political affairs and the subsequent im-prisonment of its active members Nadezhda Tolokonnikova and Maria "Masha" Alëkhina.

Global graffitied accolades, particularly across the European conti-nent, also appear for FEMEN, the Ukrainian feminist art collective that garners attention for women's issues, such as legal abortion on demand, by painting the relevant laws directly onto their bodies while topless in public venues.

Social issues that affect women disproportionately appear in graffiti across the region, especially in states where these issues are a com-mon rallying point. In Bishkek, Kyrgyzstan, the DOXA crew painted a 2018 memorial to Burulai Turdaaly Kyzy, a 19-year-old woman killed by Mars Bodoshev after he failed to abduct her for the purpose of forcing her to marry him, drawing attention to unjust incidences of violence against women. In Moscow, an artist by the name of Daria uses public art to critique sex trafficking and exploitation. She repurposes classical prostitution advertisements with tear-off phone numbers at the bottom; for example, Daria altered an ad that previously said, "Waiting for you" to instead read "Waiting to be freed." And on a mattress in the Kreuzberg neighborhood of Berlin in 2019, a third anonymous artist wrote, "Don't Tell Her How to Dress. Tell Him Not to Rape." This was specifically critiquing the societal tendency to curate women's clothing and behavior rather than transmit normative guidelines to men to only engage in consensual sexual relations. Elsewhere in Moscow, projects such as the Vagina Rules group's satirical 2015 "Husband for an Hour" advertisements that satirize the girlfriend-for-hire experience and the French artist C215's forgotten sex worker mural at the ArtPlay compound both provide commentary on prostitution, human trafficking, and the exploitation of women (see Figure 3.1 in Chapter 3).

In Osh, Kyrgyzstan, the New Rhythm crew paints graffiti about women's rights and gender inequality. Some of their work is meant to humanize the demographic of girls married off in their childhood, showing the silhouette of a woman with forty braids – a reference to an unmarried girl in Kyrgyzstan – and labeling each braid with some aspect of the child's identity, desires, and dreams outside of arranged marriage. Another stencil in Osh addresses domestic violence, showing the silhouette of a man raising his arm to hit a woman, with the words "Leave Not Endure." Other works critique family dynamics that elevate sons over daughters, elderly women over young women, and members of the "original" family unit over daughters who married into a family unit (Voices on Central Asia 2018).

Women's issues also appear further south in Kabul, Afghanistan, where female artist Shamsia Hassani has been drawing her trademark murals of modern Muslim women wearing niqabs and hijabs since 2011. Hassani paints the women lipless to demonstrate that women in Afghanistan feel like "second-class citizens, whose words are of no significance" and with their eyes closed to "symbolize the horrors in her community that were too disturbing to see, as well as the destruction that made many uncertain of their future" (Geranpayeh 2019). This work portended Kabul's extremist "vice and virtue" laws introduced in August 2024, which prohibited women from being heard speaking, singing, or reading aloud in public spaces.

While women artists fight invisibility and discrimination by painting about feminist issues, topics related to another marginalized population, the transnational LGBTQIA+ community, also appear frequently in graffiti, especially in more progressive cities in liberal democratic states.

For example, in 2014 in Berlin, shown in Figure 9.1, an artist in the upscale Mitte neighborhood painted a rainbow-colored stencil of two lanky males holding hands, while another in the then-hipster-immigrant neighborhood of Neukölln painted a mural of diverse protesters – a mother, an immigrant, men holding hands, a woman wearing a hijab – with signs such as "You are Not Alone, Together Against Homophobia" and "We are Staying," as well as "We Love Kotti" (referring to the tenant activist initiative Kotti & Co, which fights against racism and urban displacement in Berlin).[6]

In Budapest, in 2011, artists used stickers liberally throughout District VII outdoor pubs to satirize the unwelcoming atmosphere that Hungary built for its Roma, Jewish, and queer residents. Many of the stickers promoted the "Ragamuffin Collective," where these minority populations of Hungary could be celebrated. Even though people in Budapest might no longer have independent media, organize Gay Pride parades, or participate in the inclusive and sex-positive Eurovision Song Competition since Orban came to power in 2010, the physical walls of the public space continue to exist as unrestricted public domain.

Graffiti about LGBTQIA+ issues does appear outside of progressive areas, for instance, a rainbow flag that appeared during Pride Month in Minsk with the words "Minsk" and "Vilna" linked in solidarity next to stick figures denoting couples in different gender combinations,[7] or a mural of two male police officers locked in a romantic embrace in Erfurt, Germany. In 2020, Antik Danov painted a rainbow over the Kremlin in Sevastopol, a critique of Russia's attempt to ban the rainbow.[8]

In Saint Petersburg in 2021, the Russian Yav Crew collective painted a man that looks like President Putin with two fingers in his mouth, forcing himself to vomit out rainbows, satirizing the Russian leader's simultaneously homoerotic behavior and homophobic policies (Sperling 2014). Led by Anastasia Vladichkina, Yav Crew frequently paints about controversial subjects related to sex and gender, such as a 2021 Izhevsk portrait of queer icon Nadezhda Durova, who disguised herself as a man and became a decorated soldier during the war. Yav Crew also created the 2019 Saint Petersburg mural "Just a Few Scratches," which critiques laws on domestic violence in Russia by showing a man standing over a battered, bloodied, and naked woman, who is presumably dead. While these works are nuanced, topical, and thought-provoking, they are often buffed by authorities (the Moscow piece of Putin vomiting rainbows was buffed within a day of being painted) or defaced by the local population (such as the person who wrote an aggressive slur over the Erfurt stencil).[9]

Figure 9.1. Two lanky boys with a heart. 2013. Berlin, Germany.
(Photo: Alexis Lerner)

Going Green

Artists and activists also use graffiti to discuss environmental issues. For some, this means publicizing concerns about pollution, as in Anton Cheremnikh's 2018 "Lungs of the City" work in Perm, Russia, in which the lungs resemble the branches and leaves of a tree, a metaphor for the vital need for green spaces in reducing air pollution and improving air quality for city residents.[10] Others use graffiti to mobilize against climate change, as in the example of the Fridays For Future and Abby_Maybe who used street art in June 2020 to publicize an oil spill that occurred in Norilsk, Russia, ultimately obtaining more than 7,000 signatures for a petitions to hold accountable the Nornikel nickel and palladium mining corporation. In October 2020, Abby_Maybe used graffiti to mobilize for environmental concerns more generally using the hashtag #GlobalClimateAction2020 in both Russian and English. As mentioned in Chapter Five, hashtags, URLs, and QR codes are useful tools for activists that wish to link political public art to static web pages where passersby can learn more about a particular cause or event.

Others use their street art to advocate for animal rights. For example, stencils across Russia, from the side of the highway in Moscow to the exterior walls of shopping centers in Saint Petersburg, encourage passersby to forgo eating meat with slogans such as "Go Vegan!" and "Meat is Murder" (Figure 9.2). In Vilnius in 2009, an artist painted a chicken next to the words, "We are cared after worse than the worst criminals. And eventually killed." The chicken "speaks" these words from a podium which appears to have the UN logo, implying both the platform that is needed to solve issues related to animal abuse and the performative nature of the United Nations. And at the Street Art Museum of Saint Petersburg, in partnership with Berlin's Urban Nation Contemporary Art Museum, Bordalo II created a snow leopard out of repurposed garbage, not only finding a new home for local trash but also integrating animals back into urban public spaces.

ROA is a muralist from Belgium that uses street art to reintegrate animals into the urban environments from which they were once native but now displaced. He portrays these animals through the graphic lens of death and decay, intending to instigate human empathy and to encourage better treatment of living beings by humans. In Berlin and Katowice (Poland), ROA paints "deconstructed animals," which depict an animal, such as a rabbit or a bird, next to an outline of the same animal with its skeleton and innards detailed. ROA has also painted rats and decaying animal carcasses, as in the example of the 2011 mural in the Kreuzberg neighborhood of Berlin, titled *Nature Morte* which shows a rabbit, a stork,

Figure 9.2. "Meat is Murder." 2011. Saint Petersburg, Russia. (Photo: Alexis Lerner)

and a buck hanging dead on ropes above the body of a wild boar and the severed head of a pig.

Graffiti artists across the region have also used (and continue to use) street art to express their concerns about nuclear energy and its potentially deleterious consequences for the environment. Oftentimes artists refashion nature as dominated by symbols of nuclear power, linking together explicitly the advent of nuclear development with the destruction of the environment. One example is a 2009 stencil of a flower with nuclear symbols – the ones used to show the location of Cold War-era bomb shelters – instead of petals, located in Saint Petersburg. Below the stencil, the artist wrote "There's no such thing as a peaceful atom."[11] Two years later, in a sanctioned graffiti spot in residential Saint Petersburg, another artist drew a grand tree with a mushroom cloud painted to resemble its leaves and branches, shown in Figure 9.3. At the base of the tree, the artist painted a small city of homes and factories that both caused and suffered from the nuclear destruction. In 2011, on the rooftop of an abandoned parking garage in the outskirts of Minsk, an artist illustrated a dystopian future, where even aliens and their pets were required to wear gas masks to survive nuclear devastation.

After all, residents of the post-Soviet region have a unique understanding of the threat posed by nuclear energy. Most have learned about, or remember experiencing personally, the 1986 Chernobyl nuclear disaster in Pripyat, Ukraine. Reactor explosions and radiation contamination impacted the entire local ecosystem: planted food was contaminated, as were wild animals and water sources. Hundreds of workers and locals died from the immediate explosion, the fire, or acute and long-term radiation sickness. The area was almost entirely evacuated; homes and the power plant itself were abandoned, which allowed the forest to regenerate. In the abandoned town of Pripyat, graffiti of wild animals like bears and deer began to appear on the walls between Lenin Square and the amusement park. Other artists have painted flowers emerging from the cracks in the city's deserted spaces and eerie silhouettes of children playing in the old schools and apartment buildings. In 2016, Australian artist Guido Van Helten painted a photorealist mural inside Chernobyl Reactor 5 of journalist Igor Kostin, who documented the nuclear explosion as it unfolded in 1986 (Haden 2016; Meandering Wild N.D.).

City Life

Social activists use street art to communicate about societal issues, whether to influence community behavior, to unearth information about corruption, or as an attempt to ostracize a "bad actor." Moscow's

Figure 9.3. Painting depicting a nuclear factory, explosion, and spill surrounding the base of a tree. June 2011. Saint Petersburg, Russia. (Photo: Alexis Lerner)

Partizaning, discussed at length in Chapter Four, is one such street art collective that engages in what they call "guerilla art," or illicit public art meant to improve the quality of life for local residents and to encourage community members to be more intentional and introspective about their choices and interpersonal relations.

For example, in May 2012, Partizaning took the metro down to south-western end of the suburb of Troparëvo-Nikulino, where they installed a dozen yellow mailboxes. The group instructed denizens to deposit into these mailboxes their written ideas of how to improve the neighborhood, and after a few days, they received thirty suggestions about mapping initiatives, the repair of broken infrastructure such as streetlights, and creative suggestions such as the repurposing of an outdoor space with amphitheater-style seating into an outdoor community movie theater (Lerner 2013b; Malhotra 2018).

While this intervention benefited residents, it was nevertheless illicit and somewhat anarchic in its quest for civic empowerment. Partizaning is about facilitating dialogue among an estimated twelve million Muscovites, with the objective of guiding local communities to identify tangible and practical ways to reclaim their public spaces. By steering clear of political gridlock and instead addressing social issues, Partizaning can circumvent political ramifications. In recent years, they painted illegal pedestrian crossings through busy intersections, installed a series of Use/Less cycle lane signs to separate bike lanes from the high-speed traffic on the Maroseika thoroughfare in Moscow, and distributed hundreds of bright orange stickers resembling parking tickets for a day of action in 2011, hoping to shame drivers parking on the sidewalk into some sense of social responsibility.

Similarly, Czech graffiti pioneer Roman Týc also considers his work guerilla art. With his crew Ztohoven in 2007, he refashioned the figures on forty-eight Prague crosswalk signals to portray humans behaving badly – engaging in public intoxication and urination, for example – to show that people "don't have to walk or stand when the system says so" (Kirchick 2012).

Justice for All

Issues of diversity, equity, and inclusion are also prevalent in social graffiti, which refer to the needs of marginalized populations within a country, such as indigenous people and other ethnic minorities. For example, in 2017, the Russian Geographical Society commissioned a mural of an indigenous Komi-Zyryan child. The child, a boy, is shown in front of a sea in what appears to be winter; he is shielded from the cold with thick gloves and a fur coat, traditional clothing for the indigenous people living in parts of Russia, such as Komi Republic, Yamalo-Nenets Autonomous Region, and Khanti-Mansiisk Autonomous Region. On the boy's head sits a peregrine falcon. The mural is based on a photograph taken on the remote Taz Peninsula, titled "Little Varg," which the photographer Alexander Romanov explains is a reference to a fictional people in the Game of Thrones trilogy that "can merge with animals at a distance, see with their eyes, control their mind" (Romanov 2017). This mural stands in the center of Moscow, across from the Tretiakovskaia Metro, which promotes visibility for Russia's indigenous people, culture, and region in its capital city.

Graffiti also concerns those residents of a country who are unhoused or otherwise disadvantaged economically. In the Kreuzberg neighborhood of Berlin, for example, many unhoused locals woke up each morning to two large murals by Italian graffiti artist BLU. On one side was a mural the artist painted in 2008, showing a man wearing a formal dress shirt, putting on his tie while bound by a thick chain to watches on each wrist – a commentary the influence of capitalism on the measurement of both time and human worth. On the other side was a mural of two masked individuals in perceptible conflict, each a mirror image of the other and trying to unmask their opponent. One individual holds up a hand sign for *westside*, the other for *eastside*, representing differences and similarities in cultural identity between West and East Berlin, in particular, and West and East Germany, more generally.

When the tent city was evacuated in 2014 to make space for the construction of a condominium building, BLU returned to the city to buff his own work with black paint to protest the displacement and gentrification caused by the new development (Web Urbanist 2014). Anti-gentrification sentiment is prevalent across Berlin's graffiti, such as in the example shown in Figure 9.4, a satirical wheatpaste inside of an abandoned warehouse in Teufelsberg (a former US Government complex surrounding a Cold War-era listening station) that reads "Don't worry, it's just GENTRIFICATION" above a photo of a family – including at least one child – sleeping on the street (Figure 9.4). (When talking about gentrification, this is particularly apposite, as midnight graffiti [see Chapter Seven] fights the very thing that it criticizes.)

Graffiti is also used to express xenophobia, or fear of the *other*, as well as support for immigrants and migrant workers in the country. For example, the Two-Tailed Dog Party wheatpastes discussed in Chapter Eight play on Russian fears of foreign nationals with creative stories about immigrant dogs from Dagestan (a predominantly Muslim

Figure 9.4. "Don't worry, It's Just GENTRIFICATION," inside the Teufelsberg compound. December 2013. Berlin, Germany. (Photo: Alexis Lerner)

region in the North Caucasus region of Russia). However, in many other cases, this graffiti is targeted at Jews and Roma, such as in the 2011 attestation that "Jews are Vermin" on the exterior wall of the Dohany Synagogue in Budapest or "Roma, Leave" in a memorial park in Prague. Graffitied antisemitism is so common in Eastern and Central Europe that an entire chapter of this book (Chapter Ten) is dedicated to its analysis.

Finally, many works address systemic issues plaguing society, both nationals and immigrants, such as alcohol addiction. In Saint Petersburg, in 2009, a stencil on Vasilievskii Island reminded passersby to "Stop Drinking," while another in the same city in 2011 read "A Healthy Russia is a Sober Russia." Across the bridge on Nevskii Prospekt, also in 2011, another stencil depicted the double-headed eagle, a symbol of Russian national heritage looking both toward the east and west, or toward the past and the future, with a bottle of alcohol in its talons.

COVID-19 Pandemic

Many have used street art to discuss contemporary public health concerns, such as the global coronavirus (SARS-CoV-2 or, colloquially, COVID-19) pandemic caused by a highly contagious virus that resulted in millions of deaths and repeated lockdowns worldwide. Some used street art to illustrate fear over what remained unknown about the deadly airborne virus: the artist Lacuna painted a masked woman in the Prenzlauer Berg district of Berlin, staring at the outline of the coronavirus (as it is seen under a microscope) with a fearful expression. Others used public art to comment on the prevalence of norm adherence and social shaming during the pandemic: in Novosibirsk in 2020, an anonymous artist hung a bedsheet as a mock facemask over the painted face of Apple founder Steve Jobs, next to the phrase "COVID-19," signaling that even the photorealistic mural of the global technology leader needed to "cover up" (Howard 2020).

Becoming infected with the COVID-19 virus often resulted in austere isolation and quarantine restrictions, depending on state policies. Unwillingness to comply with a state's COVID-19 isolation and quarantine guidelines often resulted in not only social pressure but also often meant more formal consequences such as fines. Nevertheless, compliance with these measures often led those infected (or assumed to be infected) to be treated as societal and medical pariahs due to the high transmissibility of, and limited knowledge about, the virus. One artist in Brest, Belarus, comments on the isolating experience of the outcast coronavirus patient, wearing a straitjacket with an outline of the coronavirus molecule structure atop their head, being spoken to through a button on the wall. In Perm, authorities held a festival for residents to paint on COVID-related topics such as supporting healthcare workers and the increased isolation felt by the elderly and people with disabilities.

Other artists painted on the topic of "beating" COVID, personifying the latter as an invisible foe in a global battle. In Moscow, for example, near the gate of the Kommunarka settlement, an artist painted the word "Conquer," next to the image of a masked doctor, with a red line crossing out the COVID-19 symbol in the place of the letter "o." During the COVID-19 pandemic, doctors, nurses, and hospital staff were often referenced as being on the "frontlines" of the pandemic, again comparing the deadly virus to a wartime.

While some foreign conflicts have a national rallying effect, leading people to unify in support of their nation as it combats a real or perceived adversary, the rally-round-the-flag effect was not always the case with COVID-19. While there was initial support for so-called "stay-at-home" public health initiatives, the pandemic stretched on for several years, and so, many individuals eventually expressed concern that their state's directives regarding the freedoms of movement and assembly were restrictive, if not coercive. Artist Eme Freethinker has painted many critical and colorful murals in Berlin, illustrating these facets of isolated life throughout COVID-19.

In March 2020, he painted the Lord of the Rings character Gollum staring at a roll of toilet paper lovingly, calling it "My Precious" – satire about the difficulty of obtaining basic products such as toilet paper, infant formula, and medication during the early months of the lockdown period. In February 2021, in concurrence with the beginning of a global vaccination campaign, he painted a smirking monkey sporting a hoodie with a toilet paper logo and holding a syringe. In September 2021, with the global rollout of COVID-19 vaccines well underway, he painted a mural with the faces of two women and the words "Mandatory Vaccination? Thanks, but ... fuck you!!"

Eme Freethinker also used street art to poke fun at national leaders in the context of the COVID-19 pandemic. For example, their mural "Love in the Time of Corona," shows the former United States president Donald Trump gently nuzzling Chinese president Xi Jinping. Eme Freethinker's mural is a distinct play on Vrubel's "My God, Help me to Survive this Deadly Love" in Berlin (discussed in Chapter Two) and Mindaugas Bonanu's replica of Vrubel's piece in Lithuania, which substitutes Putin and Trump into the liplock (discussed in Chapter Eight). In Eme Freethinker's version, both world leaders are shown wearing masks, have their eyes closed, and are surrounded by sophomoric neon hearts. The pathogen that developed into the COVID-19 pandemic was first detected in Wuhan, the capital city of China's Hubei Province, a point that led the former US President to refer to COVID-19 as the "China virus" and to a subsequent rise in xenophobia and anti-Asian hate crimes across the United States in 2020. This work satirizes the tense yet codependent nature of diplomatic and economic relations between the United States and China.

Imagine Peace

Using graffiti to express antiwar sentiment and messages of tolerance, through freehand drawings of doves, olive branches, and the word "Peace," for example – is as common a practice today as it was in the late 1970s and early 1980s. Contemporary street artists continue to use these universal symbols of kindness, community, and empathy not only to promote peace but also to dwarf graffiti that glorifies racist, bigoted, or fascist ideology.

Throughout recent history, musicians have helped their fans to gather in the company of those who also desire peace. These musicians – from international superstars like the Beatles to local icons like Viktor Tsoi – have left a lasting impression on the youth of the Soviet and post-Soviet region. Musicians and the lyrics that they write not only help their listeners escape the harsh realities of the rest of the world and feel supported in their own lives, but they can also motivate the public to mobilize for or against a particular cause, promote certain values like peace or ethnocentrism, and serve as anthems for revolutionary or secessionist movements. (Consider, for example, the so-called Singing Revolution that empowered soon-to-be independent Estonia from 1987 to 1991.)

Support for certain songs and musical icons often appears in graffiti. For example, the songs and slogans of the Beatles serve as universal symbols of peace, free-spirited independence, social justice, and fair treatment of others. Across Eastern and Central Europe, artists and fans collaborate in public squares to memorialize the group's simple yet powerful messages, such as "All You Need Is Love." For example, in the alley behind the Pushkinskaia 10 artist collective in Saint Petersburg, artists have left behind many colorful references to the English rock band, including a yellow submarine (a reference to the group's song by the same name) (Figure 9.5).

In Prague, the Lennon Wall, named in honor of singer John Lennon following his death in 1980 (Figure 9.6), has long been a symbol of unrestricted expression. However, its status as a bastion of free speech has more recently come into question. For many years, it was a sightseeing destination, and tourists and locals alike would gather to add to the wall with messages in many different languages. In 2019, to curb lewd and unwanted graffiti by oft-inebriated tourists, city officials reinstalled surveillance cameras and restricted the days when graffiti could be added (Tait 2019). Despite these challenges, the Lennon Wall remains a dynamic space for free expression. Its influence even reached beyond Prague, inspiring anti-communist activists in Hong Kong to create their own "Lennon Walls" across the urban center's subway passages and underpasses (The Guardian 2019).

Back in Moscow, local legend Viktor Tsoi is memorialized on a street known as the Old Arbat, referencing its name in Russian. As I discuss in Chapter Two, the Soviet government of the early 1980s pegged rock groups as inherently anti-state, and Kino was no exception. As Gorbachev's *glasnost* and *perestroika* policies started to expose Soviet truths, Kino's frontman called for change. Tsoi was so synonymous with these calls that his face is often painted alongside his lyrics, which read, "Our hearts demand change" and "We wait for change." Several such

Figure 9.5. A yellow submarine, surrounded by Beatles tributes at Pushkinskaya 10. August 2011. Saint Petersburg, Russia. (Photo: Alexis Lerner)

examples exist across Russia: in Saint Petersburg by the Belarusian crew HoodGraff in 2014 (updated in 2019, see: HoodGraff 2019), in Moscow all along the Tsoi fan wall located on the Old Arbat, and in Yessentuki, near Mineralnie Vodi in the North Caucasus, resting in the shadow of Mount Elbrus (the tallest mountain in Europe, standing at 5642 meters).[12]

To conclude, by reading a city's walls, one can effectively understand what matters to the people living in that place and at that time. It is possible to read graffiti discourse in a place to understand popular sentiment toward, for example, policies about domestic violence in Moscow, attitudes toward the LGBTQIA+ community in Tbilisi, or unhoused people in Berlin.

While common themes – public health or climate change – appear in urban spaces across regime types, it is necessary to contextualize that work within a greater context of free speech or censorship. A graffitied call to "Go Vegan" in Berlin or Prague seems commonplace, as residents in these locales have ample and reliable outlets for free expression.

Figure 9.6. Drawings of John Lennon and lyrics to Beatles songs on Lennon Wall. 2011. Prague, Czech Republic. (Photo: Alexis Lerner)

Expressing one's opinion on social issues serves a different purpose and has a different impact under authoritarian conditions. In the latter scenario, expressing discontent on social matters (rather than overtly political themes) not only provides artists with plausible deniability of political engagement in the case that they are caught, but writing societal critiques can help artists to inspire their local communities to organize and act for the social causes that matter to them. This is best summarized by Sonya P., who spoke about guerilla art, civic duty, and societal critique in a 2012 interview in Moscow: "We try not to speak directly about Putin," Sonya explained. "Putin is not the only reason for our problems. We must change people, not Putin. People have to want change for change to happen."

Chapter Ten

Who Controls Discourse?

In the spring of 1944, my father's parents fled the Holocaust genocide on the renowned Kasztner Train. Shortly after they left their home-town of Munkács, Hungary, Nazi Germans and Arrow Cross Hungari-ans rounded up 28,587 local Jews, displaced them from their homes to temporary ghettos on the outskirts of town, and ultimately transported them to the Auschwitz-Birkenau concentration camp, where they were tortured, starved, experimented upon, and, in many cases, murdered.

Before my grandparents left Hungary, my grandfather etched his name, Leibi, onto a wall of his home which faced into the town's main square.[1] Not only did I want to see this Carpathian city (now Mukachevo, Ukraine) that mattered within my own family history, but I was also curi-ous to find out whether the graffiti that my grandfather left on the wall of his childhood home was still there in 2011. It was.

But his name was also crossed out with a large "x" and covered with new graffiti – an etching of a six-pointed Jewish star – as I show in Figure 10.1. This layered discourse illustrates a shift in content: from a name, meant to indicate presence ("I was here") or possession ("This is my home") to a symbol denoting the kind or class of person that was re-moved from a space. This writing also indicates a change in the speaker, which transitions in this case from first person to third person. This use of third-person graffiti to reveal the human contents of a private resi-dence is not unique to this situation. In New Orleans, for example, fol-lowing the devastation Hurricane Katrina left in 2005, search and rescue crews used graffiti to publicize the number of tenants (both people and animals) expected to be living in a home compared to the number for which rescue crews accounted.[2]

These multiple layers of graffiti speak about agency, discourse, and the shaping of outward-facing narratives. Graffiti is a tool for publicly shar-ing the issues that concern a community. It is a kind of public discourse

Figure 10.1. Jewish star etched onto my grandfather's former home. July 2011. Mukachevo, Ukraine. (Photo: Alexis Lerner)

available to all those who wish to participate, not only those in positions of power. Mitja Velikonja (2021, 33) writes:

> Graffitiing and street art tear down the traditional divisions between creators and public, art and general creativity, the elite and the masses. Graffiti are made **by** the people, not only **for** the people. In the same way that Benjamin characterized film long ago, graffiti and street art carry progressive and transformative potentials within themselves; [quoting art historian Véronique Plesch with the following] "every spectator is enabled to become a participant" (2007, 120).

Graffiti thus answers debates about who owns public spaces and who gets to engage in political disputes: anyone with a permanent marker or a can of paint can use those tools to express themself.

This includes not only liberal democratic content regarding democratization or social issues but also less palatable narratives such as the hate speech that favors one racial, ethnic, or national group over another. In this chapter, I discuss how narratives are shaped to benefit one actor or group, whether that is a nationalist population concerned about limited resources and unfamiliar neighbors or a state concerned with durability and instilling feelings of patriotism. In the case of the latter, I outline how authorities intervene to either remove the unwanted content (an act of censorship itself) and/or commission a self-serving narrative in its place.

What is the Purpose of Antisemitic Graffiti in Twenty-first Century Europe?

The twentieth-century history of systematic state-led oppression and mass murder has left a colossal impact on contemporary collective memory in the Eastern and Central European region. Nearly four million Ukrainian people died of hunger under the leadership of Joseph Stalin during the Holodomor (Kulchytsky 2018). During World War Two, 14 million innocent civilians in Ukraine, Belarus, much of Poland, Latvia, and Lithuania were murdered, including 6 million Jews, in the region's concentration and death camps, gas vans, and killing fields.

Graffitied references to this sweeping bloodshed appear in abundance on the region's walls. Many writers reference the Holocaust and World War Two explicitly, such as in the freehand tags of the odious Gas Chamber Crew of graffiti artists in Lviv, the laudatory phrase "Heil Hitler" on an abandoned tenement building in Łódź (Figure 10.2), or the stickered silhouette of a Holocaust victim in Warsaw, shown carrying a Torah – a sacred Jewish text – next to the Hebrew word for "alive" or "living" (Figure 10.3). Others avoid references to Hitler or Nazi-era fascism, instead painting phrases and symbols about antisemitism and white supremacy more generally.

The decision to paint antisemitic graffiti in this place is of particular interest. The Jewish communities across the region were decimated in the mid-twentieth century, and those not murdered in the Holocaust largely departed for Mandate Palestine or the West. As a result, there are relatively few Jewish residents in many of these cities, indicating that graffiti about Jews is not about living neighbors as much as it is about a theoretical bogeyman. In 2011, one mural, shown in Figure 10.4, highlights the notable absence of Jewish and Roma people in contemporary Łódź.

In Łódź, near the infamous Hospital #1, I visited a Jewish cemetery where the headstones were defaced with graffitied antisemitic vitriol. I saw the phrase "Jews are vermin" written on the exterior wall of a Jewish school in Budapest, Jewish symbols desecrated on the streets of

Figure 10.2. "Heil Hitler." 2011. Łódź, Poland. (Photo: Alexis Lerner)

Figure 10.3. Somber Jew carrying Torah. July 2011. Łódź, Poland.
(Photo: Alexis Lerner)

Minsk, and witnessed firsthand the abundance of antisemitic graffiti –
swastikas, Stars of David hanging from gallows, calls of "Jews, To the
Gas Chambers!" – in cities across Poland (see, for example, Figures
10.5 and 10.6).

This prevalence of antisemitic public art is nothing new in the region.[3]
Numerous scholars have attributed antisemitic graffiti and street art to
warring Polish football teams, Widzew and ŁKS, both of which use the
term "Jew" and symbolic references to Judaism to attack the opposing
team [for example, see Figure 10.7] (Sinnreich 2004; Lukac 2014). In
particular, Mitja Velikonja published an entire tome on this topic of foot-
baller graffiti in 2021, complete with color photos from his fieldwork.
While it is plausible that the Celtic cross or the swastika is merely a reflection of quotidian football fan rivalry, it indicates that violent hate speech,
particularly that which contains antisemitic themes, provides an effective lexicon for marking territory and delineating the boundary between
in-groups, even within the greater domain of sports rivalries. Velikonja
(2021, 98-99) writes:

Figure 10.4. Mural of former inhabitants of Poland. July 2011. Łódź, Poland. (Photo: Alexis Lerner)

> ... we cannot accept the frequently apologized use of extremist rhetoric and symbols in football fandom ... by saying "they don't really mean it" and perceiving [these hateful symbols] as a form of cheering ... they fight synonyms with antonyms: if they are A, then we are anti-A, no matter how painful the comparisons are ... however, not all signs are equally controversial: a firefighter sign or a pharmacy sign or a character from The Simpsons surely do not evoke such an uneasiness as racist or Nazi signs do ... one cannot use political signs, especially those contaminated with violence and crimes, and pretend to be apolitical.

The boundary between derogatory hooliganism and non-athletic, xenophobic epithets is further blurred when the sentiment connects a team nickname ("Jude") with the horrors of the Holocaust ("Hitler come back and finish off the Jews!"). This blurring of intention is even more complicated when the slurs appear in Jewish memorial spaces that have no explicit connection to athletics, such as the words "Zyklon B" (a reference to the poison used in the gas chambers of Nazi death camps) on the entrance to a Jewish

Figure 10.5. Swastika in Poland. July 2011. Łódź, Poland.
(Photo: Alexis Lerner)

Figure 10.6. Magan David on a noose. July 2011. Budapest, Hungary.
(Photo: Alexis Lerner)

Figure 10.7. Jude and Magan David. 2011. Łódź, Poland. (Photo: Alexis Lerner)

cemetery in Częstochowa, in 2018, or the antisemitic graffiti painted onto a Jewish memorial at a Nazi concentration camp in Płaszów (Markusz 2018).

More compelling is the assumption that symbols of hate – runes and swastikas, for example – are not intended for a Jewish audience but rather for a local or internal audience. These symbols and phrases are used intentionally to signal to an internal audience that the writer speaks the language of, and belongs to a social group with, perceived power. It is also plausible that such graffiti serves as a tool of intimidation for other locals, as a visual reminder of who holds the power over a space. There is some misguided belief that these groups are under threat from unfamiliar outsiders who wish to take resources away from a local community. Regardless of whether the intention is about loyalty, belonging, or (local) power, there is agency in the painting of hate speech.

In fact, hate speech in these situations is as often about the racial superiority of those competing for power as it is about the target of the graffiti (e.g., Jews). For example, I documented the phrase "White Power" across the region, in cities of varying sizes such as Saint Petersburg, Riga, and Mukachevo. Calls for a "Russia for Russians" (Figure 10.8) and "Love

Figure 10.8. "Hooligans, Russia for Russians, Glory to Russia, Skins." 2011. Saint Petersburg, Russia. (Photo: Alexis Lerner)

Your Own Race" in big cities in Russia imply that non-ethnic Russian inhabitants, such as migrants from Chechnya and Central Asian states, are unwelcome in these places. This connection between ethnocentrism and civic pride also appears in phrases such as "White Patriot" in Saint Petersburg and "Nationalist Patriot" with the flag of Poland in Łódź.

This language of white supremacy links back to political fascism as it is regularly observed in conjunction with phrases such as "14/88" (14 being a numerical reference to a 14-word slogan of racial purity and 88 a reference to "Heil Hitler," H being the eighth letter in the alphabet), "Heil Hitler," the white supremacist version of the Celtic Cross, and the ubiquitous "SS" bolts that reference the Schutzstaffel paramilitary organization of the Nazi era. For example, in Figure 10.9, I show the phrase "White Power" written in Mukachevo. The phrase uses a swastika to mark the dot atop the "i" and a thunderbolt for the "s" and is shown next to a rudimentary Celtic cross. Photos from the neighborhood of Bucha, the site of war crimes during the Kremlin's attack on Ukraine in 2022, show bodies lying in the street beneath graffiti of this kind ("14/88," swastikas, and other fascist symbols).

What explains this prevalence of public hate speech in this region? It is plausible that the pervasiveness of graffiti about racial superiority and antisemitism can be attributed to the continuation of social norms. Put

Figure 10.9. The words White Power, Lutsk (a city in Ukraine) with a thunderbolt S, a swastika above the "i" in White Power, and a rudimentary Celtic cross. August 2011. Mukachevo, Ukraine. (Photo: Alexis Lerner)

simply, local populations are accustomed to observing this kind of language and aesthetic, and so it continues to exist.

Alternatively, this phenomenon can be analyzed within a more contemporary perspective, considering twenty-first century liberal-democratic states. After all, some states in the region – Poland, Hungary, Lithuania, Latvia – are now full members of the EU. The fact that graffiti is an effective tool for those whose voices are marginalized from traditional outlets suggests that the prevalence of hate speech can be traced to the marginalization of supremacist and xenophobic voices from traditional outlets for information sharing.

However, even if those voices are excluded from traditional, mainstream news outlets, their durability tells a different story. Creating hateful graffiti is only one part of participating in discourse. The way that local populations and governments choose to respond to this graffiti also signals whether rhetoric is supported or opposed. While graffiti writers have the agency to paint hateful content on public walls, passersby and states also have the agency to highlight or erase it.

To Buff or Not to Buff

Painting antisemitic and hateful content requires only the right conditions and tools. Whether or not it remains in the public space depends on the tolerance of local communities and administrators. A piece may stay up for a few days or even weeks without attracting much attention, especially if it is located in a place with limited foot traffic. However, it is straightforward to take down a piece of distasteful art once it is identified. Either a passerby paints over it or crosses it out, or a local authority contracts someone to powerwash or paint over the writing.

Many motivated individuals do take down, cross out, or respond to xenophobic public art with anti-racist, anti-fascist, and anti-bigotry stencils and stickers, as those seen across Prague, Budapest, and Saint Petersburg. Two such examples are from 2014 Berlin. The first is a portrait of Anne Frank, a German-born (and eventually stateless) Jewish child diarist who famously chronicled her experience in hiding in Amsterdam (Netherlands) for two years (Figure 10.10). The diary is a canonical piece of literature, used to teach youth around the world about the Holocaust, resilience, and intolerance through the eyes of a child.

The second example, shown in Figure 10.11, is a stencil of a paper-thin woman with sunken eyes, jumping rope with barbed wire. The woman depicted resembles well-known photographs of Holocaust victims, and the piece offers commentary on the innocence and humanity stolen from oppressed minorities under the Nazi regime and its collaborators.

Figure 10.10. A portrait of Anne Frank. Jimmy C. 2013. Berlin, Germany.
(Photo: Alexis Lerner)

Figure 10.11. Holocaust victim jumps rope with barbed wire. 2013. Berlin, Germany. (Photo: Alexis Lerner)

Throughout my fieldwork, however, I have observed xenophobic and supremacist content – swastikas and verbal attacks aimed at ethnic minorities – that remains in public spaces with moderate foot traffic for seasons and, in some cases, for years. This durability implies that, in some cases, the public is apathetic or passively ambivalent to public displays of hate. In Figure 10.12, for example, I show a group of friends laughing and drinking in a high-traffic area of downtown Moscow in 2011, seemingly oblivious or apathetic to the words "Glory to Russia – SS" under their feet, illustrating how popular acquiescence to antisemitic and bigoted graffiti contributes to its durability.

While denizens of a particular place may not move to take down offensive graffiti, many local governments institute some kind of clean streets initiative, in which the city hires workers to clean or buff the streets. This is common around the world, from Los Angeles to Melbourne. Cleaning, most frequently using a powerwashing tool to wash away paint, is the most thorough way to fully remove content. However, this method can be somewhat time- and cost-prohibitive. As a result, cities most often engage in buffing as a method of removing graffiti.[4]

Figure 10.12. The words "Glory to Russia" above a thunderbolt SS. August 2011. Moscow, Russia. (Photo: Alexis Lerner)

Buffing can be seen as an act of censorship as it limits the public display of unauthorized sentiment. Often it is used to promote a seemingly "clean" or crime-free public space to put residents and tourists at ease. In practice, however, not all illegal content is buffed, and what is left behind by buffers tells us just as much about a city's political discourse as that which was originally written. What is or is not buffed reflects the state's tolerance for pluralism in discourse. Some states hurry to buff graffitied attacks on political parties or perceived corruption. In Figure 10.13, for example, I show how one artist in Budapest, commented anonymously on Hungarian prime minister Viktor Orban, whose name was left visible while the rest of the statement was powerwashed off the wall. However, those same states often refrain from buffing racist or antisemitic attacks, such as a cross on the entryway to a Jewish shop or the words "Fuck Jews →
Vermin" on the walls of the Lauder Javne Jewish Community School, both in Budapest (the latter shown in Figure 10.14). As a result, particular cities – including many of those already mentioned in this chapter – become known for their tacit approval of xenophobic and bigoted graffiti.

Figure 10.13. "Orban Viktor" midway through powerwashing. July 2011. Budapest, Hungary. (Photo: Alexis Lerner)

Figure 10.14. "Fuck the Jews → Vermin" on the door to a yeshiva, an Orthodox Jewish school. July 2011. Budapest, Hungary. (Photo: Alexis Lerner)

Other states *create* content, whether in tandem with the act of buffing, as a form of buffing itself, or to flood all subversive graffiti out of an area. For example, in Saint Petersburg, in 2009, I photographed multiple references to the historic Siege of Leningrad (1941–4). Shown in Figure 10.15, one such version of the popular stencil demarcated specific sites around the city where bombs were dropped on civilians during air raids. In Łódź, as shown in Figure 6.1 in Chapter Six, graffiti stencils outline the boundary of the Litzmannstadt Ghetto, established by the Nazis to hold Polish Jews, Roma, and other persecuted minorities.

Initiatives such as the siege stencils across Saint Petersburg may not be graffiti in the illegal and subversive sense, but they still communicate a message to the public in a way that has a rallying or memorializing effect. Regardless of current political or social differences, residents of the city generally share a collective memory of victimization, hunger, and indiscriminate violence under Nazi occupation in the early 1940s. The Kremlin, Russia's top administrative body, has taken this collective memory one step further by hiring previously critical artists to paint publicly funded murals that propel state-approved narratives about patriotism and nostalgia.

Figure 10.15. "We Remember. We Mourn." 2009. Saint Petersburg, Russia. (Photo: Alexis Lerner)

Moscow Co-opts Graffiti Art to Promote State-Approved Narratives

By spotlighting a particular issue or voice, (political) public art is used to shape narratives for some actor, institution, or policy's gain. The Russian state not only creates murals about national cultural and war heroes but also floods out subversive content from downtown public spaces. Note that I use the term narrative instead of discourse, as the state's power leaves little room for dialogism.

In the early twenty-first century, the quality of street art in Russia was largely independent, illegal, and subversive. At this time, government interference was primarily reactionary as it related to street art and graffiti culture. For example, during the 2012 Russian presidential election, Moscow's back alleys and underpasses were saturated with stencils and stickers calling for the end of frontrunner and de facto incumbent president Putin and United Russia (Zimberg 2012, 36).

The election year of 2012 represents the transition from president Medvedev, an alleged modernizer who challenged corruption and reformed Russia's police forces, to president Putin in his third term as president of the Russian Federation. It also marks a period of global unrest and weakened United States–Russia relations in the aftermath of the failed diplomatic "reset" that was initiated in 2009. At this time, Russian domestic policy was influenced by the cascading Arab Spring protests, which began at the end of 2010, the conflict in East Ukraine and the 2014 annexation of Crimea that divided public opinion domestically, and Russian involvement in the ongoing Syrian Civil War that strained its struggling and sanctioned economy (McFaul 2018). Considering these international events and domestic pressures – particularly the mass demonstrations of 2011 and 2012 and the devalued ruble – president Putin's administration promoted unity and consolidated power through campaigns of conservatism, patriotism, and nationalism (Putin 2012).

In line with this campaign, the Kremlin pivoted in its approach to the management of subversive, political graffiti. Instead of ignoring this platform and its artists, or responding with buffing as they had during the 2012 election, the state conceived of a way to harness the talent and public trust possessed by critical artists, while simultaneously shaping its public image. In short, administrative bodies ranging from the City of Moscow to the Ministry of Culture and the Ministry of the Interior began to host their own graffiti festivals. Built on the corporate model outlined by Nike and Nescafé in the 1990s, discussed in Chapter Three, state institutions invited artists to apply for the opportunity to paint large, public murals on the government's dime.

Surely, cooperation with the authorities in these venues was effectively self-censorship, as artists were repeatedly told "no politics and no porn" (Hopp 2011; Ponosov 2012), while also being guided to paint according to the Kremlin narrative of Russia's proud Soviet legacy, political spaces (such as Red Square), cultural heroes, and military triumphs. For those artists willing to abandon their criticisms and paint on Kremlin-approved themes, co-optation provided both the financial and institutional support necessary to create public art in present-day Russia. And so, motivated by regular paychecks and the promise of semi-permanence, the previously cloaked artists of the night came out of the shadows to register on the state's terms (ZUKCLUB 2012; ZUKCLUB 2017).

State co-optation of public discourse has several consequences. First, by curating the public space and its main actors, states can more efficiently track the remaining political rhetoric – whether in support of or against a state and its leadership. In short, there is less noise to navigate or to censor. Second, authoritarian leaders can use co-optation to monitor popular leaders and determine the threat that they pose to the political system, or whether they can be groomed to hold larger leadership roles, such as the talented local artists willing to pivot from oppositional sentiment to paint pro-Kremlin murals. Third, co-opted artists in Russia tend to be the most seasoned, as talent and experience influence their visibility and skill. By co-opting senior artists and pushing those unwilling to be co-opted into galleries or alternative professional ventures to avoid repressive alternatives, the state creates a discontinuity in mentorship. For example, whereas in the 1990s, graffiti artists like Basket organized workshops where senior artists taught novices the best techniques for painting subversive sentiment on a city's public spaces, novices in the contemporary age must turn to YouTube and LiveJournal for self-instruction.

Finally, autocrats can use co-optation to foster a façade of political pluralism, both domestically and internationally, to demonstrate (insincere) compliance with democratic norms (Hyde 2015a, 13; Hyde 2015b). By permitting artists a limited and controlled outlet for creative expression, the state may be able to satisfy some subversive actors, who might otherwise engage in subversive mobilization. Consider the metaphor of the safety valve on a boiler: when a boiler's temperature gets too high, there is a resulting increase in pressure in the tank. If this buildup is allowed to continue without intervention, it leads to a terrible explosion with the potential to wreak substantial damage. Because this risk is recognized, boilers have attached safety valves, which help to release excess pressure. By letting off a little steam, a boiler keeps working efficiently and the house remains intact. The same logic applies to civil society in authoritarian states: by establishing channels for subversive actors to let off a little steam, autocrats can mitigate some of the potential risk to its stability, all while shaping public narratives and fashioning an aesthetically unified contemporary urban space.

Consider, for example, the patriotic 2014 mural, photographed in 2016, shown in Figure 10.16. Here, artist Stew Lus painted a legendary Russian phoenix rising from its ashes, a symbolic reference not lost on Russian passersby. The phoenix is painted in the Socialist Realist style that was prevalent in the Soviet Union, with a long neck that cranes diagonally toward the upper right-hand corner of the six-story building's façade. Its head is enveloped in a white halo of light, as were the folkloric ikons of centuries before. Stew Lus' piece is not alone: in Moscow, for example, there are hundreds of such murals, which the Russian government approved and paid for either directly or indirectly via official festivals.

Other pieces were more overtly related to the celebration of wartime victory. For example, one mural near Red Square, photographed in 2017 and shown in Figure 10.17, shows two Russian military heroes from the so-called "Time of Troubles," a period that marked the end of the Rurik Dynasty in 1598 and the power vacuum (coupled with a famine) that existed until the beginning of the Romanov Dynasty in 1613.

Government sponsorship of these murals is made clear by an accompanying plaque and/or a painted logo. For example, the firebird mural was sponsored by the Department of Culture of the City of Moscow as part of the Best City in the World festival of 2014, and the mural of Pozharskii and Minin was sponsored by the Russian Military History Society via its "Our Heroes" initiative, a sponsorship that is indicated by the seal in the top right corner of the mural. The Russian Military History Society was sponsored by decree of president Putin in December 2012 and funded by the Ministry of Culture, with the primary aim of educating the public about Russian military history. Besides sponsorship, plaques often indicate the name of the artist and their country of origin.

Kremlin-sponsored murals also lauded contemporary wartime victories, including the Allied Powers' World War Two victory over the Axis Alliance of Nazi Germany, Italy, and Japan. For example, the decorated Soviet World War Two General Georgy Zhukov looms large over tourists on the Old Arbat, establishing to residents and visitors a narrative of continuity from Red Army victory to unified contemporary patriotism. General Zhukov, shown in Figure 10.18, led the Red Army in major wartime events, including the defense of Stalingrad and the Battle of Berlin, which led to the end of the war. North of the city, in the residential district of Marina Roshcha, murals celebrating the Red Army and World

Figure 10.16. Russian firebird rising from its ashes. Stew Lus. November 2016. Moscow, Russia. (Photo: Alexis Lerner)

Figure 10.17. Military heroes from the Time of Troubles. November 2016. Moscow, Russia. (Photo: Alexis Lerner)

Figure 10.18. The decorated World War Two military leader, General Zhukov, looms large over the tourist-heavy Old Arbat. 2017. Moscow, Russia. (Photo: Alexis Lerner)

War Two victories are ubiquitous. In Figure 10.19, I show one such mural that depicts a soldier, several military planes, and a red star that represents the Soviet Union in particular, and communist ideology more generally. Figure 10.19 also shows the words "65 years of victory," a celebratory phrase honoring both those that fought in World War Two while reinforcing the narrative of an unbroken line of military achievement for Russia from 1945 to the present day.

Between 2012 and the subsequent election year in 2018, the public art in Moscow that was once critical, satirical, and anonymous became curated and pro-Kremlin. Subversive artists were either co-opted by the state or pushed out of the city streets into private spaces, such as galleries abroad. In the case where local painters refuse to paint for the state, authorities outsource to foreign artists – for example, Brazilian-born Eduardo Kobra, the artist who painted Soviet ballerina Maya Plisetskaya on Stoleshnikov Pereulok (in English, Stoleshnikov Lane) or Valencian artist, Escif, who painted a hand raised in a nationalist salute on Zvonarskii Pereulok (Figure 10.20) (Escif 2016) – thereby further alienating those unwilling to cooperate. As a quintessential example of Moscow's post-2014 state-sponsored murals, I show Kobra's colorful tribute to

Figure 10.19. A mural in Marina Roshcha celebrates 65 years of victory for the Red Army. 2016. Moscow, Russia. (Photo: Alexis Lerner)

Figure 10.20. Saying "Hello" with a nationalist salute. Escif. 2016. Moscow, Russia. (Photo: Alexis Lerner)

Plisetskaya in Figure 10.21. Murals like Kobra's result in a more beautiful and aesthetically unified Moscow, meant to inspire national pride and a certain collective memory, but at the cost of democratic speech and free public spaces.

The top-down control of public spaces, narratives, and information – whether through public art initiatives, unpublicized excavations of public squares, or the expansion of state censorship via offerings like "free" public internet access – serves two purposes simultaneously: beautification and dominance. On one hand, the proliferation of state-sponsored murals downtown – along with the recent bolstering of Moscow's restaurant and craft beer scene, its re-visioning of public parks, and its public transit system overhaul – has surely led to a more attractive, navigable, and picturesque city. Indeed, there is a sort of plausible deniability tied to co-optation as policy; by pushing top-down sentiment via trusted social actors slowly and over the course of several years, the state distances itself from the act of co-opting and its implications. Therefore, co-optation

Figure 10.21. Ballerina Maya Plisetskaya. Eduardo Kobra. 2016. Moscow, Russia. (Photo: Alexis Lerner)

lacks a definitive pejorative quality. To co-opt controversial and subversive actors, while a variant on censorship or curation, also means identifying talent, beautifying neighborhoods, and choosing an alternative to violent repression – actions that boost popular support and keep incumbents in power.

This phenomenon extends beyond the borders of the Russian capital, and I have observed it in other Russian cities, like Vladivostok, Tyumen, and Saint Petersburg, with popular artists hired to paint large patriotic murals in highly trafficked locations, as well as in the curation of electoral ballots and social media discourse, when leaders buy off prominent candidates or public figures while saturating the remaining space with Kremlin-curated voices. The co-optation of graffiti to promote state-curated narratives also occurs in other authoritarian states. For example, fifteen large-scale murals were commissioned across Kazakhstan in 2020, depicting Soviet and Kazakh heroes such as commander Bauyrzhan Momyshuly, musician Batyrkhan Shukenov, and poet Abai, in honor of the seventy-fifth anniversary of the Great Patriotic War (Kazinform 2020). Around the globe, autocrats buy off social movement leadership and flood the streets and other public spaces that otherwise contain free political expression.

Explaining Variation in Who Controls Discourse

Political graffiti is used in similar ways and for similar purposes throughout the post-Soviet region. Ultimately, it is a way for an actor – generally one that is marginalized from the mainstream flow of information – to express political sentiment or discontent. In some situations, this may appear as activism or hate speech painted onto public walls, put there by the populations pushed out of traditional news outlets. In other cases, states understand the usefulness of graffiti as a tool for shaping public opinion. States that can effectively co-opt this artform can promote self-serving narratives, for instance, about nationalism and military victory.

What might explain these differences in who creates graffiti and about what topic? One factor is cost, as tools and labor for these multistory paintings carry a sizable expense. Further, for a state to organize a graffiti festival as a venue for painting, costs expand to include promotional materials, entertainment, refreshments, judges, and security.

Furthermore, the act of co-opting otherwise critical artists to create expansive murals that communicate a predetermined narrative requires substantial logistical attention. Not only must the state locate and commission the artists, but it must also determine the ideological narrative that it wants the artist to highlight. State-run graffiti festivals can remove some of the pressure to plan a mural from a creative or an ideological perspective, but there must still be some kind of gatekeeping committee that determines which artists are allowed to paint in the festival and about what topics.

It is also plausible that the stark contrast between hate speech and state speech can be explained by regime type, or at least by state capacity, implying that states with a more robust and centralized authority have a greater ability to manage public narratives. This implies that, as states become more consolidated autocracies, they become more likely to shape public narratives in all formats: the mainstream media, television news channels, and public art and monuments. To underscore this third hypothesis, I offer the example of a recent state-funded mural in Poland that indicates that the current Polish government has the capacity and interest in manipulating public art in a way similar to what Russia and Kazakhstan have done.

Since it first won a majority in 2015, the conservative Law and Justice political party has used its position of authority to promote a platform of rejecting liberal European ideology, adhering to Polish-Catholic values, and censoring foreign and oppositional voices in the media through institutions such as the National Media Council. It is often accused of harboring illiberal, if not authoritarian, intent and policies, though some supporters would suggest that the party's main objective is ensuring national security by any means necessary.

In 2018, in conjunction with Law and Justice's electoral success,[5] artist Jarosław Fabiś painted a large-scale mural of the fathers of Polish independence – Józef Piłsudski, Roman Dmowski, Wincenty Witos, Wojciech Korfanty, Ignacy Jan Paderewski, and Ignacy Daszyński – to celebrate the nation's 100 years of independence. The mural was commissioned by the Institute of National Remembrance, an organization established by the Parliament of Poland and widely criticized for becoming politicized on issues related to World War Two and the Holocaust under the Law and Justice administration. Overall, while Poland has demonstrated the capacity to create large-scale, nationalist murals, especially under the current administration, it does not yet appear to be a concerted campaign.

In Moscow in particular, this effort is part of a purposive Kremlin initiative to shape public narratives and to boost patriotic unity. In the Russian capital, public sentiment that was once subversive and politically combative moved away from the high-traffic, downtown area. In its place are massive murals, quite literally stamped with state approval. In practice, this means that neighborhoods previously covered with direct criticisms of Putin in 2012 – slogans like "Putin, It's Time to Go," "Putin is a Vampire," "Who, If Not Putin?" and opposition leader Alexei Navalny's popularized "United Russia is the Party of Crooks and Thieves" – are now saturated with six-story murals about patriotism, war heroes, and a Kremlin-curated collective memory. By occupying the spaces previously home to controversial political expression, the city has effectively pushed free discourse out of the public eye.

There is agency over space. Individuals and states can choose which messages they share and which they refuse to allow. Governments can control narratives selectively or as policy. Cities vary in the degree to which they permit, eradicate, or support nationalist content, and variation exists, too, in how graffiti is used both to celebrate military victories (however far in the past) and to alienate marginalized minority populations. On occasion, graffiti is used to attack religious or ethnic groups that no longer reside in an area, such as in particular Ukrainian and

Polish urban centers where references to Hitler, Nazis, and gas chambers are ubiquitous. The examples of antisemitic diatribes or symbols of white supremacy contrast with the recent authoritarian trend of co-opting critical artists to use state resources to paint curated political murals. States *do* have the power to shape narratives, and successful co-optation is evidence of that power. Yet, co-optation in practice is nothing more than a new tool for flooding the commons with controlled narratives or curated propaganda, as it aids the state in eliminating dissent and reinforcing control by rewarding shifted loyalties and punishing dogmatic adversaries by barring access to public spaces.

The Future of Political Graffiti

If Russian street art began with an illicit breakdancing video in the back room of a Saint Petersburg café, with revolutionary aesthetics that challenged existing power structures and empowered the lay person to comment on the restrictions of contemporary life, it ends with the submissive whimper of constraint and co-optation.

This is especially true in authoritarian states, such as Russia and Kazakhstan, where many paint social commentary or write on behalf of multinational corporations, local businesses, and the government. This is not to say that critique has been fully eradicated in these spaces; artists like Yav Crew, Misha Most, and Kirill Kto do still paint brave and critical works. However, state-sanctioned murals physically dwarf these subversive and unsanctioned pieces, which are also quickly buffed. This trend of flooding the public space with state-curated narratives is not limited to Russia or Kazakhstan; liberal democratic nations from Poland to the United States also leverage this tactic. The co-optation of public art may be useful for the promotion of certain values or narratives, but it undeniably inverts the Midnight Graffiti chronotope into something unrecognizable.

The Midnight Graffiti chronotope suggests images of young people – predominantly male – in New York City, in the 1980s, painting trains, running from the police (carrying backpacks of stolen paint), and crashing some kind of hip-hop or breakdancing party. These artists are perceived to be rebellious and lawless. They combine wit with bright blasts of color to express their anti-authority, anti-capitalist, and anarchical sentiment.

The Corporate Graffiti chronotope, like the Co-opted Graffiti chronotope, completely overturns the Midnight Graffiti chronotope. In the Corporate Graffiti world, graffiti is commissioned, sometimes by the owner of a building. A commissioned work is no longer illegal, and therefore, the threat of arrest or jail time is eliminated. As a result, these sanctioned pieces can be painted during the day and without hiding one's face from public scrutiny.

The absent threat of arrest leads to a second temporal shift – the departure of urgency. Consider the sticker or stencil, whose design is inherently linked to speed, as one can design the sticker or stencil at home and quickly cover an extremely large area with a uniform message, thereby having a greater likelihood of being seen. In the Corporate Graffiti chronotope, the commissioned artist's safety from the police allows them to paint a larger surface at a more leisurely pace. The previously invisible artist becomes visible and traceable, both in the act of painting a mural and in the paperwork that traces the paint purchased, the lift secured, and the permits approved.

Co-optation is pervasive in the post-Soviet region. Former warehouses and factories from Tbilisi to Łódź are now contemporary creative compounds. Historic buildings in Budapest and Saint Petersburg are gutted to make way for ostentatious condominiums. And the corporatization of graffiti means that the previously subversive art form has become a commodity that can be bought by those who wish to sell a product or an idea. Co-optation of this artform indicates that graffiti is understood by the state and corporate actors to have value as a form of communication.

What is the effect of this temporal–spatial shift? By inverting the Midnight Graffiti chronotope, commissioners have inverted not only the subversive nature of graffiti as a set of tools for expressing discontent but have also impacted *what* denizens can say and *where* they may say it. Surely artists retain agency in *whether* they will opt in at all; however, those who choose not to opt in are replaceable by artists who can be commissioned from abroad and who will paint on what a commissioner desires or deems to be appropriate. This chronotopic inversion is a form of slow censorship, not one that punishes discontent but rather one that floods a public space to the point where the discontented have no walls left that remain available to them.

At the same time, public observers likely continue to perceive these murals through the lens of the Midnight Graffiti chronotope, which means that they may believe, even if subconsciously, that this sentiment is held by subversive actors using traditionally subversive tools, and therefore, the sentiment reflects the will of the people. Even those who recognize that a mural is a hired production may agree that the commissioned work nevertheless beautifies a public space. The bright colors not only give passersby something pleasant to look at and reflect upon but also flood out non-commissioned artists, such as those who paint their bold or offensive tag, crew name, or love interest with impudence, thereby improving the quality of life for some. The commissioner – a multinational corporation or a government agency – retains some plausible deniability: in theory, they are not trying to shape public narratives and censor subversive discourse but rather attempting to build more beautiful public spaces.

In this book, I sought to accomplish three objectives: first, to revive an underexplored topic in the discipline of political science, I leverage ethnographic methods and extensive data collection to teach about the history of graffiti in the post-Soviet and post-communist region, as well as about state–society political relations under a variety of regime types. Second, I aspire for this book to encourage observers in positions of power, such as policymakers and journalists to *read the writing on the walls* when attempting to understand a society, especially a closed one (when the writing might be on the outskirts of town, fleeting, or dwarfed by large, state-sponsored murals). Third, I am hopeful that, after reading this book, you will find yourself reading graffiti as a discursive text about a place, where artists and authorities carry agency over what narratives appear in the dark corners of alleyways and on the walls of tunnels that run beneath the streets.

You can read the streets at any time: on a walk home from dinner, while waiting for a bus early in the morning, or along your daily commute. Even better – you can use graffiti to read the streets as text anywhere in the world, from Detroit and Toronto to Budapest and Tel Aviv. Every place has its own unique and discursive narrative. By reading the walls as a text, a resident can see that their privately held opinions are shared and a tourist can absorb an unfamiliar place with greater nuance.

Graffiti is powerful. It amplifies marginalized voices across regime types, from liberal-democratic to authoritarian. The issues in these states might vary: in some states, there is greater concern about voting rights while in others, it is about environmentalism or domestic violence. Yet, at least in its anonymous and accessible (Midnight Graffiti chronotope) form, graffiti remains a universal and timeless tool for expressing sentiment and circumventing censorship, one that must be recognized for its subversive political power.

In a world where voices are silenced and individual rights are threatened, graffiti stands as a resounding testament to the enduring resilience of human expression.

Appendix

The following is a guiding list of questions that I used in my interviews:

- How did you get involved with graffiti?
- Why do you paint?
- Do you ever paint political/critical art? If so, why? For shock? To mobilize? Who do you think your main audience is?
- How does graffiti benefit or hurt society?
- How did graffiti, in your opinion, first come to [your country]?
- What is your oldest/best memory of writing?
- What is the role of graffiti during this election?
- Is there a generational continuity? Do older writers teach younger writers to write?
- What is the average age/gender/socioeconomic status of a writer in [your city]?
- Do you ever write in other languages? Which ones and why?
- What is your graffiti name and how did you choose it? What does it mean?
- Why do artists write about the war?
- Are some styles more authentic than others?
- What are your opinions on legal writing/festivals?
- Who are the best writers in [your city]? Or who are your favorite writers?
- What are the best places in [your city] to see graffiti?
- Do you paint for yourself or for your viewers?
- What kinds of issues are ignored or banned by the media? What's happening right now with media freedoms in [your country]?
- Do you ever see anti-government graffiti? Do you think that anti-state graffiti changes peoples' minds about things?

- How do activists/oppositional groups use graffiti and interact with the graffiti scene?
- What are the police like? What happens if you get caught?
- When organizing or participating in a legal festival, are there certain things artists cannot write about?
- Censorship on the internet: What is the difference between writing something critical on the web vs on the walls?
- Is vandalism political?
- Which areas of (your city) do I need to visit to see graffiti?
- Who else should I be talking to?

Notes

Chapter One

1 A buffed work is covered with a coat of paint with the purpose of censoring the original work.

2 A thin, Schumpeterian definition of democracy looks mainly at electoral integrity, e.g., does the state hold elections, are said elections "free and fair," and is there some semblance of competition and enough uncertainty so that the challenger could potentially unseat the incumbent through legal means? Alternatively, a thick definition of democracy – consider for example Dahl (1998) or Freedom House's annual Freedom in the World Report – considers the existence of free and fair elections in addition to the protection of individuals rights, press freedoms, judicial independence, and general measurements of the public's ability to voice discontent or set policy items on an executive agenda.

3 I define co-optation as when a previously critical individual or group of individuals publicly trades loyalty for provisions (Lerner 2020, 5).

4 This freedom generally includes legal protections for many forms of political speech, such as on matters of government policy and decision making. However, it is frequently limited in situations involving hate speech, threats to national security, and speech that otherwise incites violence.

5 Orban first mentioned the Jewish Hungarian-American billionaire and human rights activist George Soros in conjunction with antisemitic tropes in a 2017 public speech in Băile Tuşnad, Romania, to an audience of Romanian-Hungarians (those who identify ethnically as Hungarian but civically as Romanian). During that speech, Orban said of Soros: "We are fighting an enemy that is different from us. Not open but hiding; not straightforward but crafty; not honest but base; not national but international; does not believe in working but speculates with money; does

not have its own homeland but feels it owns the whole world" (Walker 2020).

6 As I write in the Notes on the Text section at the beginning of this book, I do not discuss the states included in the Former Republic of Yugoslavia or Albania in this iteration of the project.

Chapter Two

1 *L'art pour l'art*, or art for art's sake, is a philosophy of creative expression that highlights the intrinsic and morally neutral value of art (Gautier 1835).

2 Absurdism-by-design was nothing new for Soviet artists. The Futurist movement of the early twentieth century, led by Ilya Zdanevich, Mikhail Larionov, and others, centered around the notion of challenging stale, bourgeois art and its so-called "museumification" (Ponosov 2018, 14; Gray 1962). Instead, the Futurists called for art to invade public spaces and to violate societal norms (ibid). In Chapter Four, I further discuss the impact of this and other creative movements on contemporary street art.

3 Kto is the Russian word for "Who," and this name is a self-selected pseudonym.

Chapter Three

1 I am protecting the anonymity of my source for the next few lines.

2 The practice of buffing some works and not others (e.g., buffing anti-state sentiment but not xenophobic sentiment) is common, and I address that topic in Chapter Ten.

3 This cat-and-mouse game is reminiscent of the excellent work on state–society relations in the China case (e.g., Fu 2017a and Fu 2017b), or in the Malaysia case (see Scott 1985).

4 I defined *samizdat* in Chapter Two as self-published and self-distributed written work. *Samizdat* work is often subversive and implies some ties with underground or counter-cultural communities.

5 A graffiti cap is the tip that fits on top of a spray bottle's nozzle. The size of the hole on a cap corresponds with the type of stream of paint that will emit from that can. With different sizes and styles of caps, an artist can control the width and volume of a paint blast, as well as any special effects such as calligraphy or splatter-style writing. A "fatter" cap will produce a thicker line that is good for painting quick tags, clean outlines, and for filling in large areas, whereas a small-hole opening will result in a thin line that is best for fine, detailed work.

6 Legal writing specifically indicates a commissioned graffiti job, in which a business or institution contracts with the artist to market a product or idea using graffiti.

7 I further explore the difference between traditional, subversive graffiti culture and legal writing in Chapter Seven, where I position these practices as diametrically opposed chronotopes.

8 Relations between these two states later dissolved, due to Russia's ongoing military conflict in Ukraine, its 2014 annexation of Crimea, its attempts to interfere in the 2016 and 2020 United States presidential elections, and the tit-for-tat closure of embassies and consulates in both countries. The consulate in Saint Petersburg ceased activity in 2018.

9 For more information about this festival, see their website: https://tobeawoman.az/about/.

10 Airbrushing is similar to painting with a spray can but allows the artist a great deal more control over small details and is known to be more economical and possibly better for the environment.

11 The practice of forcing activists to abandon their public displays of discontent in exchange for some kind of state or monetary benefit is not uncommon in authoritarian states. See, for example, Teets (2014).

Chapter Four

1 Graffiti is traditionally a male-dominated realm. Yarn bombing challenges that. Jessie Hemmons explains: "Yarn bombing takes that most matronly craft (knitting) and that most maternal of gestures (wrapping something cold in a warm blanket) and transfers it to the concrete and steel wilds of the urban streetscape" (Wollan 2011). Just as gangs of graffiti artists often gather to form crews, yarn bombers increasingly seem to define themselves as unified with tagging cohorts. Yet, the art form remains illicit, leading the taggers to act quickly, to wear black, and to attack at night. Learn more about Hemmons and her yarn-bombing work at ishknits.com.

2 Bombing refers to the act of covering an area with an artist's tag or throwup painting. A tag is simply a writer's chosen pseudonym, written quickly in marker or spray paint in a single layer. The word *tag* can also be used as a verb, meaning "to sign" a surface with one's pseudonym. A tag is commonly seen beside a more detailed mural, as a signature for the piece. A throwup is similar to a tag in that it is often one writer's pseudonym and signature, frequently written in bubble letters in two colors – one outline and one fill. A throwup differs from a tag in that it may be an abbreviated version of one's tag name or include more than one artist's tag in a list-like format.

3 Litvin began his career in the early 1990s, performing solo, with Group Without Name, and, after 2000, with the ESCAPE program (also called the ESCAPE group or the ESCAPE travel agency).

4 The word used here by Litvin, "meetings," comes from the Russian word used to describe rallies or even marches or demonstrations.

5 The other artists: Vladimir Arkhipov, Andrei Velikanov, Lekha Garikovich, Imperator VAVA (Vladimir Aleksandrov), Sergei Kalinin, Mikhail Kosolapov, Egor Koshelev, Pavel Kuznetsov, Polina Kulik, Ivan Lungin, Diana Machulina, Anton Nikolaev, Marina Perchikhina, Liza Plavinskaia, Aleksandr Podosinov, Ira Shteinberg, and Vlad Iurashko.

6 While the Monstrations could not exist in person in May 2020, due to social distancing rules during the global COVID-19 pandemic, Loskutov instructed his followers to participate in novel ways: by hanging a poster from a balcony or a window, attaching it to one's fence, or even writing one's message on the sidewalk using "dead mice and chocolate candies." (Loskutov 2020).

7 According to an anonymous 2012 interview with a Nashi participant, these youth were brought in to patrol any areas where military vehicles could not "fit" – the city's underground passageways, metro stations, and back streets – to "make sure nothing happened."

8 Some selections of this and the following paragraph were originally published by the author at *ForeignPolicy.com* in 2012.

9 From Lerner (2020, 16): "The concept of *sistema* originates in the Russian lexicon, but systemic opposition candidates can be found in states across the authoritarian context. Some systemic candidates are overtly affiliated with the incumbent's political party, others openly contradict themselves by advocating for the incumbent while running against him, and still others masquerade as true opposition by criticizing a soft policy of the existing regime (for example, employment policy) despite known ties to the ruling elite. Systemic candidates do not pose a realistic political threat to the incumbent; instead, they exist as mere placeholders or as tools for 'flooding' a ballot and therefore dividing the popular vote (Wood and Lerner n.d.). As representatives of a highly centralized political system, the systemic opposition is opposition only in name, and not in action."

Chapter Five

1 I focus here on physical public space, yet many of the theories presented herein apply loosely to the internet.

2 According to Article 31 of the Constitution of the Russian Federation, "Citizens of the Russian Federation have the right to assemble peacefully without arms, hold meetings, rallies and demonstrations, marches and pickets."

3 This information comes from an interviewee in Belarus in July 2011. I have agreed to keep this individual anonymous for their safety and security.

4 In 2014, the G8 became the G7 when Russia was disinvited from the political group.

Chapter Six

1 For more information on the victims of the Nazi regime and its collaborators, please see the Holocaust Encyclopedia, a set of resources compiled by the United States Holocaust Memorial Museum. For example, the articles titled "Documenting Numbers of Victims of the Holocaust and Nazi Persecution" or "Polish Victims."

2 To learn more about the Pahonia symbol, you can visit the Rada of the Belarusian Democratic Republic in Exile. https://www.radabnr.org/

3 This is reminiscent of Benedict Anderson's *Map-as-Logo* concept, first introduced in 1983, which discusses the creation of a logo that can be used to represent a nation. Even though this logo or symbol is fabricated, its repetition serves to reinforce its credibility, thereby establishing the logo as a rallying point for those including in said nation.

4 Read more about this project and others like it at the Zarya Center for Contemporary Art in Vladivostok's website: http://zaryavladivostok.ru/en/page/Russian%26English-RadyaTima.

Chapter Seven

1 Tim Frye astutely commented here, "Even Mozart and Da Vinci had patrons," implying that financial backing does not necessarily have a strong and negative correlation with the quality of one's aesthetics.

2 The author thanks Sue Vice for this fabulous insight into how Bakhtin's work connects to the Midnight Graffiti chronotope.

3 I write about this idea of co-opted graffiti in a more practical sense in an article version of this book, titled "The Co-optation of Dissent in Hybrid States: Post-Soviet Graffiti in Moscow" (2021). In particular, I discuss the phenomenon of co-optation as it relates to graffiti, asking whether co-optation in this case is a standalone method of control that is alternative to repression, a less overt type of repression, or something else altogether.

4 To learn more about this project, visit https://www.audubon.org/amp.

Chapter Eight

1 For more on analyzing the role of geographic space (e.g., densely populated city center versus abandoned parking garage on the outskirts of town), see Chapter Five.

2 Some of this content also appears in Wood and Lerner 2022.

3 Stus died in a Soviet-forced labor camp for political prisoners in 1985, and, in 2005, was posthumously named a hero of Ukraine during Viktor Yushchenko's administration.

Chapter Nine

1 To see images of Kormfox's work, visit her self-curated online gallery at https://api.flickr.com/people/kormfox/.

2 References to CCTV cameras are common in Eastern and Central Europe, from stenciled CCTV cameras in Budapest (commenting simultaneously on the pervasiveness of said cameras and the perceived unwillingness of the police to act against intolerant violence) to one 2015 sticker in Moscow, reading "Big brother is watching you… and he is bored."

3 Not to be confused with Manu Invisible, a male graffiti artist from Sardinia, who painted political commentaries in Europe around the same time.

4 Translated from the Russian: "Хватит ли этого, чтобы выразить мою политическую позицию?"

5 You can see this mural on Manu's Flickr Account at: https://www.flickr .com/photos/manuinglasses/4533321455/.

6 Learn more about this movement at: https://kottiundco.net/english/.

7 Vilna refers to modern-day Vilnius, the capital of Lithuania. The name "Vilna" and similar variants have been used in different languages. It is "Vilne" in Yiddish, "Wilno" in Polish, "Vilnia" in Belarussian, "Wilna" in German, "Vilno" in Ukrainian, and "Vilna" in Russian as well. These names reflect the city's multicultural history and its significance to various communities over time.

8 Sevastopol is a Crimean city that is both recognized as a city within sovereign Ukraine and administered by Russia since a referendum in 2014.

9 Originally shown online at http://www.lgbtgermany.com/2015/10/08/gay-graffiti-mural-defaced-in-erfurt/ in late 2021. This entire site is down as of April 2024.

10 Originally shown online at https://zvzda.ru/news/17fbd7aeb521 in late 2021. This entire site is down as of March 2024.

11 This Vasilievskii Island stencil was one of the first pieces of political graffiti that I noticed back in 2009 while living in Saint Petersburg. This piece, and others like it, inspired me to conduct a decade of subsequent fieldwork and to write this book.

12 For more photos of Moscow's Tsoi Wall, see Zimberg 2012b.

Chapter Ten

1 Vincent Vizkelety has documented this trend of writing names, dates, and short stories on bricks across Hungary. His project is called Budapest Tegali (In English, the "Bricks of Budapest"). More information is available at https://blog.nli.org.il/en/lbh_nadler_budapest/.

2 I observed this during fieldwork conducted in New Orleans in 2012. It has been corroborated by Ward 2012 and Broom 2019.

3 Historian Helene Sinnreich writes that this phenomenon has plagued Łódź since World War Two (2004).

4 I discuss the process of buffing in Chapter Three of this book.

5 In 2019, Law and Justice received the highest share of votes in Poland since the country revived democratic elections in 1989.

References

Anderson, Benedict. 1983. *Imagined Communities: Reflections on the Origin and Spread of Nationalism.* London: Verso.

Army of Discreditation. 2022. "Красноярскую активистку оштрафовали на 30 тысяч рублей за надпись «Нет войне» на снегу." *Mediazona*, March 6, 2022. https://zona.media/news/2022/03/06/fks

Austin, John Langshaw. 1962 [1955]. *How to Do Things with Words: The William James Lectures delivered at Harvard University in 1955*, edited by J. O. Urmson. Cambridge: Harvard University Press.

Baird, Jennifer and Claire Taylor, eds. 2011. *Ancient Graffiti in Context.* Oxfordshire: Routledge Press.

Baker, Mark, and Tom Balmforth. 2015. "B.B. King Wowed Soviet Audiences." *RadioFreeEurope/RadioLiberty.* May 20, 2015. https://www.rferl.org/a/bb-king-wowed-soviet-audiences/27018576.html.

Bakhtin, Mikhail Mikhailovich. 1981. "Discourse in the Novel." Translated by M. Holquist, & C. Emerson. In *The Dialogic Imagination: 4 Essays by M. M. Bakhtin*, edited by M. Holquist, 259–422. Austin: University of Texas Press.

Baku City Executive Authority. 2019. Statement. *Sputnik Azerbaijan*, September 29, 2019.

Baldini, Andrea. 2016. "Street Art: A Reply to Riggle." *Journal of Aesthetics and Art Criticism* 74, no. 2: 187–91. https://doi.org/10.1111/jaac.12261.

Banksy. 2018. "Going, Going, Gone..." Instagram post, October 5, 2018. https://www.instagram.com/p/Bokt2sEhlsu/?igsh=MWk5M29wbmNpaWty.

Bánkuti, Miklós, Gábor Halmai, and Kim Scheppele. 2012. "Hungary's Illiberal Turn: Disabling the Constitution." *Journal of Democracy* 23, no. 3 (July): 138–46. http://doi.org/10.1515/9786155225550-006

Baudrillard, Jean. 1994 [1981]. *Simulacra and Simulation.* Ann Arbor: University of Michigan Press.

Bauman, Marcy Lassota. 1987. "Literature, Repetition, and Meaning." *Language Arts* 64, no. 1: 54–60. https://doi.org/10.58680/la198725483. https://eric.ed.gov/?id=EJ345215.

BBC Monitoring. 2011. "Belarus Country Profile." *BBC.* https://www.bbc.com/news/world-europe-17941131.

– 2012. "Russia Country Profile." *BBC.* https://www.bbc.com/news/world-europe-17839672.

BBC News. 2011. "Russia election: Hundreds rally against Putin in Moscow." December 5, 2011.https://www.bbc.co.uk/news/world-europe-16042797.

Berger, John. 1972. *Ways of Seeing.* United Kingdom: Penguin Books.

Beyes, Timon, Krempl, Sophie, and Deuflhard, Amelie, eds. 2009. *Parcitypate: Art and Urban Space.* Sulgen; Zürich: Niggli.

Bown, Matthew Cullerne. 1998. *Socialist Realist Painting.* New Haven and London: Yale University Press, 1998.

Breuer, Anita. 2016. "The Role of Social Media in Mobilizing Political Protest." In *Young Generation Awakening: Economics, Society, and Policy on the Eve of the Arab Spring,* edited by Edward Sayre and Tarik Yousef, 110–31. New York: Oxford University Press.

Brooke, James. 2011. "Putin-Medvedev Job Swap Plan Draws Mixed Reaction." *Voice of America.* September 25, 2011. https://www.voanews.com/a/putin-medvedev-job-swap-plan-draws-mixed-reaction-130589908/170886.html.

Broom, Sarah M. 2019. *The Yellow House: A Memoir.* New York: Grove Press.

Bushnell, John. 1990. *Moscow Graffiti: Language and Subculture.* Australia: Allen & Unwin Pty. Limited.

Butler, Judith. 2015. *Notes Toward a Performative Theory of Assembly.* Cambridge: Harvard University Press.

Charter of Fundamental Rights of the European Union. Declared in 2000, came into force in 2009. "Charter of Fundamental Rights of the European Union, Article 11." https://eur-lex.europa.eu/legal-content/EN/TXT/?uri=CELEX%3A12012P%2FTXT.

Chenoweth, Erica, and Maria J. Stephan. 2011. *Why Civil Resistance Works: The Strategic Logic of Nonviolent Conflict.* New York City: Columbia University Press.

Clark, Katarina. 2000. *The Soviet Novel, Third Edition: History as Ritual.* Bloomington: Indiana University Press.

Daylight, Russell. 2012. "The Difference between Semiotics and Semiology." *Gramma: Journal of Theory and Criticism* 20, no. 0: 37–50. https://doi.org/10.26262/gramma.v20i0.6292.

Deibert, Ronald. 2023. "The Autocrat in Your iPhone: How Mercenary Spyware Threatens Democracy." *Foreign Affairs.* January/February 2023.

Dejevsky, Mary. 2011. "Putin's Russia: The Elections and Beyond." *The Guardian,* December 8, 2011. https://www.theguardian.com/commentisfree/2011/dec/08/putin-russia-elections.

Diamond, Larry. 2002. "Elections Without Democracy: Thinking About Hybrid Regimes." *Journal of Democracy* 13, no. 2: 21–35. https://doi.org/10.1353/jod.2002.0025

"Documenting Numbers of Victims of the Holocaust and Nazi Persecution." *Holocaust Encyclopedia*. United States Holocaust Memorial Museum.

Ellsworth-Jones, Will. 2013. "The Story Behind Banksy." *Smithsonian.com*. February 2013. https://www.smithsonianmag.com/arts-culture/the -story-behind-banksy-4310304/.

Embassy Moscow Official. 2011. Email message to Alexis Lerner (then Zimberg). "Query Regarding Saint Petersburg Legal Festival." November 9, 2011.

Erizanu, Paula. 2021. "30 Years of Independence: Is the Term 'Post-Soviet' Still in Use?" *New Eastern Europe*. August 31, 2021. https://www.new-east-archive .org/features/show/13044/30-years-independence-ussr-term-post-soviet-use.

Escif. 2016. "Heil! New Mural in Moscow." *Il Gorgo*. https://ilgorgo.com/escif -heil-new-mural-moscow/

European Parliament. 2023. "Report of the Investigation of Alleged Contraventions and Maladministration in the Application of Union Law in Relation to the Use of Pegasus and Equivalent Surveillance Spyware (A9-0189/2023)." *Committee of Inquiry to Investigate the Use of Pegasus and Equivalent Surveillance Spyware*. Rapporteur Sophie in 't Veld. May 22. https://www .europarl.europa.eu/doceo/document/A-9-2023-0189_EN.html.

European Union Agency for Fundamental Rights. 2009. "Article 11: Freedom of Expression and Information." FRA. https://fra.europa.eu/en/eu-charter /article/11-freedom-expression-and-information.

Faulconbridge, Guy, and Felix Light. 2024. "Putin foe Alexei Navalny dies in jail, West holds Russia responsible." Reuters, February 16, 2024. https://www.reuters.com/world/europe/jailed-russian-opposition-leader -navalny-dead-prison-service-2024-02-16/.

Finlayson, James Gordon and Dafydd Huw Rees. 2023. "Jürgen Habermas." *The Stanford Encyclopedia of Philosophy*. September 15, 2023. https://plato.stanford .edu/archives/fall2023/entries/habermas/.

Freedom House. 2024. "Freedom in the World 2023." FreedomHouse.org. https://freedomhouse.org/sites/default/files/2023-03/FIW_World_2023 _DigtalPDF.pdf.

– 2018. "Freedom on the Net 2018: Kazakhstan." Freedom House.org. https:// freedomhouse.org/country/kazakhstan/freedom-net/2018.

Fries, Arthur, and Nozer D. Singpurwalla. 2008. "Mimetics: Overview and Baseline Models." *Institute for Defense Analyses*. October 2008. https://apps .dtic.mil/sti/pdfs/AD1123909.pdf.

Fu, Diana. 2017a. "Disguised Collective Action in China." *Comparative Political Studies* 50, no. 4: 499–527.

– 2017b. *Mobilizing Without the Masses: Control and Contention in China*. Cambridge University Press.

Gel'man, Vladimir. 2015. "Calculus of Dissent: How the Kremlin Is Countering Its Rivals." *Russian Analytical Digest* 166 (April): 2–4.

Geranpayeh, Sarvy. 2019. "Meet Afghanistan's First Female Graffiti Artist, Who Is Risking It All for Her Murals." *The National.* April 15, 2019. https://www.thenationalnews.com/arts-culture/art/meet-afghanistan-s-first-female-graffiti-artist-who-is-risking-it-all-for-her-murals-1.848877.

Grozev, Christo. 2022. "BREAKING: Further analysis of the top secret Kremlin documents recently obtained by The Dossier Centre has revealed that a) the decision to invade Ukraine was made much earlier than publicly acknowledged; b) the KGB was deeply involved in planning the invasion." *Twitter,* March 14, 2022, 6:37 PM.

Gunitsky, Seva. 2015. "Corrupting the Cyber-Commons: Social Media as a Tool of Autocratic Stability." *Perspectives on Politics* 13, no. 1: 42–54. http://doi.org/10.1017/S1537592714003120.

Gutkin, Arina. 1999. *The Cultural Origins of the Socialist Realist Aesthetic 1890-1934.* Evanston: Northwestern University Press.

Gutterman, Steve. 2011. "Putin's approval falls to year's low: Russian poll." *Reuters,* December 16, 2011. https://www.reuters.com/article/us-russia/putins-approval-falls-to-years-low-russian-poll-idUSTRE7BF0J220111216.

Habermas, Jurgen. 1991. *The Structural Transformation of the Public Sphere: An Inquiry into a Category of Bourgeois Society.* Cambridge, MA: The MIT Press.

Haden, Donna. 2016. "Mural by Guido Van Helten for Chernobyl 30 year anniversary 2016." *Graffiti Street.* April 26, 2016.

Harvey, David. 1985. "The Marxian Theory of the State." *Antipode* 17, no. 2–3: 174–81. https://doi.org/10.1111/j.1467-8330.1985.tb00347.x.

Hodge, Robert Ian Vere, and Gunther R. Kress. 1988. *Social Semiotics.* Polity Press.

– 1997. "Social Semiotics, Style and Ideology." *Sociolinguistics,* 49–54. https://doi.org/10.1007/978-1-349-25582-5_7.

HoodGraff. 2019. "Victor Tsoi 2.0 [Video]." *YouTube.* April 29, 2019. https://www.youtube.com/watch?v=6Z9_oAWFI5g

Horsley, William. 2021. "Media Capture in Central and Eastern Europe: The Corrosive Impact on Democracy and Desecration of Journalistic Ethics." In *The Routledge Companion to Journalism Ethics,* edited by Stephen J. A. Ward, 280–8. New York: Routledge.

Howard, Caroline. 2020. "In Pictures. COVID on the Street: Pandemic Graffiti from Around the World." *Forbes.* May 30, 2020. https://www.forbes.com/sites/carolinehoward/2020/05/30/covid-on-the-street-pandemic-graffiti-from-around-the-world/?sh=f49e4bb1069f

Human Constanta Staff. 2021. "Review of the practice of using 'extremist' articles under which citizenship can be revoked." HumanConstanta.org, October 25, 2021. https://humanconstanta.org/en/review-of-the-practice-of-using-extremist-articles-under-which-citizenship-can-be-revoked/

Hyde, Susan D. 2015a. *The Pseudo-Democrat's Dilemma: Why Election Observation Became an International Norm.* New York: Cornell University Press.

– 2015b. "The Problem of Insincere Compliance in International Relations: Norms, Policy Diffusion, and International Expectations." Working Paper.

Ismailov, Hamid. 2018. *The Devils' Dance.* Translated from Uzbek to English by Donald Rayfield. Tilted Axis Press.

Johnston, Jules. 2016. "Donald Trump kisses Vladimir Putin on wall of Lithuanian restaurant." *Politico.* May 14, 2016. https://www.politico.eu/article/donald -trump-kisses-vladimir-putin-on-wall-of-lithuanian-restaurant-berlin-east-side -gallery/

Jones, James. 2011. "Putin's Youth Movement Provides a Sinister Backdrop to Russia's Protests | James Jones." *The Guardian*, December 8, 2011. https:// www.theguardian.com/commentisfree/2011/dec/08/putin-russia-elections.

Kalmar, Ivan. 2020. "Islamophobia and Anti-antisemitism: The Case of Hungary and the 'Soros plot'," *Patterns of Prejudice* 54, no. 1–2: 182–98, http://doi.org /10.1080/0031322X.2019.1705014.

Kartau, Mari, ed. 2015. "Downtown Government Fights Street Artist." ERR Kultuur. April 7, 2015. https://kultuur.err.ee/305722/kesklinna-valitsus -voitleb-tanavakunstnikuga.

Kazinform. 2020. "Mural Depicting Abai Unveiled in Aksai City." *Kazinform*, October 12, 2020. https://en.inform.kz/news/mural-depicting-abai -unveiled-in-aksai-city_a3705129/

Kirchick, James. 2012. "Brush with Controversy." *The New Republic*, March 29, 2012. https://newrepublic.com/article/102113/czech-republic -public-space-street-art-vandalism-expression-protest

Kovács, Kriszta, and Kim Lane Scheppele. 2018. "The Fragility of an Independent Judiciary: Lessons from Hungary and Poland – and the European Union." *Communist and Post-Communist Studies* 51, no. 3 (September). https://doi.org/10.1016/j.postcomstud.2018.07.005

Krastev, Ivan, "New Threats to Freedom: Democracy's Doubles," *Journal of Democracy* 17 (2006): 114. https://heinonline.org/HOL/LandingPage? handle=hein.journals/jnlodmcy17&div=28&id=&page=

Kulchytsky, Stanislav. 2018. *The Famine of 1932-1933 in Ukraine: An Anatomy of the Holodomor.* CIUS Press.

Kuran, Timur. 1991. "Now out of Never: The Element of Surprise in the East European Revolution of 1989." *World Politics* 44, no. 1: 7–48. https://doi .org/10.2307/2010422.

– 1997. *Private Truths, Public Lies: The Social Consequences of Preference Falsification.* Cambridge, MA: Harvard University Press. https://www.google.com/books /edition/Private_Truths_Public_Lies/HlKBaiCpSxYC?hl=en&gbpv =1&dq=info:Cp59QeXRlUUJ:scholar.google.com&pg=PR9&printsec =frontcover.

Kurzman, Charles. 2005. *The Unthinkable Revolution in Iran.* Cambridge, MA: Harvard University Press.

Lachapelle, Jean. 2022. "Repression Reconsidered: Bystander Effects and Legitimation in Authoritarian Regimes." *Comparative Politics* 54, no. 4 (July): 695–716. https://doi.org/10.5129/001041522X16317396828722

Lefebvre, Henri. (2003 [1970]). *The Urban Revolution.* Minneapolis: Minnesota University Press.

Lerner, Alexis, and Colleen Wood. 2019. "On the Run: Opposition Candidate Behavior in Hybrid Authoritarian Regimes." *Paper Prepared for the American Political Science Association Annual Meeting.* https://static1.squarespace .com/static/58a1878ff7e0abd069426c5d/t/5f24a3ecfb8ce430374f ccd5/1596236780466/Lerner-Wood_APSA2019_Opposition-Behavior.pdf.

Lerner, Alexis. 2012. "Moscow's Merry Pranksters." *Foreign Policy,* March 3, 2012. https://foreignpolicy.com/2012/03/03/moscows-merry-pranksters/.

– 2013a. "Flickering Flame: Remembering Street Art Pioneer Pasha 183." *The Calvert Journal.* April 3, 2013.

– 2013b. "Artful dodgers: Urban interventionists Partizaning are taking back the streets." *The Calvert Journal.* February 19, 2013. https://www.new-east-archive.org/articles/show/433/partizaning-street-art-protest

– 2014. "Off the wall: Misha Most's street art comes to London." *The Calvert Journal,* August 14, 2014. https://www.new-east-archive.org/articles/show /2993/russia-misha-most-street-art-lazarides-gallery-london

– 2020. "Authoritarian Dissent Management: Repression of the Nonsystemic Political Opposition in the Post Soviet Region." PhD thesis, University of Toronto.

– 2021. "The Co-optation of Dissent in Hybrid States: Post-Soviet Graffiti in Moscow." *Comparative Political Studies* 54, no. 10: 1757–85. https://doi .org/10.1177/0010414019879949.

Levitsky, Steven, and Lucan Way. 2002. "Elections without Democracy: The Rise of Competitive Authoritarianism." *Journal of Democracy* 13, no. 2: 51–65. https://doi.org/10.1353/jod.2002.0026.

– 2010. *Competitive Authoritarianism: Hybrid Regimes after the Cold War.* Cambridge: Cambridge University Press. http://doi.org/10.1017/CBO9780511781353.

Lipman, Masha. 2006. "Putin's 'Sovereign Democracy.'" *Washington Post.* July 15, 2006. https://www.washingtonpost.com/archive/opinions/2006/07/15 /putins-sovereign-democracy/52ce51c4-fd66-478f-af04-768ac6156f80/.

Logan, John R., and Harvey Luskin Molotch. 1987. *Urban Fortunes: The Political Economy of Place.* Berkeley and Los Angeles: University of California Press.

Lotman, Yuri M. and Boris Uspenskij. 1984. *The Semiotics of Russian Culture.* Edited by Ann Shukman. Ann Arbor: Michigan Slavic Publications.

Luhmann, Niklas. 2000 [1996]. *The Reality of the Mass Media.* Translated by Kathleen Cross. Published in German by Westdeutscher Verlag. English Translation Published by Polity Press.

Luhmann, Niklas. 2000. *Art as a Social System*. Translated by Eva M. Knodt. Stanford: Stanford University Press.

Lukac, Stanislav. 2014. "When Writing Turns Savage: Contextualizing Antisemitic Graffiti on the Streets of Krakow and Budapest." Thesis. Central European University. https://www.etd.ceu.edu/2014/lukac_stanislav.htm

Malhotra, Shriya. 2018. "In the City, Everyone Is an Artist." In *Where Strangers Meet*, edited by Claire Doherty. Published by the British Council. https://www.situations.org.uk/resources/where-strangers-meet-arts-and -the-public-realm/.

Malinova, Olga. 2021. "Framing the Collective Memory of the 1990s as a Legitimation Tool for Putin's Regime." *Problems of Post-Communism* 68 no. 5: 429–41. http://doi.org/10.1080/10758216.2020.1752732

Marjanovic-Shane, Ana, and E. J. White. 2014. "When the Footlights Are Off: A Bakhtinian Interrogation of Play as Postupok." *International Journal of Play* 3, no 2: 119–35. https://doi.org/10.1080/21594937.2014.931686.

Markusz, Katarzyna. 2018. "Antisemitic Graffiti Found on Gate of Jewish Cemetery in Poland." *The Times of Israel*. December 16, 2018. https:// www.timesofisrael.com/anti-semitic-graffiti-found-on-gate-of-jewish -cemetery-in-poland/

Martinet, André. 1964. *Elements of General Linguistics*. Translated by Elizabeth Palmer. Faber and Faber.

McDonald, Nancy. 2001. *The Graffiti Subculture: Youth, Masculinity and Identity in London and New York*. London: Palgrave Macmillan.

McLuhan, Marshall. 1964. *Understanding Media: The Extensions of Man*. New York: McGraw-Hill.

McLuhan, Marshall, and Quentin Fiore. 1967. *The Medium is the Massage: An Inventory of Effects*. New York: Penguin Books.

Meandering Wild. "Street Art Around The Abandoned City Of Pripyat." *Meandering Wild*. https://meanderingwild.com/street-art-pripyat/.

Mouzykantskii, Ilya. 2011. "In Belarus, Just Being Can Prompt an Arrest." *The New York Times*, August 13, 2011. https://www.nytimes.com/2011/07/30 /world/europe/30belarus.html.

Noir, Thierry. 2023. "The Berlin Wall." *ThierryNoir.com*. https://thierrynoir .com/biography/essays/berlin-wall/.

Oldenburg, Ray. 1989. *The Great Good Place: Cafes, Coffee Shops, Bookstores, Bars, Hair Salons and Other Hangouts at the Heart of a Community*. Paragon House.

Orbán, Viktor. 2014. "Address at Băile Tuşnad." Speech. Băile Tuşnad, Romania, July 26, 2014.

Orwell, George. 2014 [1946]. *Why I Write*. Penguin Books.

OVD-Info. 2022. "Repressions [sic] in Russia in 2022." *OVD-Info*, December 2022. *https://en.ovdinfo.org/repressions-russia-2022#1.*

Parfan, Nadiya. 2010. "Kyiv Graffiti: Production of Space in Post-Soviet City." Master's thesis. Central European University.

Pechurina, Anna. 2014. "Post-post-Soviet? Art, politics and society in Russia at the turn of the decade." *Visual Studies* 31: 1. http://doi.org/10.1080/14725 86X.2014.941601.

Peirce, Charles Sanders. 1932. *Collected Papers of Charles Sanders Peirce*, edited by Charles Hartshorne and Paul Weiss. Vols. I-II. Cambridge, MA: Harvard University Press.

– 1958. *Charles S. Peirce: Selected Writings*, edited by Philip Weiner. USA: Dover Publications.

– 1991. *Peirce on Signs: Writings on Semiotic*, edited by James Hoopes. Chapel Hill: The University of North Carolina Press.

Platt, Jonathan. 2017. *Cultural Forms of Protest in Russia*. New York: Routledge. https://doi.org/10.4324/9781315665610.

Plattner, Marc. 2019. "Illiberal Democracy and the Struggle on the Right." *Journal of Democracy* 30, no. 1 (January): 5–19. https://doi.org/10.1353 /jod.2019.0000. https://www.journalofdemocracy.org/articles /illiberal-democracy-and-the-struggle-on-the-right/.

Plesch, Véronique. 2015. "Beyond Art History: Graffiti on Freescoes." In *Understanding Multidisciplinary Studies from Prehistory to the Present*, edited by Troy Lovata and Elizabeth Olton, 47–57. New York: Routledge.

"Polish Victims." *Holocaust Encyclopedia*. United States Holocaust Memorial Museum.

Ponosov, Igor. 2008. *Russian Street Art*. Moscow: Self-published. https://issuu .com/igor_ponosov/docs/_objects-1__book

– 2010. "Objects-1: Russian Street Art by Igor Ponosov - Issuu." *Issuu.com*. April 21, 2010. https://issuu.com/igor_ponosov/docs/_objects-1__book.

– 2018. *Russian Urban Art: History and Conflicts, 2018*. Moscow: Self-published.

Putin, Vladimir Vladimirovich. 2012. Decree Number 1710. https://rvio.histrf .ru/officially/.

Radya, Tima. 2011. "Red Square (in Ekaterinburg, Russia)." *T-Radya.com*. https://square.t-radya.com/12/.

Rahman, Shameema Binte. 2021. "Edward von Lõngus: Art is a game to me, where the only rule is breaking the rules." *Medium*. October 9, 2021. https:// sbinte.medium.com/edward-von-l%C3%B5ngus-art-is-a-game-to-me-where -the-only-rule-is-breaking-the-rules-cbc26c619fe2.

Reuters Staff. 2021. "Russian authorities paint over large Navalny mural in St Petersburg." *Reuters*. April 28, 2021. https://www.reuters.com/world /russian-authorities-paint-over-large-navalny-mural-st-petersburg-2021-04-28/.

Reyburn, Scott. 2018. "Banksy Painting Self-Destructs After Fetching $1.4 Million at Sotheby's." *New York Times*. October 6, 2018. https://www.nytimes .com/2018/10/06/arts/design/uk-banksy-painting-sothebys.html.

RFE/RL. 2016. "Vladivostok Mayor Charged with Corruption, Abuse of Office." *Radio Free Europe/Radio Liberty*. June 3, 2016. https://www.rferl.org/a /vladivostok-mayor-pushkaryov-chaarged-corruptio-abuse-of-office-russian -investigative-committee-moscow-court/27776067.html.

Riggle, Nicholas Alden. 2010. "Street Art: The Transfiguration of the Commonplaces." *Journal of Aesthetics and Art Criticism* 68, no. 3: 243–57. http://www.jstor.org/stable/40793266.

Romanov, Alexander. 2017. "'Маленький варг' или 'Маленький коми-зырянин' у станции метро 'Третьяковская.'" *Website of the Zamoskvorechye District*, March 8, 2017. https://zamos.ru/news/23474/.

Russia Public Opinion Research Center. 2011. Ratings of the President and Parties: First Results After the Elections ["Рейтинги президента и партий: первые итоги после выборов."] December 15, 2011. https://wciom.ru /analytical-reviews/analiticheskii-obzor/rejtingi-prezidenta-i-partij -pervye-itogi-posle-vyborov-.

Russian Geographical Society. 2018. "Geo Graffiti Contest." *Russian Geographical Society*, June 1, 2018. https://www.rgo.ru/en/article/geo-graffiti-contest.

Saussure, Ferdinand de. 1916 [1922] *Cours de linguistique générale*, Compiled by Charles Bally and Albert Sechehaye. Payot.

Schumach, Murray. 1973. "At $10-Million, City Calls It a Losing Graffiti Fight." *New York Times*. March 28, 1973. https://www.nytimes.com/1973/03/28 /archives/at-10million-city-calls-it-a-losing-graffiti-fight-lindsay-decrying.html.

Scott, James. 1985. *Weapons of the Weak: Everyday Forms of Peasant Resistance*. Yale University Press.

Searle, John R. 1969. *Speech Acts: An Essay in the Philosophy of Language*. Cambridge: Cambridge University Press.

Shen-Bayh, Fiona. 2018. "Strategies of Repression: Judicial and Extrajudicial Methods of Autocratic Survival." *World Politics* 70 no. 3: 321–57. https://doi .org/10.1017/S0043887118000047

Shogren, Elizabeth. 1991. "Soviets Pursue an American Dream: Trends: Once cursed in the Soviet Union, U.S. pop culture–from 'Tarzan' to rap–is where it's at." *Los Angeles Times*. August 1, 1991. https://www.latimes.com/archives /la-xpm-1991-08-01-vw-107-story.html.

– 1991. "Leningrad Tunes in to Its MTV Today: Television: MTV Europe Wins the First Contract to Broadcast to the Soviet Union. About 140,000 Homes Will Get the Signal 24 Hours a Day." *Los Angeles Times*. March 8, 1991. https://www.latimes.com/archives/la-xpm-1991-03-08-ca-2723-story.html.

Sinnreich, Helene. 2004. "Reading the Writing on the Wall: A Textual Analysis of Łódź Graffiti." *Religion, State, and Society* 32, no. 1: 53–8. https://doi.org /10.1080/0963749042000182096.

Smith, Neil. 2003. "*Foreword.*" From Henri Lefebvre's *The Urban Revolution*. Minneapolis: University of Minnesota Press.

Soldatov, Andrei, and Irina Borogan. 2015. *The Red Web: The Struggle Between Russia's Digital Dictators and the New Online Revolutionaries*. New York: Public Affairs.

Sperling, Valerie. 2014. *Sex, Politics, & Putin: Political Legitimacy in Russia*. Oxford: Oxford University Press.

Stukal, Denis, Sanovich, Sergey, Bonneau, Richard, and Tucker, Joshua A. 2017. "Detecting Bots on Russian Political Twitter." *Big Data* 5, no. 4:310–24. https://doi.org/10.1089/big.2017.0038.

Svolik, Milan W. 2012. *The Politics of Authoritarian Rule*. Cambridge: Cambridge University Press.

Szopiński, Christian, Magdalena Patalong, Anna Anselm, Marina Lechleider, and Alina Kozłowska. 2014. "Street Art of the Ukrainian Revolution." *Post-Soviet Graffiti*. June 6, 2014. http://postsovietgraffiti.com/street-art-of-the-ukrainian-revolution/.

Tait, Robert. 2019. "Imagine No Graffiti: New Regulation to Fall on Prague's Lennon Wall." *The Guardian*. August 4, 2019. https://www.theguardian.com/world/2019/aug/04/imagine-no-graffiti-new-regulation-to-fall-on-pragues-lennon-wall.

Tannenbaum, Rob and Charles Marks. 2012. *I Want My MTV: The Uncensored Story of the Music Video Revolution*. New York: Plume Publishing.

Teets, Jessica. 2014. *Civil Society Under Authoritarianism: The China Model*. Cambridge University Press.

The Guardian Reporter in Hong Kong. 2019. "Hong Kong's Lennon Walls: Protest Goes on in Colourful Collages of Sticky Labels." *The Guardian*. July 11, 2019. https://www.theguardian.com/world/2019/jul/12/hong-kongs-lennon-walls-protest-goes-on-in-colourful-collages-of-sticky-labels.

Thum, Gregor. (2003) 2011. *Uprooted: How Breslau Became Wroclaw during the Century of Expulsions*. Translated by Tom Lampert and Allison Brown. Princeton and Oxford: Princeton University Press. https://www.jstor.org/stable/j.ctt7sh25.

Tilly, Charles. 2008. *Contentious Performances*. Cambridge University Press.

Topol, Sarah A. 2022. "The Battle for the Mural – and the Future of Belarus." *The New York Times*. March 30, 2022. https://www.nytimes.com/2022/03/30/magazine/belarus-mural.html.

Trickey, Eric. 2015. "The Fight over Graffiti: Banksy in Detroit." *Belt Magazine*. October 13, 2015. https://beltmag.com/the-fight-over-graffiti-banksy-in-detroit/.

Urbanist. 2014. "Blacking Out BLU: World-Famous Berlin Mural Erased in Protest." *Web Urbanist*. December 13, 2014. https://weburbanist.com/2014/12/13/blacking-out-blu-world-famous-berlin-mural-erased-in-protest/.

Velikonja, Mitja. 2021. *The Chosen Few: Aesthetics and Ideology in Football-Fan Graffiti and Street Art*. Los Angeles: DoppelHouse Press.

Vice, Sue. 1997. *Introducing Bakhtin*. Manchester: Manchester University Press.

Vizkelety, Vincent. 2020. "Graffiti in Budapest: The Mystery of Renée Nadler." *Librarians Blog, National Library of Israel.* July 8, 2020. https://blog.nli.org.il /en/lbh_nadler_budapest/.

Voices on Central Asia. 2018. "Feminism through Pictures: How Girls of South Kyrgyzstan Fight for Women's Rights." *Voices on Central Asia.* February 1, 2018. https://voicesoncentralasia.org/feminism-through-pictures-how-girls-in-the-south-of-the-kyrgyz-republic-fight-for-womens-rights/.

Von Longus, Edward (@edwardvonlongus). "Art." Instagram post, June 5, 2017. https://www.instagram.com/edwardvonlongus/.

Ward, Jesmyn. 2012. *Salvage the Bones: A Novel.* New York: Bloomsbury.

Wintrobe, Ronald. 1998. *The Political Economy of Dictatorship.* Cambridge: Cambridge University Press.

Wood, Clleen, and Alexis Lerner. 2022. "Facing severe repression, Russians are turning to antiwar graffiti." *Waging Nonviolence.* March 21. https:// wagingnonviolence.org/2022/03/facing-severe-repression-russians -turn-to-antiwar-graffiti/.

Zieleniec, Andrzej. 2016. "The Right to Write the City: Lefebvre and Graffiti." *Environnement Urbain / Urban Environment* 10 (September). https://doi .org/10.7202/1040597ar. https://journals.openedition.org/eue/1421.

Zimberg, Alexis. 2009. "Russian Revolutionary Women's Movements: Formative, Progression, and Demise, 1867–1881." *Michigan Journal of Political Science* 3, no. 2 Spring.

– 2012a. "The spray can is mightier than the sword: Street art as a medium for political discourse in the post-Soviet era." Thesis. Georgetown University. https://repository.library.georgetown.edu/bitstream/handle/10822/557900 /Zimberg_georgetown_0076M_11852.pdf?sequence=1&isAllowed=y.

– 2012b. "Цой жив! The Walls That Mourn Viktor Tsoi." *Post-Soviet Graffiti.* February 1, 2012. http://postsovietgraffiti.com/%D1%86%D0%BE%D0% B9-%D0%B6%D0%B8%D0%B2-the-walls-that-mourn-viktor-tsoi/.

– 2015. "Partizaning, Various Interventions. Moscow." In *Out of Time, Out of Place: Public Art (Now),* edited by Clare Doherty, 100–1. London: Thames and Hudson.

– "Nostalgia and Notions of False Empire: The (un)Historical Rise of the Right in Hungary." *The Hidden Transcript Foreign Affairs Magazine,* 4 (Spring): 28–31.

Index

Page reference in *italics* indicate an illustration; page references in **bold** indicate a table.

www.ingramcontent.com/pod-product-compliance
Lightning Source LLC
Chambersburg PA
CBHW071753250325
24012CB00008B/35